Curriculum and Assessment Reform

ANDY HARGREAVES

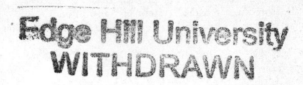

OPEN UNIVERSITY PRESS
Milton Keynes · Philadelphia

Open University Press
Celtic Court
22 Ballmoor
Buckingham MK18 1XW

and
1900 Frost Road, Suite 101
Bristol, PA 19007, USA

First published 1989
Reprinted 1990

British Library Cataloguing in Publication Data

Hargreaves, Andy
 Curriculum and Assessment reform
 1. Great Britain. Schools. Curriculum
 I. Title
 375'.00941

 ISBN 0–335–09551–8
    0–335–09550–X (pbk)

Library of Congress Cataloging-in-Publication Data

Hargreaves, Andy.
    Curriculum and assessment reform / by Andy Hargreaves.
      p.   cm. — (Modern educational thought)
    Includes index.
    ISBN 0–335–09551–8   ISBN 0–335–09550–X (pbk.)
    1. Curriculum planning.   2. Educational evaluation.   3. Education.
 Secondary—Curricula. I. Title. II. Series.
 LB1628.H334 1989   89–3323
 375' 001–dc20   CIP

Typeset by Inforum Typesetting, Portsmouth
Printed in Great Britain by
St Edmundsbury Press, Bury St Edmunds

For Stuart and Lucy

Contents

Preface and Acknowledgements

I am writing this preface on a brief return visit to England from Ontario, Canada, where I now live and work. Ontario is in the midst of a thorough review of its curricular and assessment arrangements, particularly at high school level. There is concern that the later years of high school offer too much choice and that the high school curriculum is too narrow. There has been talk of introducing province-wide benchmark-testing and even of reinstating provincial examinations for school leavers.

Across the Atlantic a National Curriculum has been legislated for England and Wales, along with sweeping reforms of the public examination system, the introduction of broader forms of assessment for recording and stimulating a wide range of pupil achievements in secondary schools, and the development of nationwide testing of pupil performance at 7, 11 and 14. Curriculum and assessment reform of this magnitude is also politically prominent in the United States, in most of Western Europe and in Labour-governed Australia too. Large scale curriculum and assessment reform is not just a local peculiarity, then, nor is it a product of national political partisanship. It is a phenomenon of international dimensions. This book sets out to explain and interpret the nature, the impact and the interrelatedness of these important and far-reaching reforms.

Over many years, I have struggled to understand and interpret these sorts of changes in curriculum and assessment policy along with all their implications. Firstly, I have done this through educational research – in particular through a study of middle school teachers' participation in school-based curriculum development and more latterly, through a study of the nature and extent of elementary school teachers' collaboration in curriculum planning outside the classroom. Secondly, my concern with curriculum and assessment reform has emerged from my practical involvement in curriculum and assessment developments, especially with local education authorities and secondary school teachers in the development of records of achievement in Britain. Thirdly, my interest and concern about curriculum and assessment reform has arisen from innumerable conversations with teachers in classrooms, staffrooms and seminar rooms, who have made me keenly aware of what motivates them, what stimulates them to change, and what helps them to deliver the practical curriculum at classroom level. Fourthly, as my practical and research-based understanding of curriculum and assessment has developed, I have spent some time studying policy documents, to try and anticipate the likely impact of new curriculum and assessment reforms.

There is also a fifth reason for my strengthening interest in curriculum and assessment reform – a more deep-seated, biographical one. It comes from that peculiarly sentimental mixture of pride, guilt and loss that we call nostalgia. As I write, I am seated in the front room of my mother's terraced house in Accrington, Lancashire, England. It is the same house, the same room where as a schoolboy plodding through my homework, I wrestled with the academic curriculum of the English grammar school. It is not a comfortable room now, nor was it then. There are no desks or tables; no dictionaries or encyclopaedias; none of the stuff of serious study or scholarship. When I was a schoolboy, its cold comforts were poor competition against the attractions of soccer and cricket 'up the park' with my non-grammar school neighbourhood 'mates'. The curriculum – what I was expected to learn, remember and revise – did little to keep me in either. My concerns about the irrelevance of the traditional academic curriculum are in this sense, far from being a recent preoccupation. Even then, the capes and bays of world geography, the five points of Stanhope's foreign policy (*only* five; no more, no less), the mysteries of electromagnetic force – these things seemed to me not to engage at all with anything I already knew or felt or understood. My drive to succeed was stimulated not by the excitement of learning, or the relevance of the curriculum to my life concerns, or the inspiration that might be drawn from expanded horizons of new knowledge and understanding. Excitement, relevance and inspiration were virtually absent features of my educational experience because of the dull, desiccated curriculum of my secondary school years. And I would not have achieved at all, were it not for the existence of more deep-seated drives for success and improvement *per se* that were rooted in certain elements of my family, my culture and myself.

In retrospect, I still resent much of my secondary school experience. I resent the wedge it struck between myself and my peers, my school and my community, my classroom and my class. I managed to make some adjustments, of course. Most commonly, I did my homework late, into the early hours of the morning, so I would not have to give up my sport and 'my mates' earlier in the evenings – a curious work habit that has stayed with me until today. But even at 14 or 15, I recall being self-consciously baffled and irritated by how disconnected the grammar-school curriculum seemed from the rest of my life and the world around me; irritated by the unacceptable cultural choices and dilemmas that the curriculum constantly pressed upon me. In a deep personal sense, therefore, it is easy for me to understand how an excessively academic, publicly examined curriculum of the kind I studied, fosters and will continue to foster only bewilderment and rejection among many working class pupils who are subject to the countervailing pressures and attractions of their class and their community. For those many working class pupils not possessing a compelling drive to achieve, the conventional secondary or high school curriculum will do little to secure that intellectual and emotional engagement and enthusiasm which can offer the possibility of success and opportunity.

These biographical experiences help explain my root concern with curriculum and assessment: the persistence, the reform or the reconstruction of a hegemonic academic curriculum, which currently helps create, sustain and reproduce widespread educational and social inequalities from one generation to the next. They help explain my particular concern with school-centred innovation as a process which seems to me usually to have operated within the broad, hegemonic limits of the academic curriculum and not to have challenged the purposes, biases and assumptions underpinning it. They help explain my interest in the relationship between curriculum and assessment reform and the culture of teaching – a culture which, with its academic preoccupations and, until recently, its unconduciveness to collaboration, has undermined attempts to broaden the curriculum beyond the conventional academic domain and prejudiced attempts to introduce different forms of assessment than those public examinations which continue to accredit and legitimate the high status subjects of the academic curriculum. My biographically rooted experiences also help explain my unease with national curriculum reform where that reform reinforces rather than redefines the hegemonic academic curriculum. For me, curriculum development and assessment development are ultimately about pupil development and teacher development. They bear on the fundamentals of the educational process – on the learning, fairness, opportunity and personal growth we offer to the generations of the future.

Through my own biographical encounters with curriculum and assessment reform as well as through my involvement in educational research, policy and practice, it seems to me that approaches to curriculum and assessment reform have usually been discussed in stereotyped, polarized terms. These approaches have usually been presented as having a mutually exclusive, either/or character. One approach is commonly represented as being school-based, local, responsive and decentralized. Negatively, the patterns of school–centred innovation found within this approach are characterized as allowing teachers excessive autonomy, creating massive inconsistencies between one school and the next, and permitting widespread mediocrity and incompetence alongside only occasional excellence. In this book, we shall see that this view of school-centred innovation as a process unleashing unregulated excesses of teacher autonomy is much exaggerated and that the historical legacy of school subjects and the academic curriculum, the continuing pressures of public examinations and the trenchant influence of the academically inclined culture of teaching have placed strong limits on the scope of school-centred innovation and on its capacity to challenge and reshape the hegemonic academic curriculum.

The approach most commonly counterposed to school-centred innovation is centralized curriculum reform. It too is frequently stereotyped. Its advocates point to the advantages of consistency, accountability and control in the service of the public interest. Opponents point to the centralized curriculum's vulnerability to political partisanship and to the threat it poses to the professional discretion and development of the teaching force. Both groups we shall find, however, commonly underestimate the extent to which the culture of teaching allows and encourages teachers to vote with their feet behind their own classroom doors, when central curriculum imperatives are at odds with their own wishes and ambitions. They underestimate the fact that central curriculum policy does not translate at all easily into local curriculum practice.

This book therefore seeks to move beyond the common, stereotypical alternatives to school-centred innovation and centralized curriculum reform. It recognizes that there are strong possibilities but also serious limitations in each pattern of change. Further, in the closing chapters, it sketches out the beginnings of a reform model which might permit redefinition of the hegemonic academic curriculum as a basis for enhanced teacher development and improved educational opportunity for young people.

In effect, the book draws together and in some places develops a number of papers representing my engagement with curriculum and assessment reform over recent years. Most of the papers appear much as originally published. I have not made strong attempts to update all the material. I have learned that it is futile to try and keep pace with the glut of educational reforms being implemented even in those countries with which I am most familiar. Books with an excessive concentration on the particular and the very recent become outdated even over the short period required to process the text for publication. This book is most concerned with modern generic themes and issues in curriculum and assessment development such as school-centred innovation, national curriculum reform, curriculum change and the culture of teaching, the persistence or redefinition of the academic curriculum, alternative patterns of assessment and so forth. These themes, I believe, carry very well across the range of recent initiatives, whatever their specific detail – and would benefit little from frantic attempts to connect them to the very latest reform proposals. Furthermore, since all but two of the chapters were originally published from 1985, the vast majority of the material and argument is very recent anyway. However, although I have made little attempt to update specific detail, I have endeavoured to show the continuity and interrelationship between different chapters and themes within the book as a prelude to a new final chapter which proposes a fresh approach to curriculum and assessment reform.

Acknowledgements

I am grateful to Ivor Goodson for engaging with the work represented in this volume, and for the stimulating discussion and debate we have had about the nature of curriculum over the years. Few have a better understanding than he of the ways in which a sense of history can undermine claims to curricular absolutes. During the years I spent at Oxford, my near namesake, David Hargreaves, with his powerful grasp of the nature of curriculum and the process of teaching, undoubtedly influenced my developing views of these subjects – not just as academic issues but as profoundly practical ones too. He would not agree with all I have to say here, but discussions with him have certainly helped frame the agenda from which my arguments proceed.

I am indebted to John Skelton and Open University Press for their kind support in publishing this book and the wider series of which it is a part.

Acknowledgements and thanks for permission to reprint are also due to the original publishers of the material on which I have drawn in putting together this book. These are Taylor and Francis and the *Journal of Curriculum Studies* for material in Chapters 1 and 4, Falmer Press for material in Chapters 2, 3, and 5, the American Sociological Association and the journal *Sociology of Education* for material in Chapter 2, Basil Blackwells of Oxford for material in Chapter 6, Cassells for material in Chapter 7, and Kogan Page with the World Wildlife Fund for material in Chapter 8.

Although I say it at the beginning of every book, and it is rapidly becoming something of a cliché, my wife Pauline has been as outstandingly supportive as ever while I have been writing this. Her remarkable human virtues are diminished no less by my repeating them once more. Lastly, I am especially grateful to my children, Stuart and Lucy, to whom this book is dedicated, for the joy they give to my life, the purpose and meaning they give to my craft, and the living example they show me of how exciting and inspirational learning and growing can be. Through them, I have a heartening practical glimpse of what might be possible for and what should be the entitlement of all young people in their education.

Andy Hargreaves

Critical Introduction: Understanding/Undermining Hierarchy and Hegemony

IVOR GOODSON

In a way our lives are the instruments through which we come to understand (or misunderstand) the world. In this sense an initial commentary about the academic terrain on which Andy Hargreaves and I have encountered each other might serve a dual purpose. Firstly it might shed some light on aspects of the social construction of knowledge, on the social milieu in which these essays are embedded and from which they emanate. Secondly, and in a more specific and limited sense, it should provide a background against which the essays might be read and indeed against which my own comments might be scrutinized.

I first met Andy Hargreaves at a conference in 1978. In Britain at this time, conferences of social scientists, sociologists, school ethnographers and interactionists and the like were frequently funded by the Social Science Research Council. This being the case at this conference there was a very conscious sense of taking part in a social scientific enterprise of finding ways to explore and understand the social world. To reach back to these conferences of social scientists in the 1970s is to be urgently aware of a 'lost discourse' in Britain – some might argue a discourse that was systematically destroyed. Certainly the Social Science Research Council was in due course replaced by the Economic and Social Research Council and much of the kind of social science work that Hargreaves and I were engaged in became essentially unfundable.

The last conference which Hargreaves and I attended together in Britain was at St Hilda's, Oxford in September 1985. Many of the scholars present were, I think, sharply aware of the deterioration in the conditions of work and funding for social scientists. A decade ago such conferences had comprised many 'work-in-progress' accounts – laying out the empirical data generated in research studies and developing theoretical connections and speculations. This time much of the commentary was inevitably anecdotal since so few research studies were being funded – people talked instead rather more about courses they were teaching. The only paper to speculate from the basis of empirical work was a valuable retrospective piece looking at some work the scholar had conducted on a project which had finished in 1974, more than a decade before.

My own contribution at the conference speculated pessimistically about the kind of work in research and evaluation which was now fundable and argued that the very focus of the work implied a high degree of political co-option to ideological purposes. I remember making cautionary comments about the new fashion of collaborative research. Whilst convinced of the virtues of collaboration I was uneasy about the timing of this tendency.[1] Promoting collaboration and action-research at a time of centralization and increasing state control might, I thought, have undesirable consequences. The methodologies are intrusive to the teachers' work process. The results though unintended could well implement and extend new modes of surveillance (interestingly these points are extended in the concluding chapter of this volume). At the conference Hargreaves took a similar line in his evaluation of some work undertaken under the auspices of the new ESRC. The result, as I recall, was a very heated exchange.

In the informal sessions at the conference – notably being punted down the River Cherwell by Hargreaves (not a relaxing experience!) – he and I talked a good deal about the 'climate' of social science work. I had just returned from a summer school at the University of British Columbia and confided to him that I had been offered a Professorship in Canada and was sorely tempted to accept. He, who had two brothers in Canada and knew the universities there after a visit in 1983, argued it would be a sensible move. In due course I accepted. A few months after my arrival Hargreaves himself applied for, and was offered, a job nearby in Toronto and in the summer of 1987 he likewise moved to Canada.

The act of migration and settlement heightens one's awareness of identity, but also of roots. We have resumed our intellectual dialogue in Canada but much of the discussion is about the 'lost discourse' in Britain and about ways in which that discourse can be revived and reconstituted. For both of us our sense of Britishness is I think substantial, so also is our debt to the British academic community where many of our best friends remain. The task we all share is how to revive and reconstitute the social science enterprise and how to build on some of the vital work carried out in the 1960s and 1970s (and, of course, how to broaden and deepen some of the work which continues in the more hostile 1980s). This essay, and indeed the whole volume, should be read, then, as part of a broader project of revival and reconstitution.

But I think this biographical prologue argues for a further act of sociological imagination in the way that we scrutinize and locate our social science work. In seeking revival and reconstitution we have to sharply learn the political lessons of the past decade. For the restructuring of social science is part of a much broader restructuration. As social scientists concerned to understand schooling we are driven to investigate the wider politics of schooling as it impinges upon our sociological study. Specifically this means we must build on the micro and mezo level studies that were so generative in the 1960s and 1970s and reconnect them to macro concerns, to ways of understanding structural changes and structural redefinitions and reconstructions.

For this reason, above all, this collection of Hargreaves essays seems to me important. Of all the sociological work in Britain in the 1970s I have long felt that his work has produced some of the most interesting insights and data at the mezo level. These middle level conceptual frameworks – coping strategies, contrastive rhetoric, etc. – have themselves provided the stimulus for further work. In addition they have provided us with those vital 'glimpses of structure' which are the perennially elusive pursuit of any *bona fide* social scientist.

'Glimpses of structure'

In this introductory essay I want to take a couple of examples to indicate the value of Hargreaves' work and more generally to indicate how the work of the 1970s – my 'lost discourse' if you will – can be revived, reconstituted and re-connected to a broader investigation of the structure and politics of social change. My own biography has provided a number of standpoints from which to investigate questions of agency and structure. I suppose these biographical standpoints have also offered certain bridging points into Hargreaves' work. As his introduction elegantly indicates, his class upbringing and his retrospective analysis of the lived experiences of that upbringing are unerringly similar to my own (a comparison of his introduction to my previous musings on this topic would catch these resonances in full).[2] But from similar class origins our paths have diverged considerably before settling on some kind of intellectual convergence in recent years.

Firstly my experience in school teaching has afforded a way of reading these essays as a past participant in the processes Hargreaves describes. His paper on contrastive rhetoric draws by chance on the instance of Countesthorpe school in Leicestershire. This was the school in which I spent my first years in teaching – a fairly fiery initiation into the politics and pedagogy of curriculum innovation.

Secondly my work on the history and politics of curriculum covers a very similar terrain to that which Hargreaves covers in this book. But though the focus is similar and in the end the understandings somewhat convergent, the route has been different. I have arrived through a process of historical scholarship, studying the history and emergence of curriculum and schooling. Hargreaves has similarly served his empirical apprenticeship but has arrived through a sustained use of sociological theorizing.

One of the more important movements in the school curriculum in the 1970s was school-centred innovation (SCI). In his review of this movement in Chapter 1, Hargreaves reminds us of another 'lost discourse' from a previous period. In attempting revival and reconstitution it is enormously important to fully grasp the politics of this truncated movement for curriculum innovation. In this chapter Hargreaves indicts the SCI movement, rightly in my view, for its 'micropolitical naivete, timidity and evasiveness.' He argues that the failure of the movement in this regard 'almost certainly holds some responsibility for producing the educational inconclusiveness within school-based curriculum development which has created some of the pretext for central intervention'.

In this micropolitical sense Hargreaves is absolutely correct. But in exploring the limits of political possibility at particular historical moments it is also important to focus on certain schools-based initiatives which exhibited greater political dexterity. For such initiatives reveal at another level the 'glimpses of structure' which are so important. Let me give an example.

The Hertfordshire 'A' Level in Environmental Studies was a deliberate attempt 'to create a discipline from below', to define a high-status examinable subject from a school-base. The originator was absolutely clear about his political intentions: 'I would like to have seen this piece of work as a school-based 'A' level, if only to show that a school can put an 'A' level up and get it accepted.' At the time a number of important official documents were arguing that this was a viable strategy for innovation, notably the Schools Council publication on sixth form work *Growth and Response*.[3] The Hertfordshire pioneers explicitly followed this alternative route. Their curriculum development at 'A' level was 'schools based and is the result of initiatives taken together by practising teachers with the support of their local authority. Such self-generated work offers a viable way of developing an area of curriculum'. Thus in this school-based strategy the academic discipline is developed because classroom teachers perceived the need for a new area of knowledge for their pupils and set about constructing it.

On the face of it this all seems sensible and viable but what about the 'politics of feasibility'; who, in short, exercises power in these matters? Will such strategies for curriculum development collide with 'the politics of school knowledge'?

In the case of the Hertfordshire initiative I have documented the answer in some detail elsewhere.[4] In summary the answer was that the schools-based initiatives were firstly redefined; then strangled to death. The redirection took place because initially the schools-based definitions of the 'A' level in Environmental Studies were turned down by the Examination Boards to which they were submitted.

Hertfordshire then employed a strategy which in effect sought to gain the sponsorship and involvement of certain university personnel without accepting a wholesale defeat for the schools-based initiative. But how substantial had the 'involvement' to be? Or put another way, how much control would universities have to exert before a *bone fide* discipline could emerge? The question 'is it a discipline' thereby poses the surrogate question 'who has defined this' and 'who controls this knowledge'. Interestingly the major opponent in the Examination Board posed the problem in exactly these terms: 'This conference must ask itself the question – what is it that we see as fundamentally an 'A' level discipline and does the subject "environmental studies" satisfy our criteria?'

Later on when the negotiations for the 'A' level became protracted the same man argued 'the study must be a discipline, a coherent body of facts and concepts demanding an ordered mind for its appreciation'. The thorough renunciation of pedagogic schools-based concerns was perhaps reflected in his statement that the discipline should be recognizable in this manner 'even by the student'.

As the negotiations for the 'A' level dragged on for more than five years, slowly but surely the landscape of power with regard to 'A' level school knowledge was explored and exposed. In its final form the 'A' level syllabus defined by the Hertfordshire teachers and their university sympathizers had to pass through Schools Council committees. But the subject syllabus went not to a committee for new subjects or interdisciplinary studies but to existing subject committees. Not surprisingly these committees, notably Geography and Science, defended their own subject terrain against the newcomer. The strategy employed was an elegant two-stage filibuster. Firstly the committees demanded more geographical content or more science. Then in the second stage the committees turned down the redrafts because they were so similar to Geography or Science syllabuses as they existed. These committees were able to insist on prohibitive restrictions on the new syllabus. The subject could not be offered with Geography (a most likely partner subject); it was only passed for a five year 'experimental period'; only pilot schools were allowed to take it up. By ensuring these obstacles faced the new subject in the early years when the momentum for change was strong, the opponents to the new subject effectively extinguished the chances of its establishment in the school curriculum.

This extended example, I think, shows that SCI faced major structural barriers to its development, extension and take-up. In some cases, micropolitical naivete, timidity and evasiveness ensured that these barriers were not seriously investigated, that the limits were untested and blame could therefore be placed easily on the 'incompetent' school-based personnel. But in other cases this convenient version of events was transcended because SCI's initiatives were pursued with remarkable political tenacity and dexterity. In these cases, some of the political 'high ground' of curriculum power was fitfully exposed. But this example also serves to illustrate that even when schools-based groups pursued their cause with political acumen they were most often defeated. The structural location of other interest groups – notably universities and established subject associations and groups – offered them a position of considerable control and superiority. The outmanoeuvring of schools-based groups in such a situation was successfully accomplished and the attempt to innovate 'from below' effectively frustrated. A hierarchical subject-based pattern of curriculum and assessment was thereby defended and reasserted. In this situation SCI was not so much presented as 'incompetent' as rendered 'inappropriate'. But the defence of hierarchical subject-based structures once again left the way open for a reassertion of established patterns of knowledge and ultimately for the extension of such control: in the British situation this took form of the new National Curriculum.

In Chapter 2 Hargreaves extends his analysis of SCI to look at curriculum decision-making – the practical process of curriculum deliberation as it is developed and experienced by the teachers themselves. He claims that this will allow us:

> to appreciate the significance of the distribution of power in the curriculum decision-making process, the different kinds of knowledge and experience on which various participants draw during that process, and the ways in which these distributions of knowledge, experience and power profoundly affect the course and consequence of schools-based curricula development.

In this chapter Hargreaves elegantly shows the kinds of exclusion which are practised in curriculum decision-making. In particular, he shows how education theory is deemed 'culturally inadmissible' by the teachers: 'they rejected it in their initial training and they continued to have little acquaintance with it and make little use of it in their current practice'. But other kinds of exclusion are practised. These emerged particularly in setting the parameters and agendas for debate when full-scale discussion is allowed. It is here that he develops the generative concept of 'contrastive rhetoric' where he argues that 'the culturally based over-reliance by teachers on classroom experience as a basis for searching and wide-ranging curriculum debate creates ample opportunities for powerful members of senior management to draw up the boundaries of such debate.' Contrastive rhetoric works by introducing into the debate the possibility of undesired alternative practices – they are introduced in 'stylized, trivialized and generally perjorative terms which connotes, and we might add confirms and ensures, their unacceptability'.

In this instance Countesthorpe College is introduced into the debate and this immediately led to a 'heightened emotional response' and a collective confirmation that the various tendencies represented by that school were viewed as unacceptable. But the interesting aspect of the debate transcript is the way that many of the real challenges of the Countesthorpe structure of decision-making and pedagogy were themselves hidden from view in the discussion. The emphasis was retained on the changes of curriculum and in classroom life and on recognizable signs of classroom deviance, 'smoking, reading comics, eating crisps, calling staff by first names'. The debate therefore, as Hargreaves argues, was substantially defined by the culturally based over-reliance of teachers on classroom issues. This made it easy for the school hierarchy to damn the whole Countesthorpe experiment without even dealing with what was arguably its main challenge, and source of fear, namely the issues of *governance*. By confirming the teachers in their self-created *lager* of classroom experience it was relatively easy to disvalue

Countesthorpe and all it stood for – without needing to even examine 'all it stood for'.

Let me say a little more about what Countesthorpe stood for in terms of alternative strategies for curriculum decision-making, and indeed general decision-making. The first package of materials sent to new staff contained the following statement from the headmaster:

> Countesthorpe College exists in a normal elective authoritarian society. However, the practice of that society makes it possible for us to introduce a wide measure of participation into our management. It is the practice for the central government to interfere comparatively little in the local practice of education, its control being largely with finance on the one hand and with the overall organisation on the other. The practice of local governments is variable but theoretically at the secondary level, the policy within the school, and the executive practice adopted, has been left to the Headmaster subject to a variable checking system by means of governors who usually represent mostly the county education committee and the urban and rural district government. In practice, a number of authorities, including the one in which Countesthorpe is, leave much autonomy to the headmaster. The chief control is of the quantity of resource made available, in terms of staff and money.[5]

Essentially the arguments that followed this statement indicated that the headmaster planned to exploit the precedents and patterns of control and to introduce participatory democracy. It was in short a plan for 'democracy in one school'. The substantial nature of the reforms in decision-making are best summarized in Figure 1.

Plainly at Countesthorpe the staff were to be fully involved in discussing and participating in *all* aspects of governance. This I think adds a new urgency to the concerns of the hierarchy in Hargreaves case study school as they employed contrastive rhetoric to disvalue the range of practices at Countesthorpe. Reviewing the *Times Educational Supplement* at the time I find a wide coverage of the new Countesthorpe view of governance. It seems reasonable to assume that the hierarchy of the case study school knew the real nature of the challenge and sought to employ contrastive rhetoric *at the level of classroom anecdote* to disvalue the whole enterprise. Moreover this disvaluing was made more urgent by the character of the rank and file staff in the case study school: young, inexperienced and potentially amenable to new modes of participatory decision-making.

In Chapter 3 Hargreaves speculates about the hegemonic crises in the 1970s, particularly with regard to the academic subject-based curriculum. The crisis took the form of a challenge to extend entitlements to education and to develop a broader range of educational experiences and assessments. I have scrutinized in some detail two case studies of this kind of challenge: the Hertfordshire 'A' level initiatives and the evolution of Countesthorpe College. In both cases a challenge to existing patterns of educational entitlement

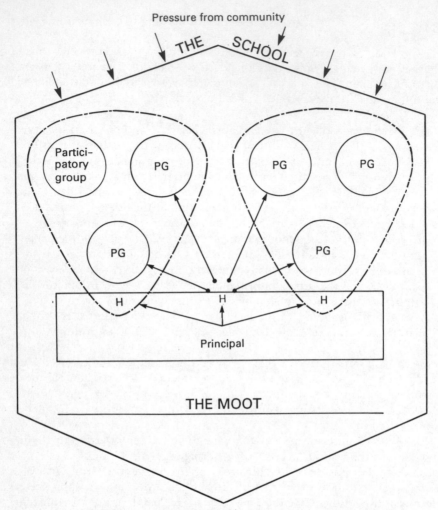

Figure 1   A possible organization for improved creativity in the school

PRESSURE FROM COMMUNITY

DEFINITIONS AND POWERS

Participatory Groups (PG)
Consists of 3–4 teachers and students who work together.
Have power to make policy decisions within a policy framework laid down by the Principal/Hierarchy group.
Power to take executive action.

Principal Hierarchy
Consists of principal and those with direct delegated powers – heads of department, or sections, houses or deputies. Have power to make the overall framework policy – subject only to MOOT veto.

as evidenced in traditional patterns of curriculum and assessment was promulgated and promoted. Both cases in their different ways and at different levels consciously sought some kind of structural redefinition.

At Countesthorpe the opponents of this challenge employed a variety of strategies to unravel what was clearly a well thought-out campaign for change. The story has been told in fascinating detail in Tuula Gordon's study *Democracy in One School*.[6] But the ingredients of the 'counter revolution' are important for the arguments in this book. Firstly the whole pattern of governance by the school community via 'the moot' was attacked. The most recent head 'had to be pressured to even have a *staff meeting*.' The local education authority then re-established the old pattern of authority and hierarchy in the school with the headmaster and the governor having full executive control. Secondly at the level of curriculum there were echoes of the Hertfordshire story. Many of the new Mode 3 'O' levels so crucial to the school's view of student learning were attacked and discontinued. This in many ways was the most serious body blow to the whole ethos of the school, because 'interdisciplinary teams' teaching in 'home bases' and employing individualized learning and project work were the central agency of work in the school. Assessment strategies had to respect these objectives – whilst Mode 3s were in existence this was possible. With their progressive closure a substantial alternative view of schooling was at risk and in due course was conclusively defeated.

I have deliberately chosen two instances of a complex pattern of challenge and response. Both instances indicate the way that the limits to structural redefinition were explored and ultimately clarified. And both instances offer full confirmation of the interlinked nature of curriculum and assessment and of the need to address this linkage in my future attempts at educational reform. In a sense these examples should therefore highlight the significance of the sequence Hargreaves has chosen in presenting his essays in this volume.

Responsible for executive action subject to appeal to MOOT.

H
Member of hierarchy (could be principal) responsible for innovation.
Has resources but no power.

The Moot
Consists of all staff, with or without students or student representation.
Has powers to veto on a two-thirds majority any policy decision but not to initiate policy.
Acts as Appeal Court against executive action.

(Broken line)
Area of close co-operation and communication between participatory groups and including member of hierarchy.

In the second half of the book Hargreaves therefore moves to a consideration of curriculum assessment. Here he develops in a strikingly original
manner his argument for the essential interlinkedness of curriculum development, assessment development and teacher development. In this he is
undoubtedly right and in causing us to focus on 'glimpses of structure' from
previous periods of contestation he serves to sharpen our political knowledge. As we have seen, the lessons of the 1960s and 1970s are clear about the
need for structural redefinition of both curriculum and assessment if there are
to be changes in the teachers' and pupils' culture and work.

The strategy of employing assessment reform to restructure the culture
and work of teachers and pupils is clearly defined in Part II. In particular the
investigation of pupil-centred assessment procedure is valuable for our
analysis of new policy directions. The use of pupil records of achievement
and pupil profiles offer a way of partially disestablishing the hegemonic
academic curriculum. In his concluding chapter Hargreaves pushes the
argument towards its logical end and defines a valuable alternative strategy
for curriculum and assessment reform. Here above all is a message of hope for
those concerned with the anti-educational implications of traditional
academic curriculum and assessment.

However, what is less clear is where the countervailing political forces are
to be found which will support such structural redefinition, particularly as we
enter the 1990s. Future attempts at structural redefinition will require the
integrated approaches in curriculum and assessment reform and teacher and
pupil development which Hargreaves defines, but they will also require a
major shift in political forces. Only then can we hope for a shift in the political
economy of schooling and for a renewal of debate about educational entitlement and social justice.

We are in the midst of an epoch in Western countries where our accumulated knowledge about schooling and social justice is often so discounted as to
seem marginal and meaningless. This is what the lost discourse in Britain was
much concerned to understand and address. In other countries the current
silence in these matters is also deafening. Throughout the Western world new
notions of modernization and technologization seem temporarily to cover
the deep structures of inequity embedded in schooling and to drive us in other
directions in the search for better schooling. As I recently argued in *The
Making of Curriculum*:

> In such a situation it is quite possible to develop an ideology as in current
> times where our gaze is directed to individual classrooms and schools
> since they are thought to have 'autonomy'. The search is on for 'efficient'
> teaching . . . 'better schools'. The researcher is guided towards the
> individual classroom or school in a quest for the ingredients of the more
> successful practice. The differentials of success become paramount, i.e.
> why is one classroom better than another? why do parents choose one
> school rather than another? This all restores attention to the individual
> practice of school and classroom.

Of course the other side of the coin of this current range of policy foci is what is not scrutinized, what is missing, what was once present in our 'lost discourse'.

Conversely our gaze is directed away from the parameters of practice, the commonalities of success and failure in schooling: from the historical analysis of the social construction of the curriculum. Yet this is part of the story of the 'good' classroom or the 'better' school: for this is the story of how this particular range of goals was established and enshrined.[7]

The focus on individual schools and classrooms diverts our attention from fundamentals and commonalities. Yet it is to these that our research should return and refocus if a democratic and socially just society is our concern. The rapidly expanding field of curriculum history has explored a terrain similar to that covered in this volume. A wide variety of studies in different countries have pointed to commonalities in the social construction of hierarchies through schooling and to the salient role of curriculum and assessment in this process.

I have previously pointed to the crucial role of the academic tradition which is found at the apex of school hierarchies in curriculum and assessment. I argued that in English comprehensive schools in the 1970s:

The deep structures of curriculum differentiation are historically linked to different educational sectors, to different social class clienteles and occupational destinations, to different status hierarchies. Differentiated curricula and the (existing) social structure are matched on very firm foundations: by building on these foundations comprehensive re-organisation has had to accept the antecedent structures which contradict its stated ideal.[8]

In this way antecedent structures of curriculum and assessment (related to antecedent social hierarchies) posed an insuperable barrier to attempts to socially reconstruct schooling towards a less hierarchical order. In this contestation the 'hegemonic academic curriculum' acted as the bastion of existing patterns of social hierarchy.

In the United States Kliebard's epic curriculum history has shown how the academic subject proved to be 'an impregnable fortress'.[9] Likewise Labaree has shown the role of the academic curriculum in the history of 'Central High School' in Philadelphia. Again academic subjects sat at the apex of social hierarchy within the school. By 1900, in Central High School, the new curriculum was established in a formal pattern that remained stable for twenty years:

The college preparatory, academic course, which was broken into three strata, was on top, and the commercial course, which was more explicitly vocational than the earlier scientific course, fell below. The courses chosen by the students who entered in 1900 show a pattern of lessening interest in the academic course at each step down the class scale: This course was chosen by 72.2 percent of the students from the proprietary middle class, by 66.7 percent of the students from the employed middle class, by 55.2 percent of the students from the skilled working class and 14.3 percent of the students from the unskilled working class. The top track of the high school's newly stratified curriculum was most popular among the most privileged students, for whom it was a special school within the school. The new academic diploma provided these students with an exclusive and marketable piece of cultural property that enabled them to maintain their class position.[10]

In Canada, Tomkins has discerned similar patterns of academic dominance in his recent comprehensive curriculum history[11] and likewise in contemporary Australia, particularly as detailed in Connell's most recent work on schools in South Australia. In *Teachers' Work* Connell focuses on the consequences of curriculum construction for teachers for 'as well as being a definition of the pupils' learning, "the curriculum" is also a definition of the teacher's work. The way it is organized and the social practices that surround it, have profound consequences for teachers'. Connell found that in all the schools studied 'a particular way of organizing knowledge and learning was hegemonic'.

I will call this the 'competitive academic curriculum'. To say it is hegemonic is not to say it is the only curriculum in those schools. It is to say that this pattern has pride of place in those schools; it dominates most people's ideas of what real learning is about – its logic has the most powerful influence on the organization of the school, and of the education system generally; and it is able to marginalize or subordinate the other curricula that are present.[12]

The competitive academic curriculum alienates and eventually excludes the majority of children. This poses a harsh dilemma for the teachers: a dedicated group who do not willingly wish to fail the majority year in and year out. But, says Connell, 'the competitive academic curriculum makes the sorting and the hardening of hearts a central reality of contemporary school life'. This stiffens the dilemma for teachers, for most of them do not need researchers to tell them that the testing and streaming system has ill-effects on school life.

As a result, the persistent failing of the majority through the academic curriculum leads to recurrent calls for reform: particularly attempts at unstreaming. Connell describes one such initiative where a new social science curriculum was introduced to unstreamed classes. Far too many problems arose, however, for the experiment to be sustained. A range of 'behaviour problems' arose, particularly problematic was that the top ability children needed 'more reward'. The teachers concluded that since children are not 'equal' you cannot teach them as if they were. So, says Connell, runs the argument but he judges that it misses two vital ingredients.

> One is the politics of the situation where unstreamed classes have been tried . . . generally introduced in the face of scepticism and resistance lacking support staff and relevant training, short on appropriate and varied materials.

The second,

> more subtle but perhaps more basic, is the question of where these conceptual categories of ability and pace, this unit of teaching, and this conception of learning, actually come from. They do not fall from the sky. . . . I would argue that they arise from particular educational practices; specifically that they are generated by, or at least strongly shaped by, the competitive academic curriculum. It is the kids ease and skill with this particular organization of learning that is constantly at issue in the 'streaming' debates. To the extent that the school defines its offer of teaching in terms of this curriculum, 'mixed ability' becomes a problem and streaming a resolution of it. The connections are so close that streaming can virtually be regarded as the institutionalized form of the competitive academic curriculum. It is very difficult to run that sort of curriculum without a streamed school.[13]

Throughout the Western world the hegemonic academic curriculum plays a central role in schooling. Our historical study has shown that the relationship between curriculum, class and credentials is tightly patrolled, because here we are in the heartland of the production and reproduction of social hierarchy. The defence of these structures of curriculum differentiation and assessment ensures that educational reforms are persistently frustrated if they seek to challenge social hierarchies. Likewise the culture of teachers and pupils, the work process of both, derives from these structures. Academic subjects make academic subjectivities – a patterning of consciousness as to what schooling and ability are about. Only curriculum and assessment reform therefore, of the substantial sort that Hargreaves defines, could transcend existing patterns of educational achievement.

Concluding remarks

In reading and rereading the essays in this volume, and in focusing on Hargreaves' work, what I have found fascinating is the manner in which my immersion in historical data and the analysis of that data has led me to a similar point in the understanding of patterns of hierarchy and hegemony. This point of convergence with Hargreaves has not been easily reached. On

the way I have at times disagreed with the tone of some of his arguments –
perhaps most notably in his debate with scholars from the Centre for
Contemporary Cultural Studies at the University of Birmingham. But if I
have at times been uncertain of tone and tenor, over the years I have become
convinced, to quote Hemingway, of his 'purity of line'. For in part the focus
of our investigation as well as our tenacity of purpose is a statement not about
our disinterested scholarship but about what our scholarship is interested in:
in short about values and commitments. In this sense Hargreaves' return to
his room in Accrington is of more than symbolic significance, more than an
act of nostalgia and self-indulgence. It may of course be all those things but at
the end of the day his work is driven by a desire to understand patterns of
hierarchy and hegemony. I am ultimately convinced that he follows the ideal
that to understand may be to begin to undermine. If that be so there is no
better way to position the revival and reconstitution of the social scientific
investigation of schooling.

PART 1

Curriculum Reform

1 The Rhetoric of School-Centred Innovation

Introduction

Two very different movements have been present in recent patterns of curriculum development and change in Britain. On the face of it, they are worlds apart, diametrically opposed even. The first concerns the growing involvement of the Centre, of National Government and the Department of Education and Science (DES) in the direct control, administration and monitoring of the school curriculum. Because of wide media coverage of the host of official educational documents and measures which have marked the state's long and sustained endeavour to exercise greater control over what is learned and by whom in schools – its attempt to bind schools more firmly in the service of society – this movement has become the best-known one to the public at large and the most contentious among professional educators. The teaching profession – raised on a tradition of school and classroom autonomy – has been voluble in its protests against moves towards greater central control of the curriculum; and academics of different persuasions have registered their own dissatisfactions about the secret activities of the 'mandarins' of the DES,[1] about their attempt, with parliamentary government, to control the educational system by much closer regulation of the school curriculum and teacher practice than the broader and looser *licensed* autonomy that had been granted to teachers during the era of educational and economic expansion.[2] And they have shown themselves to be wary of the ideologically loaded language in which HMI and DES documents have been couched.[3] Publicly, the centralizing tendency of curriculum change, culminating in the introduction of a National Curriculum, has been the most visible and best-known one, and professionally it has certainly been the most contentious, occasioning the greatest amount of controversy and dissent. I shall return to the issues surrounding centralized curriculum control and the development of a National Curriculum a little later in the book. My immediate concern is with what was for some time an equally profound and vigorous, if less clearly defined movement of curriculum change: that of a more school-based nature. An inspection of the fate and fortunes of this second, more localized mode of curriculum innovation is interesting and valuable in itself. Such an examination will also highlight some of the more important factors underlying the remarkable surge of interest in and pressure towards the alternative pattern of curriculum development which has now become familiar to us – that comprising a National Curriculum. In some respects, within the failures and limitations of school-based curriculum development can be read the origins of National Curriculum control.

The decentralizing or localizing tendency towards innovation in curriculum provision and in-service training (these things have tended to be linked) at the level of the school has been not so well known to those outside schooling. Yet it has until recently pervaded the everyday experience of many teachers. This pattern has been variously referred to as school-based curriculum development, school-focused curriculum development, school-based in-service education and training (INSET) and school-focused INSET. I shall refer to them all as school-centred innovation (SCI) for short, since it is their common localizing tendency rather than the fine distinctions which separate them that concerns me here.

The proponents of SCI have claimed that it has had a staggering impact on the educational system far in excess of the amount of public recognition accorded it.[4] In part, this suggested strength and novelty of SCI has possibly been overrated by its advocates because the processes to which it refers had been going on unnoticed many years before the advent of the 'school-based'/ 'school-focused' label. However, the movement has not, as some writers have implied,[5] simply been a modest extension of a long-established trend, but has been shaped through definite, concerted and co-ordinated initiatives, that together far outweigh the previously disparate activities of thoughtful and enlightened teachers and heads in separate schools. That concerted effort can be seen in the very sizeable body of literature on SCI – in primers and readers for those new to the field,[6] as well as in well-known educational journals,[7] especially those which have published special issues on the subject.[8] In addition, conferences on different aspects of SCI have been held,[9] and various initiatives of some magnitude have been taken to generate, co-ordinate and evaluate large-scale programmes of school-centred work across the country.[10] All this frenetic activity might in one sense be viewed as an elaborate smokescreen to disguise the more overtly and politically contentious efforts of the state to exercise central direction over the curriculum. While there is some truth in this, SCI has been more than just talk and rhetoric. A good deal of real and consequential work has been going on within the schools themselves. This appears, in fact, to be one of those proverbial cases where there is no smoke without fire.

When one peers into the flames of SCI, though, the most discomforting fact is the absence of that scepticism and watchfulness among academics and practitioners which so strongly characterizes the debate surrounding the centralizing tendency of curriculum change. In effect, SCI has been optimistically and zealously advanced as both guardian, if not modern patron, of teacher autonomy and professionalism and as a likely cure for much of the current educational malaise. This is not to deride the *principles* of SCI; principles which, in large part, accounted for its emergence. Against the backdrop of the failure of nationally based programmes of curriculum change, and the difficulties that teachers commonly experience when trying to apply the insights of university, college and LEA provided courses to the everyday demands of school life, SCI undoubtedly offered the very real hope that curriculum development and in-service training could be successfully related to the particular needs of each school for which it catered. And into the bargain, it promised to achieve these ends at considerably less expense than non-school-centred programmes.[11] Moreover, in an educational system beleaguered by falling rolls and economic cuts, SCI has also been viewed as a way of compensating for the erosion of career opportunities by involving teachers in school decision-making processes. Thus, SCI has come to be regarded as a way of allowing innovation to 'take' at low cost while maintaining motivation and morale among teachers.[12] It is not the least bit surprising, then, that so much hope, faith, time and energy should have been invested in it.

However, what gives cause for concern is the fact that hope, faith and optimism have not so much permeated the discussions and evaluations of SCI as consumed them. In these discussions and commentaries, the virtues and successes of SCI appear to have been legion; its drawbacks and failures few. Such a heavy skewing of discussion away from sharp and constructively critical analysis of SCI has created quite serious and widespread misunderstandings of the actuality of decision-making processes and their consequences at the level of the school. Given that strong wave of optimism, sometimes amounting to only mildly restrained self-congratulation on the part of those involved as leading participants in SCI, those misunderstandings may, in the short run, have been politically apposite ones, confirming an optimistic democratic and 'sensibly' pragmatic ideology of SCI which served to direct professional attention away from those things which other educational researchers have long held to be at the heart of the schooling process and which give it life – processes of conflict and struggle, power and constraint, domination and persuasion, the creation of consent and the suppression of opposition, and so forth. A proper appraisal of SCI and the likelihood of its long-term success should at all times embrace these other, less obviously appealing and benign aspects of formally democratic and collaborative decision-making processes. Such micropolitical realities of curriculum change must be subject to the most rigorous scrutiny. In the discussions of SCI, that task has scarcely been dealt with. And that is a pity. Perhaps if the micropolitical realities of SCI had been properly grappled with in the first instance, if some short term political discomfort had been tolerated, then the pretext for the superimposed introduction of a National Curriculum upon a school system perceived to have failed in reforming itself may have been avoided – or even if that pretext had not been avoided, its case may at least not have been so easily made.

Telling it like it ought to be: accounts of SCI

When one surveys the SCI literature, the dearth of rigorous, critical and empirically grounded accounts of particular schemes and projects is most striking. It is hard to find dispassionate studies of the actuality of decision-making processes, the particular forms that participation in decision-making takes and the effects that such participation has in the moment-by-moment process of deliberation. As Reid reminds us, curriculum decision-making is a process of eminently *practical* deliberation made in an institutional context and within a formal distribution of power and experience between teachers and heads that places constraints on the sorts of decisions that are and can be made, and on the kind of accounts that teachers and heads tend to put forward to justify those decisions.[13] It is disappointing, then, that so little of the SCI literature has given any sense of the dynamics of the decision-making process and its effects on the perceptions, motivation and morale of those involved. Instead, most writers in this field have been concerned either to persuade people of the importance of SCI, to outline the many possible forms it might take, or, somewhat anecdotally, to assert its success in particular cases. These kinds of accounts I call *exhortatory, taxonomic* and *reflective*.

Exhortatory accounts

Exhortatory accounts seek to persuade people that SCI *should* take place.[14] Like most statements published during the early stages of educational movements, these accounts are both intensely programmatic, issuing spirited moral and professional injunctions about the importance of school-centred work, and also rather vague, providing little guidance about the forms SCI might take, and the problems that might be encountered along the way. After identifying the failure of centralized and non-school-based forms of curriculum development and in-service training in the past, and outlining the challenge that a contracting school system presents to the educational imagination in the present, the authors of exhortatory accounts have fervently recommended the participation and collaboration of teachers in SCI. But the way in which 'participation' has been advocated has done little to further people's understandings or expectations of the particular forms that participation might take. Thus, in answer to the question 'what kind of a context is best for promoting teacher development?' Eraut includes 'participative decision-making and flexible policies' as one of the five defining characteristics of such a context, but never explains what these things mean.[15] Similarly, Sayer proclaims that:

a strategy of INSET which has the school as its starting point, is likely to encourage groups of teachers to do things themselves: the initiative is theirs, the exercise becomes one of self-development and active participation rather than 'being sent' on a course.[16]

Once again, though, what such participation would look like in practice and whether it would then be endorsed by all concerned is never specified. In this sense, terms like 'participation' and 'self-development' have barely any explanatory value at all. Their role in the SCI discourse is largely symbolic, their purpose being to arouse sympathy and support by locating SCI within the cherished tenets of social democratic thought and practice. Few could demur from the principle of participation advocated in this way, since all it seems to be doing is extolling virtue and pronouncing against sin.

Like primary school teachers who speak to each other as if they all know and agree what 'progressive education' means, then go away to operate widely different teaching styles in their own classrooms,[17] the enthusiastic proponents of 'participation' have almost certainly been hiding more than they reveal. Although, temporarily, this might have helped secure professional commitment to the cause of SCI, it is also probable that those who have then embarked on such schemes will as a result have been ill-prepared for the difficulties they would be likely to encounter in the process of deliberation.

In a period of relative contraction, with all the problems that this presents for the internal management of schools, the need to be cautious about advancing overly simplistic internal solutions to large-scale problems that affect the educational system as a whole is especially great, because the collapse of these proposals may not only fail to *raise* staff motivation and morale, but might actually *depress* it still further. Indeed, we will see evidence of such dangers in the next chapter. The recommendations of those who see SCI as a useful strategy for dealing with the effects of contraction should therefore be treated very warily. Claims about enlightened yet cautious advances towards democracy in school decision-making of the kind outlined by one headteacher, for instance, might fall into this category.

> I feel that we are moving steadily towards the position where primary schools will see it to be highly desirable, if not essential, to function as a team of professionals sharing fully in the decision-making. The day of the autocratic head setting his personal thumb-print clearly on his school is almost over.[18]

Now, it would be as churlish to dismiss out of hand such optimism about the growth of enlightened forms of school management, as it would be naive to accept it on trust. However, there does appear to be a danger that bland advocacy of increased participation in school decision-making or, even further, claims that such a trend is already well under way, might lead specialists in school-based INSET and curriculum innovation to embrace dangerously simplistic panaceas. What is required is close examination of the

forms that participation takes when it is implemented in particular programmes of staff development and curriculum change. In particular it needs to be
adduced whether teacher participation leads them at present to being *in control*
of the curriculum or to their remaining *in service* to ends formulated by
others. 'In service' or 'in control'? Paternalistic consultation or radical staff
democracy? These are just some of the alternative meanings of teacher
participation that need to be identified and examined in actual cases of
school–centred educational change, for the consequences are likely to be very
different in each case.

Taxonomic accounts

Taxonomic accounts are also programmatic, but more elaborately so. In
meticulous detail, they outline the many different kinds of SCI that might, in
theory, be developed. Such schemes are described in a hypothetical and
conditional language of the possible. The authors of taxonomic accounts
have taken it for granted that SCI *should* take place. Their more precise
purpose has been to specify the different conceivable ways in which it *could* be
organized, and their repetitive use of 'could', 'might' and 'may' has reflected
this. A good example of the genre is Henderson and Perry's work on
school-focused in-service education. In it, they have suggested that:

> Some needs *may* be met within the school, through staff conferences,
> curriculum development activities or personal study. Some *may* involve
> short-term visits to other schools, longer-term exchanges of staff be-
> tween schools, or study groups involving two or more schools in a
> locality. . . . Other types of need *may* be met by a consultancy approach;
> by the school inviting, say a local authority advisor, a training institution
> lecturer, or a teacher from elsewhere into the school to work with the
> whole staff, a small group of teachers, or an individual teacher. . . . One
> mode of consultancy operation *might* be the school-based course. An
> extension of this, when the same needs are being felt by a number of
> neighbouring schools, is a locally-based course or study group on a
> more conventional pattern, based in one of the schools concerned, a
> teachers' centre, or a local institution. [my italics].[19]

Though writers such as Henderson and Perry have drawn a number of
important fine conceptual distinctions within SCI (for example, between
school-based and school-focused work), the more powerful theme pervad-
ing their accounts has been that of the immensely, almost infinitely diverse
forms that SCI *might* take.

This celebration of an open horizon of possibilies for SCI has been taken
one stage further by a small but influential group of writers who have
constructed formidably complex taxonomies in an attempt to illustrate all the
possible intersections between the many different dimensions along which
varieties of SCI might be arranged. Bolam, for instance, devised an analytic

framework for classifying different ways of evaluating INSET programmes.[20] Here, the particular nature of an INSET evaluation activity was defined in a three-dimensional matrix at the intersection of the type of INSET evaluator (school, LEA, etc. – four types in all); the nature of the evaluation task (negotiating access, disseminating findings etc. – six types in all); and the target of the evaluation (school, LEA, etc. – five types in all). This created a total of 120 possible varieties of evaluation activity. Alexander presented an even more complex framework than this, which extended into four dimensions.[21] Perhaps because this would have been rather diffiult to represent diagrammatically, he opted to collapse two of the dimensions – the mode of the INSET programme (course-based, non-course-based, etc.), and the location of the programme (school, teachers' centre etc.), – into one. But even with this simplified framework, the matrix still generated as many as 486 permutations of possible kinds of school-focused INSET.

Undoubtedly these armchair exercises are very impressive undertakings. For all their taxonomic grandeur, though, their major effect was to draw attention away from the actual and patterned differences that could in practice be found between real, rather than hypothetical instances of SCI. Just as importantly, they led to a neglect of those common difficulties and constraints that *all* SCI schemes are likely to face within the confines of the wider educational, economic and political situation. The conjuring up of potentially relevant indices and dimensions 'in the air', as it were, aside from the everyday situational demands that teachers and heads face in different kinds of schools, creates a pluralistic and individualistic image of SCI which makes it look *as though* there were as many kinds of SCI as there were intersections of variables, and *as though* these intersections were in every case almost random, determined by the particular nature and needs of each school in its own specific locality. Thus while the fascination for constructing elaborate taxonomies – one great strength of curriculum theory – has certainly given a sense of the diversity of SCI, it has, at the very same time, precluded the careful description, explanation and evaluation of the nature and effects of teacher participation in different schemes. What it did, in effect, was to place the extremely important work of SCI outside the explanatory embrace of social science.

Reflective accounts

In contrast to the speculative and hypothetical character of exhortatory and taxonomic accounts, reflective accounts do at least present reports on actual instances of SCI. However, instead of being presented as carefully constructed research-based analyses, reflective accounts normally take the form of journalistic recollections authored by leading participants in or instigators of the programmes that are being described. Though the reports are not always unreservedly flattering about the schemes concerned, criticism is rarely more than mild or sporadic. Any reservations that are expressed are usually rather brief and placed in parentheses. For the most part, the dominant interest is in providing an account of 'how it was done' as a contribution to the overall pool of professional experience of those involved in SCI in order to develop and enhance a tradition of 'good practice' in the area.[22]

While I would not wish to impugn the honesty and integrity of these story-tellers, the accuracy of their accounts is always bound to be open to a number of substantial doubts. Firstly, this is because of the mode of reporting. Reflective accounts, rather like HMI reports, are presented as somewhat loose forms of description that do not allow the reader to check out the data on which that description is based, and therefore to assess its accuracy. The second problem concerns the status and interests of the reporter. Because of their commitment to particular projects, the authors of reflective accounts have a strong stake in witnessing them reach a satisfactory conclusion and may therefore be unreceptive to evidence to the contrary. Furthermore, given their relatively senior position within the school or the project team, contrary evidence may simply be withheld from them. They are unlikely, for instance, to be fully cognizant of the perspectives and reactions of all their staff, especially those of their more junior colleagues, or of any teachers who nurture hidden reservations and resentments about the change.

It is not unreasonable, then, to ask for accounts that are more open to checking and scrutiny. There are many ways in which greater openness could be secured, but some might include giving examples of the kinds of data on which accounts are based, identifying the people whose perspectives have been elicited, noting what kind of interaction processes have been observed, indicating how accurately these have been documented, and so forth. Certainly, a wider range of accounts than those offered by leading and committed participants need to be sampled. Only when these kinds of precautionary measures have been taken, might it then be possible to determine whether any administrative raconteur is an astutely observant participant, or an imaginatively unobservant one.

An ideology of SCI

The overall outcome of the speculative outlines and retrospective views contained in exhortatory, taxonomic and reflective accounts, has been an ideology of SCI which has given a distorted picture of the practice that occurs in many schools and of the consequences of that practice. That ideology has emphasized and encouraged increased teacher participation in SCI, but has not assessed the different forms that participation actually takes, nor the uses to which it tends to be put. In particular, it has failed to acknowledge the resistance of many teachers, especially probationers, to the very idea of participation,[23] or to recognize the ways in which senior staff often use a range of strategies in the decision-making process which have the effect of frustrating the involvement and undercutting the contributions of other

enthusiastic teachers within the school (see Chapter 2). Secondly, the ideology of SCI has stressed the value of collaboration between teachers, but has
neither examined the ways in which such *collaboration* is secured nor admitted
the presence and importance of conflict and struggle between different
teachers, subject departments and so on, in the process of educational
innovation.[24] Thirdly, the ideology has celebrated the evolution of SCI as an
instance of *grass-roots democracy*, which presents an important alternative and
counterbalance to the encroachment of centrally generated curriculum initiatives, but in so opposing these movements it has failed to examine the extent
to which the educational rhetoric and curriculum categories of 'standards',
'accountability', 'differentiation', and so forth, employed in local discussions
are themselves central in origin.[25] Attention has been focused so heavily on
the centre's unsubtle attempts to storm the front gates of the citadel of teacher
autonomy, that its quiet entry through the back door of SCI has gone
virtually undetected. This is an important oversight, for the centrally provided ideology may well, through the co-operative process of SCI, have laid
the discursive groundwork for later national intervention. It may have helped
generate and disseminate a language, a way of thinking about education,
among the teaching community, in which the ensuing case for national
co-ordination and control could be understood – a language that could not be
argued with insofar as it was, to some extent, already owned by teachers and
heads themselves. Fourthly, the ideology has posited a virtually infinite range
of different possible kinds of SCI, according to the needs and demands of
particular schools, but has not matched this elusive *diversity* against any
substantive study of existing practice. In other words, SCI writing has not
demonstrated the presence of value-pluralism. It has simply been predicated on
the assumption of that pluralism's existence.

Overall, then, the SCI literature has encapsulated the highest ideals of
liberal democracy as worthy and readily attainable goals in the management
of schools. In effect, it has promised no less than the realization of liberty
(individual diversity), equality (participation and grass-roots democracy),
and fraternity (collaboration).[26] Cast in these terms, it is not surprising,
therefore, that the ideology of SCI should have been imbued throughout
with a widespread *optimism* about the necessity and impending success of the
venture. In the light of the above observations, though, and with the added
advantages of hindsight, this optimism seems to have been less than fully
warranted. However, just as disconcerting as the distortions created by the
'hard sell' approach of much of the SCI literature is the fact that most of the
rather limited amount of empirical research in this area has tended, because of
its methodological orientation, to reinforce rather than dispel the myths that
programmatic and retrospective accounts have generated. This research will
now be examined carefully in order to elucidate the exact ways in which
it has tended to confirm rather than challenge existing professional assumptions.

Research on SCI

In the modest amount of research that has been conducted on SCI, two strands are dominant. These are the traditions of survey research and 'tied' evaluation. Though the merits and demerits of each of these traditions are now reasonably well known, appreciation of their limitations has not really penetrated into the SCI literature. For that reason, while the following points are hardly 'news' in the most general sense, they are worth reiterating in this particular context.

The survey tradition

A small number of studies of involvement in school decision-making have tried to discover staff perceptions of the decision-making process on the basis of questionnaires administered to a large sample of teachers. One of the largest surveys of this kind was Cohen and Harrison's study of decision-making in Australian schools.[27] Amongst other things, they were interested in who participates in making curriculum decisions. As part of their research, they carried out a national survey of the principal, three heads of departments and ten teachers in each of 98 secondary schools. One of their findings – for them a lamentable one – was that only 24 per cent of the sample considered that school objectives were written by the total staff. The researchers then claimed that this finding – an alleged indicator of low rates of teacher participation – was, as the others, 'generalizable to all Australian secondary schools because of the rigorous method of sampling' (a stratified random sample). This led them to bemoan the widespread absence of systems of participatory decision-making in Australian secondary schools.

In advancing strong claims for the generalizability of their findings about school decision-making, Cohen and Harrison were drawing sensibly on the traditional strength of survey research – its capacity to generate findings which are broadly applicable to a large number of people and institutions. But the crucial question which is begged in research which tries to get at people's perspectives on social life, via the survey method, is not the generalizability of the findings but their validity. Simply put, what people write 'in the cold' as a response to a brief item on a questionnaire, is often a poor document of their everyday working perspectives. If researchers want to examine the complexity of decision-making processes and people's perceptions of those processes, the questionnaire is therefore likely to prove a rather clumsy, inaccurate and imprecise tool. For instance, Cohen and Harrison give no indication of what 'participation' means to the participants; nor is their indicator of teacher participation – the staff's inclusion in writing curriculum objectives – a self-evidently valid one. The writing of curriculum objectives may be only one small part of the curriculum decision-making process and an unimportant one at that. Nowhere is it stated that teachers attribute any great importance to formally written objectives. For them, this may be only a nominal exercise, 'real' participation taking other forms.

Furthermore, the statement that objectives were written by 'the whole staff' may mean a host of different things. Written simultaneously? Written by a working party chairperson then co-ordinated with the statements of other working party chairpersons? Written by the headteacher after canvassing the views of individual members of staff? With or without their knowledge? Or what?

The overall consequence of such survey studies of teacher participation in curriculum decision-making is that unwarranted claims are made about allegedly generalized features of the decision-making process on the basis of what, given the methodology, are unavoidable simplifications and misunderstandings of the nature, process and meaning of participation. Such misunderstandings usually lead to shoring up rather than questioning of existing political and professional values and assumptions about school decision-making. This is not because of what is asserted, but more because of what is left out – because of certain possible meanings of participation and collaboration that are kept off the agenda.

A good illustration of this is the influential research of Rutter *et al.* on secondary schools and their effects.[28] In their survey of twelve secondary schools, Rutter and his colleagues found that one of the variables correlating with favourable pupil outcomes was the existence of a curriculum in the school that was group-planned rather than fragmented according to the interests and whims of individual teachers. 'Schools where most teachers planned jointly', they argued, tended to have better attendance and less delinquency. They acknowledged that 'group planning took many different forms', but emphasized that 'in less successful schools teachers were often left completely alone to plan what to teach with little guidance or supervision from their senior colleagues and little co-ordination with other teachers to ensure a coherent course from year to year'. The pattern of decision-making that was found to be most closely correlated with favourable outcomes was one where 'decisions were made at a senior level rather than in the staff room but where teacher's own views were represented at the appropriate decision-making level'.[29] The conclusion the authors drew on the basis of these findings amounts to a vindication of democracy by consultation: 'The combination of decision-making by senior staff, after consideration of the views of the whole staff', they suggest, 'may be a good one'.[30] In the light of 'findings' such as these, it is not difficult to see why many critics have discerned a 'tight ship' philosophy in Rutter's model of the good school. And yet the basis on which that model rests is exceedingly fragile. In effect, the most important distinctions – between different kinds of consultation – are not made in the study. It is a banal truism that most headteachers and departmental heads consult their staff about curriculum decisions, at some level, in one form or another. What it is more important to know is the particular forms that such consultation takes and which of those forms are more effective. All that Rutter and his team have done, though, is to oppose a self-evidently virtuous model of order (group-planned curriculum, teachers' views taken into account) against an equally self-evidently unacceptable model of chaos (individually determined curriculum, teachers' views not represented). All the vital distinctions that separate 'ordered' schools from one another are glossed by unhelpfully vague phrases which refer to things like consultation at the 'appropriate decision-making level'. The most crucial and contentious questions concerning the *kinds* of consultation that are most effective – for instance, whether a consistently pursued policy of 'left-radical' staff democracy of the kind seen at William Tyndale school or Countesthorpe College is better or worse than an occasional series of paternalistic (or maternalistic) chats between heads of departments and their junior staff – are never asked. The fact that these kinds of distinction are not drawn and cannot be drawn because of the rather bland and undiscriminating kinds of questions that teachers are asked, and the fact that unusual schools are not included in study samples precisely so that those very distinctions might be highlighted, then enables the researchers to preach a homogenous philosophy of consultation, and to give that philosophy one particular interpretation. That interpretation – which as the HMI document *Ten Good Schools* also makes clear, views consultation as taking place within a framework of firm but humane leadership – therefore serves to reinforce rather than question by close comparison what is claimed to be existing 'good practice'.[31]

The tied-evaluation tradition

Much closer insights into the fine details of school-centred decision-making have been provided by curriculum and INSET evaluators. The great merit of their work is that, in comparison to survey research, it certainly enriches our understanding of the dynamics of the curriculum decision-making process and of the perceptions of those who participate in that process. A strong sense is given of what actually happens during the long and tortuous process of deliberation, and in some of the very best accounts, as in much of the work produced by the Centre for Applied Research in Education (CARE) at the University of East Anglia, the authors have shown a commendable capacity to carry the reader along with the drama of innovation as it unfolds. Here, the power of human observation is sensitively put to work so as to bring alive the dynamics of decision-making among teachers. It is not without some justification that this tradition has often been termed *illuminative* evaluation.[32] However, the immense potential of first-hand observation, as a resource for explaining complex processes of social interaction in the schooling system, has never really been fully harnessed because of the use to which that observation has been put – *evaluating* rather than *explaining* school-centred innovation. Of course, evaluation does not exist apart from explanation; indeed the two are highly inter-dependent. The problem, though, is that the quality of the explanation in terms of its *accuracy*, its *scope* and its possible *generalizability* to institutions beyond the ones being studied is severely restricted by its subordination to the requirements of evaluation. This is especially true in those forms of 'democratic' evaluation[33] where the subjects of the evaluation are involved all along the line in the process of evaluation to the extent of exerting a large influence over the collection of data, the production of explanations and the release of research reports. A flavour of this tradition is given in Henderson's work on school-focused INSET, though other examples would serve just as well. Henderson's argument is that:

> evaluation should be a co-operative activity undertaken as an integral part of the INSET activities by the participants themselves. Information thus collected might then be collated by the LEA or local training institution (and thereafter, perhaps, at the regional and national levels) in order that experience can be distilled and fed back to the schools.[34]

As with other SCI literature this writing is redolent with the irresistibly appealing symbols of participation, collaboration and grassroots democracy. If Henderson's prescriptions were acted upon, though (and in many places they have been), it is difficult to see just how any generalized and rigorous explanations of SCI could be produced when the evaluation is explicitly consumer-serving, internal, informal and judgemental.[35] Why is this?

The most central and obvious point is that the very existence of evaluation and evaluators in a school has an immense impact on the process being evaluated. Often, this is precisely what is wanted since one clear purpose of evaluation is the improvement of existing practice. In one sense, there is nothing wrong with this. Few people would wish to impede the process of bringing about change for the better in schools. But it is not possible to have it both ways – to change the decision-making process under review even as it proceeds *and* to produce potentially generalizable explanations of the dynamics of the process as it would have unfolded had no evaluators been present. In this sense, the distillation of *experience* (in the manner suggested by Henderson), important as it is, is a poor substitute for the generation and accumulation of rigorous *knowledge*. Of course, some evaluators might attempt to get round this problem by delaying the feedback of results to the schools concerned, but, even here, their very presence in the school as evaluators who are known as such is still likely to have a restricting effect on the sorts of knowledge and practices that teachers are prepared to disclose.

The very nature of evaluation (as opposed to research), therefore, makes it almost impossible for its proponents to tell either the truth (the problem of accuracy) or the whole truth (the problems of scope and generalizability). The latter difficulty is further exacerbated by the tendency of school-centred evaluation to be, in Henderson's words, both internal and consumer-serving. In short, school-centred evaluators tend to tie the analysis, findings and recommendations of the evaluation to a programme of change that can be practically carried out within the context of the school. This means that, while issues such as the time allowed for decision-making and the way in which working parties are composed often receive full attention,[36] rather grander interpretations of the dynamics of school decision-making, the implications of which might extend beyond the problems of particular schools to things like the desirability of the very institution of headship, or the level of financing of the educational system, tend to be ignored. These are just not 'practical' issues for any one school. Yet while such problems may be the least tractable ones, they could well be the most crucial. By keeping them off the agenda, the tradition of 'tied' evaluation may therefore be doing the cause of school-centred innovation a considerable disservice.

The failure of tied evaluation to question or challenge the boundaries of school-based decision-making is particularly important where school-centred innovation is stimulated by national government initiatives which carry with them the added incentive of financial support from the Centre. In the 1980s, governments have shown an increasing tendency to provide earmarked funding for particular initiatives like the Technical and Vocational Education Initiative (TVEI), the Lower Attaining Pupils' Project (LAPP) and Records of Achievement, where broad criteria have been set down which schools and LEAs have had to meet in order to receive the money, but where those schools and LEAs have still been allowed considerable latitude to develop the initiative concerned in ways that meet their own local circumstances and priorities. A requirement to undertake evaluation of the initiatives has usually formed part of the contract agreed between the LEA and the government providers. While this has opened the locally variable initiatives to a valuable process of continuous monitoring and review, such evaluation, however, has also tended to take a predominantly formative mode: being concerned more with helping the innovation as it proceeds rather than with producing generalizable findings about the initiative itself. Under circumstances such as these, where the evaluations are sponsored by those responsible for implementing the initiative, there are very serious doubts as to how far such tied evaluations of government initiatives are likely to challenge the boundaries, the very purpose, worth and validity of the initiatives in the first place, or whether they will be confined to more locally manageable questions of technical means. On broadly favourable evaluations of a practical sort, the renewal of contracts depends. In a climate of desperately scarce research funding, this kind of dependence raises profound questions about the capacity and willingness of the research community to challenge the political boundaries and context of school-focused curriculum development where necessary, rather than merely restricting itself to the more technical, managerial and immediately 'practical' aspects of the development process.

One particular strand of 'tied' evaluation, the 'theorizing practice' tradition, has attempted to make a virtue out of these fundamental weaknesses by pursuing a programme of action where 'the analysis of practice is followed by the application of relevant theory'.[37] This theory is not introduced from the outside, as it were, but is based on the already existing organizing categories of the practising teacher.[38] The aim, then, is to theorize teachers' existing craft knowledge for them (or, rather, with them) in order to help them cope better with their professional work.[39] The act of theorizing practice is therefore consciously related to the immediate practical needs of the classroom and, to that extent, is seen to be superior to the formal teaching of educational theory through the disciplines in a way that subsequently proves frustrating.[40]

This is not to deny the much under-valued qualities of teachers' practical reasoning, to which I shall return in later chapters. But there are also fundamental drawbacks to this eminently practical approach; and ones which have a certain political attractiveness too. The approach isolates the classroom from its wider determinants, whether these are in the authority structure of the school or in the economics and politics of education, and treats existing practice more or less as a given, attempting only to identify and theorize its 'best' features. Alternative educational practices, the political and economic conditions that might be needed to establish them, the social values that would be needed to support them, are therefore precluded from consideration. Furthermore, the use of teachers' present experience as the mainstay of the explanation of classroom practice, offers little hope of moving beyond the bounds of existing practice, of constructing collective and critical revisions of the nature of teaching. While teachers are left to innovate in this way by drawing on their experience alone, it is difficult to see, in the absence of any dialogue with other kinds of experience (not least with that of educational researchers, who have undertaken rigorous observations of school life elsewhere) how that experience can be extended or transcended. How, under these conditions, does one get to create innovative and imaginative curricula? How does one develop alternative pedagogies?

In the confines of the present schooling system, then, the truth of SCI is neither 'democratic' nor is it 'plain-tongued', as the theorizers of practice and advocates of CARE seem to imply.[41] It is not 'democratic' because, in the present system, teachers have particular interests to defend, especially those that attach to their subject identities. The prospect of establishing truth through free, open and undistorted dialogue between researcher and researched,[42] therefore, seems a remote one at present. Nor is the teacher necessarily the most likely party to breach the terms of the democratic bargain between researcher and researched. The researcher, while advocating plain-speaking at one level, also retains unequal access to the world of formal theory and its concepts at another, introducing these concepts into discussion in a way that leaves their origins and contentious nature unclear to teachers.[43] To withhold such theoretical knowledge during discussions and collaboration with teaching colleagues is, in fact, to engage in a kind of patronising disingenuousness. It is to indulge in an ethically worrying sort of personal inauthenticity with one's educational fellows. Moreover, researchers may also exercise indirect control over the release of findings by drawing on their own privileged knowledge about tight publishing schedules and so on.[44] Despite their claims to the contrary, therefore, it would seem that the theorizers of practice are not at all the simple, anti-intellectual men and women of practice they profess.

When taken together, these various difficulties – the distorting effects of evaluation on the processes being observed, the limiting effects of teachers' experience as a main platform for the generation of theory, and the covert importation by researchers of additional assumptions and unspecified theoretical and practical knowledge into the process of 'democratic' evaluation of collaborative research – are not conducive to the production of theoretically rigorous, methodologically cautious and potentially generalizable under-standings of the nature and consequences of SCI. For these reasons, it is therefore somewhat regrettable that the very great capacity of first-hand observational research to get to the heart of the actuality of school decision-making has barely been exploited because of its containment within a widespread programme of 'applied' educational research and evaluation. This is not to deride the undeniable value of applied research in other respects, especially as a device for changing the particular schools under scrutiny; but it does cast doubt on its worth as a means of producing valid and potentially generalizable understandings of the everyday dynamics of SCI.

Conclusion

To sum up, it would appear that while great amounts of time, energy and resources, and not a little hope and optimism, have been invested in SCI, its success has by no means been demonstrated. Nor, as we shall see, has its effectiveness in raising (or even maintaining) staff motivation and morale been evident either. In effect, despite the heady rhetoric of SCI, promising everything from an effective method of managing innovation in schools, to the realization of staff democracy, fraternity and liberty, its practical success in actual instances of school change has, judging by the very limited amount of research available to date, been questionable. Centralized curriculum reform, epitomized in the National Curriculum, the development of ear-marked government initiatives, and the abolition of the Schools Council, has come about for a number of reasons, many of which have nothing to do with the politics and practicalities of school-centred innovation. But the micro-political naivete, timidity and evasiveness of much of the SCI movement almost certainly holds some responsibility for producing that educational inconclusiveness within school-based curriculum development which has created some of the pretext for central intervention.

Some features of that micropolitical naivete and inconclusiveness have already been referred to in this chapter: not least the failure to address political differences and conflicts of interest within the teaching community, along with the wider structures of power and control in education which support and sustain these differences. The next chapter looks at one particular example of school-centred innovation in some detail from an observationally based research perspective, and finds in it a further explanation for inconclu-siveness in school-centred decision-making. This explanation looks deep into the culture of teaching and factors within it which inhibit and undermine school-centred curriculum change on a broad front, even when many of the teachers involved are, in principle, deeply committed to such change.

2 The Practice of School-Centred Innovation: A Case Study

The course of school-centred innovation is best described not through ideal models of implementation, nor through retrospective appraisals by involved advocates, but through first-hand observation by researchers who have had no direct involvement in the process itself. This chapter provides evidence from one of the few observational studies of school-centred innovation which describes and deals with detailed aspects of the decision-making process. It is a study which deals not with the ideal ambitions of school-centred innovation, but with the practical process of curriculum deliberation as it is developed and experienced by teachers themselves. Studies such as this enable one to grasp the less commonly recognized micropolitical aspects of school-based curriculum decision-making – to appreciate the significance of the distribution of power in the curriculum decision-making process, the different kinds of knowledge and experience on which the various participants draw during that process, and the ways in which these distributions of knowledge, experience and power profoundly affect the course and consequences of school-centred innovation.

The study focuses on curriculum decision-making in an open-plan suburban, 9–13 middle school. It is based on two kinds of data: transcribed tape recordings of a series of weekly curriculum decision-making meetings held after school in the summer term in which the head, his deputy and the staff of thirteen sought to decide on a curriculum for the following year; and one to two-hour interviews with all the teachers concerned. The meetings were instigated by the head and his deputy – the deputy nearing the end of one year full-time study for a higher degree at a nearby university where curriculum studies was one of his main courses. The first meeting commenced with the deputy head using the overhead projector (to appropriate theatrically orchestrated gasps of astonishment from the rest of the staff) to outline a model of curriculum planning. The early meetings (from which the data here were drawn) were then devoted to questions of a general nature, concerning the purposes of education, choice and responsibility, moral education, areas of knowledge, and so on. These were the sessions in which discussion was most wide-ranging and most vigorous, the ones in which teachers might be expected to be at their most reflective.

I do not claim that the processes observed in this case are representative of staff decision-making processes elsewhere. Any claims for generalizability must, in this respect, await further case studies. However, although the case may not be typical, it is in many respects an extreme case, a place where one might most expect teachers' thinking and their contribution to debate to be rigorous and reflective. The staff were young and energetic, the school itself was little more than a year old, and, as we have seen, the young deputy head had the recent experience of full-time in-service education to feed into the curriculum process. Participation was enthusiastic, and the response to the early discussions animated. Furthermore, in terms of topics selected and issues raised, the discussions were far from superficial. The teachers often touched on some of the deepest and most complex social issues with which schooling is concerned – for instance, whether it fosters the development of individuals or secures social order; whether it is a potent agent of social change, or whether its influence in this respect is minimal. The meetings therefore occasioned not only critical and vigorous staff involvement, but also consideration of serious, indeed fundamental social and educational questions. If one wants to find rigorous reflective thought in collective staff discussion, then this is the kind of place where one might most expect to find it.

It will therefore be revealing to examine the character of the actual discussion in that context. What range of curriculum policies and practices were discussed? How were those policies and practices introduced? Who introduced them? What kinds of knowledge and experience were used to support and justify those decisions? And what do the identified decision-making practices reveal about teachers' and headteachers' knowledge and about the exercise of power and control in the decision-making process? Let us look first at the kinds of knowledge and experience on which teachers drew during the curriculum planning process.

The use of classroom experience

When teachers accounted for their practice, they drew overwhelmingly not on the logic and principles of formal educational theory but on their own experience. This is not perhaps all that surprising. Writers like Lortie and Jackson also found this to be true with the teachers they studied.[1] But of all the different kinds of experience that the case study teachers may have cited, it was their experience with pupils in the classroom that seemed to count most and that provided their most common source of justifications. The particular *kind* of cases that teachers cited is of special interest, though. They were not just any old cases. The experiences on which teachers were drawing were experiences of a particular kind – a selection from a whole range of possible experiences on which they might in principle have drawn. It was their experience of the classroom, and especially of *their* classroom, present or past, which teachers cited most extensively.

The specific examples teachers used were often populated by some of the school's more colourful characters, sometimes to provide support for a proposal (if pupil X can do this, then anyone can) and sometimes to pour cold water on it (you could not do it with pupils like X). But in either case they played a crucial role in staff discussion.

> *Mr Banks*: May I just bring in Stuart Madison [subdued laughter] at this stage who's making paper with me? Now I know he can't make paper and he probably doesn't know it, but he's doing various experiments and I think he's learning far more because he's following his own line of thought and he realizes what works and what doesn't work than if he was guided more strongly, to be merely told what exactly to do and what to do next.

On other occasions, no background information was supplied; the mere mention of a pupil's name was sufficient. Staff only had to fill in all their relevant, shared knowledge about the pupil concerned to know without hesitation that the proposal was unworkable with pupils like this.

> *Mr Banks*: I think to some extent schools ought to teach manners, but you can't teach them to children like Simon Watson, for instance.

Particular cases might concern events just as much as specific pupils:

> *Mr Button*: I mean, there's some children – I know when I was in the third year, we literally had to write out timetables for them because they couldn't do it [organize their time].

The cases might have a comparative reference point with schools that the teachers have visited or worked in, in the past:

> *Mr Button*: I notice [name of school] do CSE work with children and they had to choose topic work. Well, very well, they – they would choose any old thing and very soon they – they would realize that what they've chosen is beyond them or it's not interesting enough for them.

Often, the examples cited were more general than this, amounting to claims – empirical generalizations in fact – about typical kinds of learning and behaviour in typical situations. The data base, though, was still very much confined to personal classroom (or playground) experience.

> *Mr Pool*: Well, what about some decisions as to how they organize themselves in the break time?

Mr Banks: Well they should – they should do that from their own initiative in the playground.

Mr Pool: What about this organization in the club – in the club atmosphere which they do after school?

Mr Banks: We see very little of that I'm afraid.

Mr Pool: Sorry, I missed that, Edgar.

Mr Banks: I said, you will see that *normally* in the playground of the school and you see very little of that when there's – There's very, very little organized games in the playground. You look along . . .

Occasionally, particularly when alternative possibilities were being presented, some of these claims were given the status of universal 'laws' of pupil behaviour.

Mr Button: Kids are gonna be kids. I mean, no matter how hard we try, they're still gonna cheek the dinner ladies at the end of the day.

More usually, the particular and the general were intricately woven together into a tight web of experience-based explanation. In one instance, Mr Kitchen, the head, addressed one of the school's central dilemmas – choice versus constraint in particular areas of the school curriculum in which certain pupils may lack confidence and therefore need the teacher's guidance – by pointing to the example of swimming:

Mr Banks: But if a child is frightened of something, it doesn't matter how you approach it, you find it very difficult to overcome this fear.

Mr Kitchen: Oh, I don't know. Uh – certainly in swimming, I've seen kids terrified and in a week or two they're swimming with the best of them. If you'd given way to that fear at first and not tried to bring them in, you'd never . . .

Mr Banks: Well you've go to be very, very gentle.

Mr Kitchen: You've got to be *very* gentle, yes.

Mr Banks: I mean, as soon as you force it, you might spoil it for life.

Mr Kitchen: It took Richard Shoulder three weeks to get into the water and the rest of the term before he finally got up to his ears. He was hanging on to the side. But, eventually, he was swimming a few strokes.

In some cases, such experience was explicitly drawn on to evaluate possible changes in educational practice. The likely consequences of innovation could be estimated by reference to teachers' existing knowledge about pupils and how they respond to different situations, such as making choices.

Mrs Fletcher: In any topic or project work where you allow a choice, you wouldn't allow a child to choose absolutely anything because *you'll all know* there are some children, for instance there are some girls who every term would do a project on horses. Or some children would do something fairly uninteresting perhaps on animals or something because they've either not got the confidence or they haven't had their eyes opened.

Note again here how the teacher trades on and indeed appeals to a shared cultural assumption among her colleagues that the meaning, the point of her example, is obvious, agreed, uncontentious. Indeed, when she punctuates her remarks with 'you'll all know', she actually helps reinforce that public cultural consensus about the meaning of their classroom experience. In the process, disagreement is made more difficult, for were it expressed, it would not merely be just another point of view but a challenge to a publicly asserted, yet taken-for-granted, educational consensus.

Looking at the decision-making process as a whole, the form of teachers' thinking and reasoning here shares very similar properties with that of recognized educational theorists. They made empirical generalizations, they tested general claims against the evidence of their own experience, they hypothesized about the implications of possible innovations, and so on. In this sense, the differences in thinking and reasoning between classroom teachers and recognized educational theorists are less great than is commonly imagined. But while the *form* of teachers' reasoning was similar to that of educational theorists, the data base on which teachers repeatedly drew was very different. It was a base of personal classroom experience. Like the elementary teachers Jackson interviewed, it seems that the case study teachers 'rarely . . . turn to evidence beyond their own personal experience to justify their professional preferences.'[2] That judgement is supported by some of the responses the teachers made in interview to questions about the kinds of factors that had influenced their present teaching style. Like the teachers interviewed by Lortie, the case study teachers, in almost all instances, were influenced by experience, not theory.[3]

internal factors, sheer hard experience, finding what works with certain groups of children, what doesn't, what falls flat on its face, what sparks enthusiasm, what doesn't, what gets the best response, what doesn't. Really, experience – the hard graft of doing the job (Mrs Speaker, third-year teacher).

experience in comprehensive schools. I was so repelled by some of them that I tended to go the other way (Mr Driver, third and fourth-year leader).

I've picked up a lot of tips from other people that I've watched teaching. Obviously, when you come straight out of college, you're raw and you're not fully aware of proper ways to teach and you pick up from people around you virtually (Mr Home, craft teacher).

Force of circumstances [laugh!] – just kind of physical factors of the group you've been given to teach, the other teachers you're working with (Miss Rogers, fourth-year teacher).

I have this sort of horror from . . . my probationary year, which was sort of a traumatic experience in this awful school . . . My probationary year was a great influence on me (Mrs Littlejohn, part-time French teacher).

You naturally learn from experience (Mr Banks, third and fourth-year teacher).

I think observation of other people at my last school. Particular teachers seemed to get what they wanted by teaching in a particular way and obviously I tried to copy that style with my own ideas of differences, slight differences (Mr Button, second-year teacher).

Other people and the way they teach, they way they talk about what they do, which I suppose just ultimately made me think about the things I do. I started off teaching very much with the idea of what I thought a teacher should do and found that it wasn't anywhere near as much as was needed (Mrs Gough, first-year teacher).

Variety of experience! Because I've been in various set-ups and seen things to commend them and things that you make a note to avoid (Mrs Weaver, acting deputy head).

Predictably, perhaps, the major exceptions to the rule that teachers are influenced most by classroom experience were the two novice, probationary teachers. Only two terms out of their initial training, they had barely had the time to accumulate the kind of experience their colleagues rated so highly. College was still the important thing for them, though interestingly, the tone in which it was mentioned was now almost apologetic, as if more worthwhile justifications were not yet available: 'I should think one of the major factors would have been my college,' said Mrs Raines tentatively. Mrs Home, the other probationary teacher, said, 'I suppose at the moment, I've *only* got my college to fall back on'. But even though these novice teachers were not yet out of their probationary year, the experience principle was already beginning to make its mark, as Mrs Raines made clear when she stated, 'I do observe other people's methods and try to adapt the successes they have to my situation'. Furthermore, when asked what it was about college that they valued, they mentioned not the educational theory but the more practical side of initial training, particularly the experience of teaching practice.

So, judging by what the teachers said in these interviews and in discussions with one another, they did not value educational theory as a systematic, coherent, and authoritative body of knowledge and insights that might have some relevance for their classroom practice. They rejected it in their initial training, and they continued to have little acquaintance with it and make little use of it in their current practice. Few teachers claimed to have much interest in contemporary writings on education. Mrs Littlejohn and Mrs Fletcher were sometimes given relevant articles – morsels of educational wisdom – by their husbands, who lectured in the nearby college of education. But with one exception, which I shall turn to shortly, the rest claimed that the most they could manage was a cursory glance at the educational press, a look at magazines that offered specific tips on subject teaching (for example, craft teaching, in Mr Home's case) or, as in Miss Rogers' case, an occasional thumb through a small education paperback, although even here there was the problem that 'it was very often hard reading, you know, and after a bit, you got fed up with it'.

These findings about teachers' responses to educational theory and educational theorists are not unusual. Teachers have little time (in both senses of that phrase) for the latest revelations of educational research. 'Fine words', they might say, 'butter, no parsnips!' When teachers are chained to the incessant routines and strictures of classroom life, as writers like Lortie and Jackson suggest, this is perhaps excusable. But when teachers such as the ones studied here become engaged in an educational activity whose central purpose is the reshaping of the whole curriculum in relation to high-level aims concerning the contribution of school to society, we should perhaps worry that they do not consider or refer to what some of the most careful and detailed educational scholarship has produced in response to these very questions. We should be concerned that they draw so little on the experience, understanding and insight of others outside their own school community. If teachers are discussing education and moral development, for instance, would they not benefit from consulting the works of writers like Kohlberg or Durkheim, who devoted much of their intellectual energies to this very problem? If they are trying to define areas of knowledge for a school curriculum, would they not do well to examine what sociologists and philosophers have had to say about such matters?

That teachers do not do so when their specific purpose is to question and analyse the very foundations of the school curriculum and education in general might appear to be the height of either arrogance or ignorance on their part. I want to suggest, however, that their public disregard for or indifference to formal education theory, although perhaps regrettable, is not indicative of any illogic and irrationality; nor does it indicate that they are bad learners, an 'occupational disease' that Waller alleged afflicts most teachers.[4] Rather, I want to propose that educational theory and other non–classroom-based explanations are excluded from discussions primarily because teachers deem them to be culturally inadmissible.

Non-classroom experience

There are two sorts of evidence to support this *cultural exclusion* thesis. The first concerns the one teacher (other than the deputy head) who did have demonstrably broad access to current educational theory: Mr Button. Mr

Button was an Open University student, who, at the time of the research, was taking a sociology of education course. Though he said he was taking the course 'purely for the money', to give him graduate status and therefore a higher salary, it had clearly made him familiar with a number of sociological critiques of schooling, which arose from competing 'definitions of the situation' (a phrase that he himself used) held by teachers and pupils; and he was evidently familiar with some of the Marxist arguments concerning the structural constraints on and contradictions of schooling as manifested in 'the liberal dichotomy' of education.

Elsewhere, I have described Mr Button as an extremist talker – as someone who, with his radical interpretations of schooling, constantly challenged and questioned the broad liberal consensus within which the rest of the staff aired their differences.[5] The effect of his contributions was to provoke strong disagreement from the rest of the staff, particularly from the head. He made them work hard at defending the boundaries of their practice. But even so, it is interesting that Mr Button's contributions came in short snatches. He made no attempt to mount a systematic sociological critique of schooling or to indicate the formal theoretical reference points, the names, and the traditions that he was using as a basis for such a critique. Presumably, any such frontal assault, any such clear opposition between school practice and scientific theory, and between their competing claims to truth, would have done even less for his credibility among school staff than the attritional build-up of extremist criticism he mounted instead. That Mr Button toned down his theoretical knowledge in staff discussions adds weight to the thesis that what we are primarily dealing with here in analysing the experience-based character of staffroom debate is not merely a question of cultural awareness of competence, but one of cultural exclusion too – a kind of exclusion that on some occasions appears to necessitate a measure of strategic compliance on the part of some of the teachers involved; a holding back of valuable inputs and theoretically knowledgeable contributions that might otherwise be made in the planning and decision-making process.[6]

The second form of support for the cultural exclusion thesis requires more extensive discussion. The case study teachers not only screened reference to formal educational theory out of their discussions but they also excluded references to many other kinds of non-classroom experience. In interview, the case study teachers often talked privately and extensively about a whole range of biographical influences they felt had had some bearing on their current approach to teaching. Seven of the teachers had spent a considerable part of their careers after leaving school outside the formal educational system. In interview, six of them spoke unprompted and at some length about the impact of such things as parenthood and other work experience upon their current approach to teaching.

Two of the female members of the staff who had taken time out from teaching at some point to care for their small children referred to the effect of these family responsibilities upon their present work. Mrs Raines, a mature entrant to teaching, stated that one of her strengths as a teacher came from maturity and from having children of her own.

> I do feel that I understand children better than, say, some people who have not got the experience of having children of their own. I know that children can be absolutely horrible and nice at the next moment. I don't expect them to be on a level all the time. I can take them at their worst and at their best and I think this gives me an advantage in some respects over people who may have been teaching for a long time but haven't gone through the same thing with children of their own.

Similarly, Mrs Weaver, the acting deputy head, listed among the variety of experiences that had affected her current approach to teaching the influence of her own children: 'What I want for them eventually in life influences me a lot in what I expect from these people, particularly my own year.'

Two other teachers mentioned that early childhood and their own schooling influenced their work. Interestingly, these were the other two female teachers who had spent some time as full-time housewives. Mrs Fletcher, for instance, remarked:

> I owe a lot to the way I teach – to my own sort of personal background before I was in teaching and the fact that I was brought up in such a strict regimented family, such a strict Christian background, that in order to become a sort of person in my own right, I had to question things and this, this has continued with me; my own sort of questioning mind of why, and is it worth it, and is this the best way of doing things, or what's the value? And because of the way educational trends are very much geared to questioning, and to children questioning things, I think it suits my personality.

Mrs Littlejohn, the part-time French teacher, also drew on her childhood experiences, this time as a pupil.

> When I was at school, I used to have to work to get anywhere because I'm not habitually sort of brilliant. At least, I wasn't. I always think I've developed later and I sort of think I've gradually got brainier as I've gone along. But it's taken me a long time and I've always had to work very hard. So what influenced me most is that I've tried to understand that here are a lot of children who are also like that. I've tried to make sure that when I explain things, I *do* explain things so that they can understand them. So that my own sort of difficulites at school have influenced my attitude to children there.

Mrs Speaker, who had not only looked after her children full-time for several years but who had also gained extensive experience in secretarial and clerical work before entering teaching, suggested that those parts of her career that had required her to combine home and work responsibilities may have coloured what she thought about children, homes, mothers, and work because, she said, 'I've done it.'

Of the men (three of whom had reasonably extensive work experience outside teaching), only Mr Driver saw the relevance of non-classroom experience for his current approach to teaching. Though he had been a laboratory technician, a Capstan lathe operator, a clerk and a foreman in the past, it was the experience of doing research for a higher degree that he felt was particularly influential.

> I realized that my first degree was a waste of time, that formal learning was by itself a waste of time, and that the important thing was under-standing, originality of mind, and the determination to see a thing through, rather than specific knowledge. From that has stemmed my dislike of exams, my dislike of assessment, and my dislike of too much formality, because I don't think they actually achieve anything. None of the things I learned for exams, for formal assessment, were ever any use for research. Valueless!

There are a number of implications one might draw from these citations of non-classroom experience among certain members of the case study staff. The preponderance of such comments among the female staff, but not among the male staff, is certainly a matter of some interest. It may say something about the kinds of roles that professional men and women respectively play in the domestic labour of family life, for example. Equally, it may be an indicator of women's greater readiness to speak in interview about the more personal aspects of their lives and careers. Important as they are, not least in pointing out the much-neglected influence of domestic and child-rearing experiences on the professional competence of many female teachers, there is not the space to pursue such topics here.

The crucial point for our present purposes is that although some of the case study staff were prepared to speak in interview about the relevance of their role as parents, their work experience outside teaching, and so on, these influences were virtually invisible in collective staff discussions. Compara-tive experiences were hardly mentioned here – be this the experience of training (mentioned only once and then only to exemplify the problems that teachers experienced as learners in the college environment), their own experience as pupils and its relevance to what they currently demand of their own children (mentioned twice), experience of school inspectors (mentioned twice), experience of parents (normally mentioned by the head who had most contact with them), and experience of colleagues (raised not in a context of criticism or collaboration but in connection with quite mundane issues such as the particular contribution the part-time French teacher might make to the curriculum). Thus, as a group, the case study teachers not only gave little credence to formal educational theory, but they also excluded from debate all those non-classroom experiences that might be relevant to educational discussion. If we go by the interviews, this was not for want of awareness and appreciation of their importance. The exclusion of non-classroom experience, it seems, derived not only from ignorance of the relevance of non-classroom matters, but also from cultural pressures and assumptions as to what constituted an acceptable account in staffroom discussion. In *that* context, it was the immediate, practical situation of the classroom that mattered most of all. This was the testing ground, the court of appeal against which claims to truth and feasibility were publicly measured.

This absence or cultural exclusion of formal theory and non-classroom experience has important implications for the conduct and consequences of school-based curriculum planning. Of course, in some circumstances, the absence or exclusion of non-classroom experience may not be especially important. As Jackson suggests, experiential knowledge of the classroom may in fact be highly functional for competent performance when applied to practical routines and familiar procedures in that environment.[7] Moreover, as Elbaz notes, 'to reflect constantly on one's teaching acts while they are going on would be to destroy the coherence of teaching and perhaps render it impossible.'[8] The value of teachers' practical knowledge, itself a kind of theorizing, within the classroom setting and the planning and evaluation that immediately affect it, should not be underrated. But when classroom-based knowledge alone is applied to very general questions concerning the aims, context and functions of education, the effects may not be quite so beneficial.

In the case study school, the absence of references to researching findings, formal theory and comparative cases in general discussions of the curriculum meant that the legitimate resources for debating questions of general social and educational importance became limited, in the main, to teachers' class-room experience and to their collectively uncontested assumptions about pupil learning.

The experience-based nature of teacher accounts had two major sets of consequences for the course and outcomes of the curriculum decision-making process. Firstly, it reinforced the capacity of senior management to set boundaries and limits to the curriculum agenda, to decide what the range of acceptable curricular practice was to be, to determine what was worthy of serious discussion and what was not. Secondly, the experience-based character of teacher contributions helped to sustain a substantial measure of inconclusiveness in curricular discussions, which in turn created a pretext for managerial intervention. Both these things had important implications for the actual value of teacher participation in school-centred innovation and for the forms of staff motivation (or their absence) that were associated with it. I shall now examine each of these effects in turn.

Limiting curriculum debate: the use of contrastive rhetoric

Fixing the agenda, setting limits beforehand to what will be discussed, is increasingly acknowledged as one of the most important ways that power is exercised through the decision-making process.[9] Those who have the power to define the agenda of debate also wield considerable power in influencing the decisions that arise from that debate. The decisions most prejudicial to participants' interests or aspirations are excised even before debate begins. A few writers have drawn attention to the limits that such processes place on collaborative decision-making in schools; on the ways in which participation can easily be converted into pseudo-participation when some of the most important educational decisions have in fact already been taken beforehand, or are made elsewhere; when much that is educationally important does not even appear on the agenda for discussion.[10]

There is less understanding, however, of the ways in which holders of power are able to draw in, define and defend the boundaries of discussion within the collaborative decision-making process itself. From the evidence of this study, it is my argument that the culturally based over-reliance by teachers on classroom experience as a basis for searching and wide-ranging curriculum debate creates ample opportunities for powerful members of senior management to draw in the boundaries of such debate. The strategy by which they do this, I call contrastive rhetoric. One of the most important conditions of existence for the successful deployment of such contrastive rhetoric, I want to argue, is the high priority accorded to classroom experience within the culture of teaching. This, along with the strategic intervention of senior management, places important restrictions on the rigour and scope of curricular debate at school level.

Contrastive rhetoric refers to that interactional strategy whereby the boundaries of normal and acceptable practice are defined by institutionally and/or interactionally dominant individuals or groups through the introduction into discussion of alternative practices and social forms in stylized, trivialized and generally pejorative terms which connote their unacceptability. The concept is in part derived from research on interactional practices among professional groups and from the sociology of mass media and deviance; but in the main it is a *grounded concept* formulated from the research as the most satisfactory method I could evolve of explaining the data to hand.[11]

One of the clearest and most lengthy instances of the use of contrastive rhetoric took the form of a discussion about Countesthorpe College, a well-known and much publicized comprehensive school standing very much outside the mainstream of educational practice. The discussion was initiated by the deputy head.

> *Mr Pool*: Perhaps I could quote an example where they took it [pupil choice] not only on an individual, intuitive basis of what's right and wrong, but at Countesthorpe . . . I don't know if you've heard of this school in Leicestershire? [Laughter] You have. Yeah. Well, you know what happened there. They gave the kids an awful lot of choice.
> *Mr Stones*: I've been there.
> *Mr Pool*: You went, Alan?
> *Mr Stones*: Well, my friend lives in Countesthorpe and she's . . . um . . .

Mr Pool: Well, can you tell us more about it? You'll know more than I do.

Mr Stones: Well, she's one of . . . she's a twenty-five year old who goes in with the kids to do her 'O' levels. She doing 'O' level biology and they just sort . . . well, I've not actually been round while it's working. I've been to have a look at it. But from what she says, you know, they're given free choice that the pupils . . . on what they want to do . . . you know . . . they can walk out half way through a lesson if they're bored and all this sort of thing. There are grown-ups and children in together on 'O' levels and 'A' levels and it's all sort of first name terms with staff. She only knows the two that are taking her for biology as Jim and Bill. It's that sort of set up.

Mr Pool: Mmm . . . And did she approve of it, or . . . or what? What kind of benefits or . . . or . . .

Mr Stones: She doesn't . . . doesn't like it. She doesn't like it. But then she's been brought up in a formal atmosphere.

Mr Pool: On what grounds? Just because it's different, you know, or has she got some sort of thing that she's got against it?

Mr Stones: Well, she doesn't like the way they can sort of just walk in and walk out and come in at any time and all this sort of thing.

Mr Pool: Yeah, yeah.

Mr Stones: She doesn't think that should happen. I don't know, she's got a bit of . . .

Mr Pool: The bits . . . the bits that I read the reports about it was that the kids were appointed to a . . . a home basis and then there were a variety of choices which they could make, whether they went and did . . . uh . . . 'O' level science courses or whether they went and did CSE science courses, or just a general thing anyway, or whether they didn't do science in fact. This went through a whole load of things. These specialist things were provided for them and whether they chose these was a matter of counselling on the part of the staff for the kids, and the parents' pressure and their own wishes of course. But apart from that, there was no . . . compulsion to go. In fact, stay in home base all day and read . . . just read comics until they got so bored with it, in theory, that they wanted to do something else. And if you walked around the school, you could see kids eating crisps and sitting around, you know. But that's right at the far end of what we're talking about.

Mr Stones: A long way [muttered]. [Concurring laughter.]

Mrs Home: A very long way. [More laughter.] Cos I can see the kids that once they get bored sitting around and eating crisps and reading comics, will just go out of the school and find something more . . . more exciting.

Mr Stones: Oh, they had the . . . trouble with the smokers' room, didn't they, which . . . there was a great big kick up about under fourteen . . . over fourteens select smokers' room. The headmaster there was

the headmaster at my school, Mr X in Southshire. He was the
headmaster for the first term that I was there and he tried to get
something off the ground like that, but it . . . he couldn't. It's a bit of a
stronghold.

Mr Pool: Really, I think it's . . . it's worth looking at these things when
you know . . . you do hand things right over to the kids and see what
happens.

As some of the better known and more unconventional features of Countesthorpe were introduced into discussion, laughter broke out. This was made
possible because potentially serious (and conceivably threatening) educational questions and practices were reduced to trivial, peculiar and highly visible
features of Countesthorpe culture – smoking, reading comics, eating crisps,
calling staff by first names, etc. There is much in common here with what
Cohen observes to be the usual way in which instances of deviance and
dissent are portrayed in the mass media. In such coverage, Cohen argues,

> Symbolization and the presentation of 'the facts' in the most simplified
> and melodramatic manner possible leave little room for interpretation,
> the presentation of competing perspectives on the same event or in-
> formation which would allow the audience to see the event in context. [12]

What Cohen means by symbolization is a process whereby,

> Communication . . . of stereotypes, depends on the symbolic power of
> words and images. Neutral words such as place names can be made to
> symbolize complex ideas and emotions: for example, Pearl Harbour,
> Hiroshima, Dallas and Aberfan. [13]

Even though it cannot be shown that it was anyone's particular intention to
introduce 'Countesthorpe' into debate for just these reasons, the effect of the
mere mention of the name – the evoking of a heightened emotional response
(in this case through the medium of laughter) – is undeniable. In the world of
teachers, certain schools like 'Countesthorpe' or 'Tyndale' become epony-
mous. Their very mention triggers off a vast array of educational fears and
uncertainties and symbolizes the threatened extension and incursion of
extreme or unreasonable educational practices. In the terse though graphic
descriptions of such schools, particular words and phrases are selected out to
conjure up generalized images of apparently anarchic and bizarre educational
practices. These images become so strongly embedded in teacher folklore,
that they need no detailed elaboration, only the merest allusion to exert their
emotive effect. Thus, after noting that his friend knows only the first names
of her biology teachers, Mr Stones adds without further explanation, 'It's
that sort of set up'. As with some of his other statements, the rest of the staff
are simply left to 'fill in' most of the additional and presumably obvious
details of 'this sort of thing' and 'that sort of set-up' themselves. The

statements are taken to be and treated as if they were self-explanatory. The interchangeability of teachers' standpoints is assumed.

The elements of exaggeration and stylization that permeate the discussion of Countesthorpe College add to the humour of the account and to the laughter it evokes. Like much routine staffroom humour, this serves to neutralize the threats presented by alternative practices and thus implicitly reaffirms the teachers' broadly shared existing conceptions of good versus bad teaching. An important feature of contrastive rhetoric, therefore, is the sometimes humorous but always dramatic definition of normality by reference to its opposite, deviance; and thus the demarcation (albeit a hazy one) of the outer limits of existing practice.[14]

Secondly, contrastive rhetoric demarcated the boundaries of existing practice at *both* ends of the educational spectrum. In other words, by excluding extreme and unacceptable alternatives of both progressive and traditional kinds, contrastive rhetoric specified the *range* of acceptable practice. It was by no means the case that contrasts were made solely with reference to extreme progressivism. Archaic traditionalism was just as much a *bête noire* for the head and his deputy. Thus, in the case of traditional schools, Mr Kitchen argued that

If we took conformity, a way to make them conform would be to blow a whistle and they'd stand still. Blow another whistle and they'd move into a line and the teacher would move them in. And I know a school that was like that. They conformed! But, my God, I wouldn't like it here!

And Mr Pool spun out a favourite haberdashery metaphor of his:

Many tight schools tell the kids what they have to do from thread to needle. They don't have to do any of that kind of [independent] thinking at all.

Very occasionally, the extremes at each end of the spectrum were highlighted by their juxtaposition in a single dramatic paradox which showed them to be only different sides of the same rather grubby coin. Thus, at one point, as when the headteachers combined the worst of two twilight worlds, mixing together dark visions of pupil anarchy with salutary images of headteacher despotism.

I mean, one of my lines has always been I want people to have as much choice as possible – that is, staff to be able to use their expertise, to feel that, 'Yes, I would like to try this out. I've got reasons for doing this'. [Mmm] Because in many, many places . . . I've been in so many places where . . . where they go on this choice business. Uh . . . one in particular I can think of in Halford where choice is the thing running across everything in that the children choose the colours the loo doors will be painted – and, you know, there's rainbow colours of them. They

choose a lot of pencils they'll have in school. They go to the County
Supplies Link and choose the type of books they'll have. It goes to these
lengths. And yet the head has got a most rigid grip on the staff, really and
truly. They have no choice at all! He's got this choice firmly fixed in his
mind and he jolly well makes sure they carry it out to give children
choice. And this is my big criticism of the place, you know, the staff
have no choice at all. And he . . . he boasts that he always takes
probationers. Now I know, he always . . . *always* takes probationers.
[Laughter] That's right. That's why he does it!

In this expertly constructed paradox signalled by the grammatical force of
what Smith calls a contrast structure ('And yet . . .'),[15] many of the same
elements were presented as in the Countesthorpe case – the laughter (the
meaning of which is taken to be obvious – 'that's right'), the indications that
the case being discussed was an extreme one ('It goes to these lengths'), the
introduction of graphic images of the trivial and outrageous (loo doors,
choice of pencils, etc.). Progressivism and traditionalism were, therefore,
simultaneously united and distilled into a single fearful phenomenon, ex-
tremism: something to be avoided at all costs.

Contrastive rhetoric, therefore, presented stylized and trivalized images of
alternative practices, characterizing them as unacceptable extremes and
thereby implicitly drawing the boundaries around the permissible range of
present practice. Nor was this power to define the boundaries of existing
practice exercised by just anyone. In all cases, the contrasts were introduced
by either the head or his deputy; the instigators of curriculum change. In the
Countesthorpe case, for instance, it was Mr Pool who initiated discussion
and later reminded everyone of the extreme character of the cited example
('That's right at the far end of what we're talking about'). The contrasts, that
is, were introduced by the more senior members of the school hierarchy, the
holders of formally designated institutional power. Contrastive rhetoric was
a major part of their strategic repertoire; a crucial means by which they
translated institutional power into interactional power and thus exercised
control over the decision-making process.

That they were able to do this was in part due to the capacity of other
teachers to recognize the messages connoted by the particular images and
symbols the head and deputy presented and the trivialized and stylized mode
of description in which those symbols were enshrouded. The success of
contrastive rhetoric in screening out undesirable alternatives was therefore
contingent on the kinds of knowledge, experience and interpretative schemes
that teachers brought to the interaction, and on the capacity of its users – the
head and deputy – to trade on these components of teachers' culture.

The presence of considerable laughter was one testimony to the existence
of shared understandings of the symbols and descriptions in contrastive
rhetoric. Perhaps the most telling illustration of the kinds of response
generated by contrastive rhetoric, though, is to be found in the extended
contribution of Mr Stones to the Countesthorpe debate. This is an excep-

tional piece of data, for at no other time did anyone respond to the use of contrastive rhetoric as he did. Furthermore, he not only reacted to contrastive rhetoric, thus indicating his ability to interpret its symbols and mode of description, but formulated a considerable part of it himself. Much of the description of Countesthorpe College was indeed his. If we examine this case closely, we might be able to determine what it is that makes the case an exceptional one; why, that is, Mr Stones was able to contribute to the extent that he did. Accordingly, this might also tell us something about the normal pattern; about why other teachers made no such contribution. In short, why were most teachers receivers and not producers of contrastive rhetoric?

The reason, I want to propose, is to be found in the way that teachers draw on their own experience in educational discussion. As I have already explained, experience, especially classroom experience, lay at the heart of virtually all the contributions that teachers made to discussion. It supplied most of the justifications for the accounts they presented. But since most teachers' experience excluded even the most fleeting of encounters with educational alternatives, it is hardly surprising that they made little or no contribution of their own when the question of such alternatives were raised. Like Mrs Home, who speculated that 'the kids . . . will just go out of the school and find something more exciting' after they have got bored with 'eating crisps and reading comics', the teachers could only take the sketchy images with which they were presented at face value and react accordingly within the conceptual limits of their shared interpretative scheme. Since, in their experience, they had no previous acquaintance with the particular reality to which the image referred, they could not substantially elaborate on the image or dispute its accuracy. In this case, it was the absence of particular knowledge and experience rather than its cultural suppression that appeared to be the operative factor.

Mr Stones was no exception to the rule of experience. What distinguished him from the rest of the staff was not that he used criteria other than experiential ones to present and justify his accounts but that one fragment of the *content* of his experience – the Countesthorpe connection – was different. It was this that enabled him to talk about that particular alternative at unusual length; to produce his own formulation, that is. The *fact* that he produced a formulation was a mark of the atypical nature of his experience; but the fact that his formulation was consistent in form with the other instances of contrastive rhetoric used by the head and deputy was indicative of the sort of cultural resources on which he drew. In effect, Mr Stones constructed his unflattering description of Countesthorpe College by drawing on a standard repertoire of symbols of outrageous progressivism that carried the appropriate pejorative connotations; 'they can walk out if they're bored', 'all sort of first name terms with the staff', 'they can sort of just walk in and walk out and come in at any time'. To these symbols of first naming of staff, walking in and out and so on were added important descriptive and indeed implicitly contrastive qualifiers. Thus, the fact that 'first name terms' are, in effect, '*all sort of* first name terms' established that the first naming of staff is but the

visible tip of an enormous and dangerous iceberg of unacceptable pedagogical relationships. And the fact that pupils do not simply 'walk in and walk out'
but *'just* walk in and walk out . . . *at any time*' reflects on the shared
assumption that, in *normal* classroom relationships there are appropriate and
inappropriate occasions and reasons for this action. No-one *just* walks in and
out. Entry into and exit from the classroom are rule-governed affairs and
these rules are in large part enforced and interpreted by the teacher.[16] The
absence of such rules, therefore, entails the suspension of normal teacher–
pupil relationships. Mr Stones drew on those shared interpretative schemes
concerning alternative practices which normally enabled staff to interpret
contrastive rhetoric when it was employed by others but which, given his
incidental and somewhat second-hand experience of Countesthorpe, also
enabled him to produce contrastive rhetoric of his own on this one occasion.
What analysis of this initially discrepant case reveals, therefore, is that the
routine responses of the staff to contrastive rhetoric and Mr Stones's own
production of it were each the product of their drawing on a dual repertoire:
of professional experience on the one hand, and of a shared interpretative
scheme for dealing with educational alternatives on the other.

But why was it that the head and deputy produced contrastive rhetoric
when the rest of the staff, with one exception, did not? In my view, the reason
once more has to do with the different nature of their experience. Such
experiences are normally distributed very unequally between ordinary and
senior staff. In the main, regular teachers have little continuing access to
educational theory or detailed comparative knowledge of other schools and
practices. Heads and deputies on the other hand, while not necessarily
possessing sophisticated knowledge of educational theory or detailed familiarity with the administration of the schooling system, do move more
widely in these circles than their fellow teachers. This differential access to the
cultural resources underlying decision-making, therefore, means that the
head and deputy hold not only *de jure* institutional power, but also tend to
possess *de facto* interactional power. It is they who have the necessary
familiarity with educational alternatives such that they can introduce them in
an extreme way that resonates suitably with teachers' own conceptions of
present practice and its enemies.

The maintenance of the boundaries of permissible practice is therefore
achieved through a combination of three things: head and deputy headteacher
strategy in the form of contrastice rhetoric, the cultural resources which
teachers bring to the interaction (these consist of professional experiences and
shared interpretative schemes), and the influences of the institutional distribution of power on the content of those resources. Teachers' work and
headteachers' work, as it is presently defined, is fundamentally different. One
revolves immediately around classroom work and experience. The other
does not. This creates profoundly different structurings of knowledge and
experience between them and with it, serious imbalances of input and
influence in processes of whole-school curriculum planning. In some cases,
initiators of programmes of school-centred innovation actually build these

imbalances into the design of the decision-making process – by giving headteachers or designated senior teachers access to relevant pieces of educational theory, but not their colleagues.[17] Contrastive rhetoric with all its implications for the restriction of curriculum debate is one of the more managerially interesting realizations of this imbalance.

Inconclusiveness and intervention

Given teachers' extensive and almost exclusive reliance on classroom experience as the basis for their contribution to curricular debate, it is not surprising that the discussions often became inconclusive, speculative and tangential. The data at hand were simply not suited to the kinds of broad questions the teachers were addressing. At times, the teachers themselves seemed to be aware of this inconclusiveness and passed comment on the circularity of the discussion even as it is proceeded:

> *Mr Pool*: I'm a bit confused.
> *Mrs Fletcher*: This is all very vague.
> *Miss Gough*: How many times have we been round in a circle, John?

To some extent this uncertainty and inconclusiveness was itself prompted by the head and deputy, as when Mr Pool asked very early on in discussions if anybody had 'any things [ideas] they'd like to throw out'. The intention here, perhaps, was a pooling of ideas and experiences, but the effect was more like a whirlpooling, or 'pooled ignorance', as two critics of this process have called it.[18] This circularity and inconclusiveness provided ripe opportunities for the head and deputy to redefine, sum up, and close different parts of the discussion.

Despite such interactions, though, the process as a whole was generally exhausting and time-consuming. Thus, by the end of the school term, there was still little sign of a complete curriculum for the following term. Staff unease mounted. Even the deputy seemed anxious and uncertain when he confided, 'I don't know what level of [curriculum] integration there's going to be. Are they going to have class teachers or what?'

Matters came to a crescendo on the penultimate Monday of term. The head, who, in his deputy's subsequent judgement, had panicked, felt bound to produce the curriculum that the staff had been unable to devise for themselves. Entering the staffroom, he placed a pile of teachers' individual timetables for the following year on one of the tables. My field notes record the scene that took place almost immediately afterwards:

> As I entered the staffroom at 3.45, it was quite clear there was an 'atmosphere'. My own presence was hardly noticed, the air was so hot.
>
> *Mr Pool*: I wanted to integrate more. I thought we were, but that's been stamped on!

Mr Driver [furiously]: I've been given all science throughout the school.
I wanted at least to retain some maths.
Mrs Home: You never know where you are. The timetable's changing
all the time.   .
Mr Button: Well, I'm renewing my subscription to the *Times Ed* [the
London Times Educational Supplement presumably to scan the job
pages!].
Me [naively]: What's the problem?
Mr Button: Autocracy [accompanied by an exaggerated 'v' sign towards
the headmaster's office].

There may, of course, be a number of reasons why the curricular discussions at Riverdale should have been terminated so abruptly. Time, as other
researchers and commentators have noted, is clearly one important factor.[19]
The task of constructing an entire school curriculum is undoubtedly a
daunting one, and it is most unlikely that it will be brought to a satisfactory
conclusion in a period as short as one school term (the time allowed in this
case).[20] Nevertheless, it is reasonable to conjecture that even if greater time
had been available, as long as the teachers remained tied to their classroom
experience as a basis for decision-making, they might still have found great
difficulty in resolving or in dealing precisely with general and challenging
questions concerning the very nature and purpose of the education they
wished to offer in their school. Whether in the short or long term, then,
overreliance on classroom experience as an approved data base for staff
discussion has real material consequences for that discussion and for the role
of teachers within in. Classroom experience is of itself insufficient to deal
with broad questions about the nature and purposes of education, the place of
the school curriculum in community and society, and so on. The result in the
case study (though there may have been other contributory factors too) was
inconclusiveness. That very inconclusiveness in turn offered occasions for
the head and deputy to intervene and tie up the proceedings. Staff morale
plummeted, since their intensive contribution to curriculum decision-
making was apparently overruled by the head. Ironically, then, the process
that was in part designed to *raise* staff morale and increase their involvement –
a common aim of school-centred innovation – demoralized the staff and
dissociated them from the collective affairs of school life. The failure of
democratic staff involvement, due in part to the overemphasis on personal
classroom experience and the cultural exclusion of other kinds of experience
as a basis for collective curriculum planning, therefore created the very
circumstances that increased headteacher domination still further.

Conclusions and implications

The exclusion of non-classroom experience by teachers from the process of
school-centred innovation, we have seen, leaves teachers vulnerable to

manipulation and intervention by senior colleagues as they draw in the boundaries of debate or bring inconclusive parts of the discussion to a close. Given these consequences, it is perhaps worth considering why such exclusion occurs and how it might be remedied. Lortie argued that teachers retreat to the classroom because they can draw greater rewards for greater effort there than they can in the school as a whole.[21] Other writers argue that teachers and administrators divide the issues of school life into zones of control.[22] Teachers control curricular issues in the classroom and administrators control most extra-classroom and logistical matters, such as timetables. Because they are unfamiliar with the administrative zone and with the politics of controlling matters within it, schoolteachers are likely to be unsuccessful on those occasions when they do participate in schoolwide decision-making. The failure and disappointment that commonly results will then only serve to reinforce their existing commitment to the classroom above all other aspects of school life. If this explanation sounds circular – teachers are preoccupied with classroom affairs, which makes them fare badly in schoolwide decision-making, which makes them concentrate on classroom affairs still more – this is in part because the actual process it describes is circular too – perhaps viciously so!

A second and not incompatible explanation is that once the worlds of classroom teaching on the one hand and school administration, educational politics, or educational theory on the other *are* segregated in this way, teachers can then privilege the former against the latter as a way of defending their own competence and expertise and of undermining challenges to it from elsewhere. Hammersley, for example, interprets staffroom debunking of educational research and educational researchers as a cultural strategy for neutralizing threats to and criticism of teachers' existing routines.[23]

Either way, this culture of teaching with its privileging of classroom experience, presents such an historically entrenched obstacle to curriculum innovation that any policy of simple exhortation to teachers to draw on and accept wider experience and perspectives is unlikely to prove effective. In this sense, curriculum change strategies which address themselves to raising or altering teacher consciousness (either through formal teaching of the educational disciplines in initial or in-service training or through collaborative attempts to engage with teachers in theorizing about their existing practice) are unlikely to meet with much success as long as they ignore the conditions, demands and constraints that give rise to and provide continued support for the culture of teaching in the first place.

Instead, if we accept the general point that in cultural terms, teachers, like other workers, are creatures of their occupational situation, then we might do better to address ourselves to how the circumstances of the occupation might be modified so as to elicit a different kind of cultural response. In other words, if we want to change the culture of teaching as a basis for more open and rigorous curriculum planning we might do well to start with the structures that support it.

3 National Curriculum Policy and the Culture of Teaching

This chapter is concerned with different approaches to curriculum change. It starts from the central precept, advanced by Lawrence Stenhouse, that curriculum development is ultimately about teacher development.[1] Change in the curriculum is not effected without some concomitant change in the teacher. After all, it is the teacher who is responsible for presenting or 'delivering' the curriculum at classroom level. What the teacher thinks, what the teacher believes, what the teacher assumes – all these things have powerful implications for the change process, for the ways in which curriculum policy is translated into curriculum practice. Some of these patterns of thinking, belief and assumption are so widely shared among the community of teachers that they amount to what might be called a broad occupational culture of teaching. This culture of teaching, I shall argue, seriously inhibits practical curriculum change at school and classroom level.

Two widely adopted strategies of curriculum change – *cultural interruption* and *structural reinforcement* – at best ignore and at worst merely shore up this existing culture of teaching, thereby frustrating the achievement of substantial curriculum innovation. It is only through a third strategy, I shall propose – one of *structural redefinition* – that the culture of teaching can be successfully reshaped and the practical school curriculum be improved.

The cultural reproduction of teaching

Many of the dominant features of the culture of teaching are now reasonably well known, even if their range, consistency and origins remain matters of dispute. Teachers, it seems, are present-oriented, conservative and individualistic. They tend to avoid long-term planning and collaboration with their colleagues, and to resist involvement in whole school decision-making in favour of gaining marginal improvements in time and resources to make their own individual classroom work easier.[2] This classroom-centredness is indeed one of the overriding characteristics of the teaching profession;[3] a characteristic which arises from and is in turn fed by the daily, recurring experience of classroom isolation. That isolation is itself a product of what Lortie called the 'egg crate structure' of schooling: the fact that schools are segmented into isolated and insulated classroom compartments which divide teachers from one another and make comparison and collaboration between them difficult.[4]

Possibly this assessment applies more closely to the US elementary school teachers studied by writers like Lortie and Jackson, than, say, to high schoolteachers or to teachers in other nations. But it is interesting to note that writers on the culture of secondary school teaching in Britain have reached conclusions not all that dissimilar from those of their American colleagues. Thus, David Hargreaves has complained that the collective capacities of British secondary school teachers

> are distressingly weak. . . . The culture of individualism is by no means confined to pupils; there is a parallel culture of individualism among teachers. . . . In its ultimate expression, this culture of individualism among teachers produces a teacher who restricts his role very sharply to what he does within the privacy of the classroom. The general determination and direction of educational policy, both within the school and within society is someone else's business: he is simply a teacher doing his job.[5]

Add to this general orientation the necessities of coping daily with classroom constraints of low resources, poor buildings and large class sizes,[6] along with the strains that arise from the conflict-based character of the teacher–pupil relationship,[7] and one can understand why teachers become not just concerned with but also confined to classroom life and its problems. In circumstances such as these, it is hardly surprising that most teachers show little interest in becoming involved in extra-classroom activities such as whole-school curriculum planning.

For those seeking increased teacher involvement in school-wide curriculum change, the reproduction of this culture of teaching has a depressingly circular quality about it. The classroom isolation of teachers cultivates a preoccupation with classroom affairs, with those matters over which teachers have direct and immediate control and which consume the major part of their time and energy. This, in turn, discourages their involvement in school-wide decision-making. Moreover, on the occasions when they do make occasional forays into that wider sphere, teachers' inexperience and unfamiliarity with many of the issues and procedures is likely only to reinforce their view that their competence and expertise really resides in their own classroom, and that other matters are ultimately best dealt with in the principal's office.[8] In this sense, it is interesting to note that it is those teachers whose experience of extra-classroom duties is most limited and whose classroom survival problems and control anxieties[9] are most intense – novice probationary teachers, that is – who appear to be among the most unsympathetic to the idea of being involved in school–wide decision–making.[10]

The culture of teaching, then, is a culture in which classroom experience is exalted above all else in collective discussions of educational matters. It is a culture whose conditions of existence in the pressing and recurring immediacy of classroom work and in the isolated context of classroom performance make sustained and shared reflection of a rigorous nature difficult. And it is a culture whose conditions in the allocation of time to different areas of the teacher's task, place the classroom at the centre and all else at the periphery of this work. Once in motion, the culture of teaching is reproductive and self-generating, but only as long as the conditions of its existence – the isolation and constraints of the classroom, the limited opportunities for reflection, the minimal allocation of statutory time to non–classroom work – persist and continue to sustain it.

This relationship between the culture of teaching and the conditions of its existence can be further illustrated by examining one more feature of that culture – its division and fragmentation, especially at the secondary or high school level, along academic lines. School subjects are more than just groupings of intellectual thought. They are social systems also. They compete for power, prestige, recognition and reward within the secondary or high school system. Historically, Goodson has shown how school and university geography, for instance, first established itself through a process of upward assertion against the claims of other subject communities, then, by a converse process of downward domination, resisted the incursions of environmental studies into its newly won academic territory.[11] At school level, Ball has recorded how attitudes and responses to a school-wide innovation – the implementation of mixed ability grouping – were defined very much on subject departmental lines, occasioning conflict and competition between those departments.[12] Moreover, as both Goodson and Cooper point out, the subject department provides one of the major routes for improved prospects, pay and promotion within the secondary sector.[13] It is one of the major avenues for the pursuit of teacher self-interest, for the improvement of status, and the maximization of economic reward. As such, it is likely to act as a powerful source of resistance to any school-wide innovations which threaten its position through attempts to disband it, to amalgamate it with other departments, or to reduce its timetable allocation and thereby the size and scope of its influence on the curriculum along with the promotion prospects of its teachers. In such vipers' nests of vested interest, it is scarcely likely that attempts to secure an agreed whole school policy will meet with anything more than paper success.[14]

A second contributory factor to this process of conflict and division among secondary or high school teachers in particular resides in the fact that even at their point of entry to teaching, the identities of many teachers have already been formed predominantly on subject lines. This socialization of teachers into subject loyalty stretches back to their own experience as successful pupils, is reinforced through the specialist pattern of most undergraduate education and is virtually completed with exposure to a subject-divided and also subject-biased pattern of teacher-training.[15] This again has implications for the creation of loyalties and attachments among teachers to separate communities of interest within a school rather than the school community as a whole. It divides members of the subject community from one another, and also members within that academic community from those outside it, especially those within the pastoral and counselling systems.[16]

Thirdly, membership of subject communities, of different subcultures within the more general culture of teaching, usually carries with it a set of beliefs, assumptions and practices shared with other members of that subculture about how that subject is best delivered in the classroom. Subject subcultures therefore serve as a grounding for pedagogical subcultures. Classroom pedagogy – assumed best ways of teaching and relating to children – therefore tends to vary on subject lines.[17] This has been found to make teachers' experiences of teaching outside their subject difficult. Not only have they had to come to terms with different subject matter, but different pedagogical assumptions and practices, different ways of teaching too.[18]

These subject divisions, along with the differences they embody in attitudes to children and learning and in approaches to pedagogy, further reinforce those tendencies towards conservatism and individualism that characterize the culture of teaching more generally. When curriculum policy is intended to transform curriculum practice, it is this culture of teaching that strikes wedges through that relationship. Curriculum policy does not correspond with curriculum practice. The intended curriculum is cast adrift from the curriculum-in-use. The implication for anyone seeking to bring about radical curriculum reform is that they must face the formidable challenge of fundamentally reshaping this culture of teaching, and therefore of interrupting its reproductive processes. In the remainder of this chapter, I want to examine how well various curriculum change strategies have met that particular challenge.

Cultural interruption

The first strategy for breaking the cultural reproduction of teaching is that of cultural interruption. This is a process designed to develop, refine and transform the language and categories in which teachers think about their work. It seeks to infuse the teaching profession with a new set of insights and understandings about the schooling process. It proposes to lay the conceptual groundwork for a new, more educationally worthwhile and enlightened culture of teaching. There are two broad ways in which this can be done.

The traditional version of this strategy in teacher education can be found in academic, award-bearing programmes which draw widely on the educational sciences of sociology, psychology and philosophy, and, more recently, of management theory. Undoubtedly, in a personal sense, many students and in-service teachers have found such courses invigorating and exciting. The evidence available, however, suggests that on their entry or re-entry to practical classroom teaching, those teachers have quickly pushed aside or 'forgotten' these more general aspects of their educational studies.[19] Such studies have not easily meshed with their daily practical concerns, with the limitations and realities of their existing surroundings, or with the suspicion of change and cynicism about theory among their present colleagues. However enlightened they may be, individual teachers are in a weak position to combat the wider culture of teaching with all its resistance to educational theory and school-wide change that persists among those colleagues whose company they must keep when they return to school.

Academic programmes of initial training, taught courses of in-service training, and the stated aims and objectives of curriculum policy documents have therefore tended to expose teachers to theories, categories and principles which have often struck them as unhelpfully remote and disconnected from the particular needs of their immediate classroom and school situation. The gap between presented theory and experienced practice has commonly seemed too great.

In this context, the movements towards school-centred innovation discussed in Chapter 1 have offered a most attractive alternative. Such patterns of innovation have adopted a more pragmatic and appreciative stance towards teachers and their thinking. The advocates of school-centred innovation recognize that teachers already possess a wide range of categories for theorizing about their work. This existing knowledge and awareness lays the basis for researchers and evaluators to collaborate with teachers in extending that ability still further. As we saw in Chapter 1, relevant theory is not imperialistically shipped in from elsewhere, though, but is based on and built upon the already existing 'craft knowledge' and 'personal, practical knowledge' of the classroom teacher.[20]

This principle of working *with* teachers and not just preaching *at* them may be vital to the task of securing effective curriculum development in any particular school. It is sensible that curriculum research should treat teachers with seriousness and get a sense of the classroom and school world as they see it, of the meanings and frameworks of their actions. Without that understanding, it is likely that curriculum developments will be misconceived for want of knowing how teachers will interpret, transform and possibly even resist them at classroom level. But the difficulty is that while the existing qualities of teacher thinking are certainly received much more warmly by the school-centred pragmatists than by their more traditional academic counterparts, there is a strong tendency for theory to be applied and developed only to those things which teachers already value, to practical classroom issues, that is. Given what we know about the culture of teaching, particularly as we witnessed it in operation in the previous chapter, the use of teachers' present experience as the mainstay of explanations of classroom practice raises serious doubts about whether it will be possible to move beyond the bounds of existing practice to construct critical and collective revisions of the nature of teaching, still less to develop school-wide, state-wide or nation-wide policies of change. The likely consequence of much school-centred innovation, then, is that in the main, it will endorse and gloss what teachers already think and do. It will reinforce and rationalize the exsting culture of teaching, not transform it.

Of course, there is in principle no reason why the process of collaboration and engagement between teachers and researchers should not extend to inquiring into issues of power and constraint and their effects upon the classroom process. In principle, the consciousness of teachers can be heightened in relation to such issues as assessment constraints, subject status hierarchies, the effects of cutbacks in educational expenditure and so on just as easily as it can be raised in connection with more specifically 'micro' questions to do with the development of listening skills, pupil-centred group work and the like.[21] In practice, though, the policy initiatives and practical recommendations of curriculum collaborators tend to run in one of these directions only – the one most immediately and practically amenable to *individual* teacher intervention. The work of writers like Olson exemplifies this tendency and the pragmatic, humanistic approach towards changing curriculum practice, on which it rests.

Olson draws upon his research into how teachers respond at classroom level to the principles and intentions built into the British Schools Council Integrated Science Project (SCISP), to point to the recurrent failure of curriculum developers to take account of the language and daily working problems of teachers. Innovators, he argues,

> need to learn more about the theories teachers have about their work, and to learn the language teachers use to describe and explain their actions. Such knowledge can then become the starting point for effective curriculum renewal – by paying attention to problems of communication.[22]

Olson goes on to refer, if somewhat *en passant*, to the difficult constraints and dilemmas with which teachers have to cope during the course of their work – with examination constraints, for instance. But overall, he seems much less interested in the nature of those constraints, or indeed in their relative tractability or intractability, than in how teachers *perceive* them. This leads to some intriguing policy recommendations. For after noting that, for example, science teachers twist SCISP material to suit the constraints and demands of the existing examination system, Olson does not then advocate the reform, still less the abolition of those examinations. Instead, he notes only that 'the person who wishes to communicate ideas to teachers is going to have to understand the network of beliefs that teachers hold and what particular terms mean within such networks'.[23] The language of innovations, that is, 'is in need of translation into practitioner language' if the 'innovative ideas are to be understood'.[24] The basic problem of teacher reception of innovation, then, is ultimately perceived not as one of social constriction and constraint which might suggest a contentious need for organizational and structural reform of the education service, but as essentially one of language and communication.

Interesting as this analysis is, and important though its recommendations are in emphasizing the need to understand teachers' own perspectives on innovation and classroom life, it has to be said that in stressing the importance of teachers' own language and thinking on curriculum matters, it does not really deal with the conditions and constraints which sustain that culture of teaching. In effect, Olson converts a sound interpretive principle of innovation (it is important to appreciate and take account of the teacher's initial viewpoint) into a dubious practical endorsement and embellishment of the existing culture of teaching (let us translate our curriculum materials so that they mesh with teachers' existing language and concerns!) If indeed this emphasis on teachers' existing language truly is the prime course of action being recommended by Olson, he would do well to recall the debate which took place in connection with another kind of language use, that of working class pupils in classrooms, some twenty years ago.

Like Bernstein's widely known early work on working class children's use of what he called restricted linguistic codes,[25] many curriculum packages of a mechanistic kind, employing a model of technical efficiency, have been predicated on a deficit view of teachers' language and thinking.[26] This sometimes led to curriculum developers specifying their curricular and pedagogic instructions to teachers in insultingly laborious detail, to try and make their packages as 'teacher proof' as possible. As Apple has pointed out, though, the untenability of this position is demonstrated by the fact that teachers using such packages have stubbornly insisted on going on thinking for themselves all the same: adapting, reshaping and redefining the package materials to suit their own continuing purposes in ways that the package developers could scarcely have predicted.[27]

Writers in the humanistic tradition, like Olson, have tried to remedy the defects of this approach by pointing to the rich store of personal constructs and forms of practical reasoning which teachers possess, constructs which, in their own way, are every bit as sophisticated (if not quite so pretentious) as the forms of reasoning expounded by curriculum developers and academic educationists.[28] To put it another way, humanistic writers seem to be saying that teachers do not use a 'restricted' form of theoretical language compared to the more 'elaborate' forms of their academic counterparts, but that both teachers and academics employ forms of reasoning which are appropriate to the respective contexts in which they operate. The two groups are in that sense neither better nor worse than one another – merely different. It is therefore incumbent upon the academic educator to evaluate teachers' language and thinking on its own merits, in terms of the practical contexts for which it is best suited, rather than measuring it by the yardsticks of intellectual coherence and fluency more appropriate for the university seminar.

All this is reminiscent of the responses made by cultural difference theorists to Bernstein's 'deficit' model of working class language in the early 1970s –

for they too insisted it is possible to identify a richness, worthwhileness and inner coherence in the language used by hitherto sociologically stigmatized groups (in their case working class and ethnic minority pupils) if trouble is taken to evaluate it in its own terms and in terms of its appropriateness for the context in which it is normally used.[29]

In either case – pupils' language and culture, or teachers' language and culture – much time and energy has, in fact, been needlessly wasted on the polarized questions of deficit and difference; on the issue of whether the language and culture of teachers or of working class/ethnic minority pupils is really worthwhile or not. The important point is not that language and thinking are appropriate to social context, but that they are fundamentally shaped by the *particular kinds* of context which people routinely experience on a day-to-day basis. For working class and black people these contexts are repeatedly either ones of informality or powerlessness.[30] The contexts of power, assertiveness and rational argument calling for the exercise of 'elaborated codes' are not a routine part of working class life. A change in the language would therefore require changing the contexts that call for its use.

So it is with teachers. Their language and thinking is indeed usually appropriate to the social contexts in which it is applied. But to understand and intervene in that relationship we clearly need to study not only the language and the thinking, but the context too. The influence of examinations or standardized testing on classroom pedagogy, the effects of tightly bounded subject communities on attempts to implement cross-curricular change, the heavy imbalance in teachers' timetable allocations towards classroom duties and responsibilities as against non-classroom ones, and the limited amount of statutory time available for rigorous, sustained and collective reflection about educational issues – all these things are indispensable items on any agenda for substantial innovation. Since it is conditions of just this kind that confine teachers' concerns to the realm of the classroom, sustain their pedagogical conservatism and make collaboration between them difficult – that, in short, help reproduce the existing culture of teaching – it is precisely these conditions, and not just the cultural responses to them that should, perhaps, be made the prime target of curriculm reform.

Consequently, while sustained, rigorous reflection and the opportunities to engage in it are necessary for transforming the culture of teaching, there would also be much to be gained by transferring much of our innovatory energies away from the individual teacher in the individual classroom towards creating school-wide, state-wide and even nation-wide structures of an enabling kind which would provide a more welcoming and supportive environment in which a reshaped culture of teaching could grow and prosper. Currently, there are a number of far-reaching structural changes already underway in the official policy sphere which are reshaping the context of teaching in fundamental ways, and whatever we might think of the directions in which these changes are moving, it seems to me important that we begin to engage with them on their own level, and not just focus our energies on helping teachers cope with their effects in the classroom.

Structural reinforcement: the National Curriculum

Towards the close of the 1980s, some of the major patterns of educational reform across a range of Western societies seem to be creating educational structures which look likely to reinforce rather than reshape the existing culture of teaching. This pattern of structural reinforcement can be evidenced by considering one national case in detail: Great Britain. In British society, recent years have witnessed educational policy changes of national scope and significance which have reinforced the existing culture of teaching in three ways: through the entrenchment and extension of the academic subject-based curriculum; through the intensification of pressure and constraint upon teachers' work which has bound teachers more closely to the immediacy of the classroom environment; and through reduction of teachers' in-service opportunities for extended reflection about the fundamental purposes and parameters of educational change, in exchange for short-term programmes of non-reflective training designed to adapt the teaching force to the efficient technical delivery of programmes and purposes decided elsewhere. For reasons of space, I shall discuss only the first of these in detail.

In the case of the subject-based academic curriculum, it is interesting that following what amounted to something of a hegemonic crisis in the early 1980s, that kind of curriculum has emerged strengthened, reconstructed and refurbished. Until the late 1970s, in Britain, as indeed in many other countries, the pre-eminence of the high status subject-based academic curriculum was virtually unquestioned. As in many other countries, the academic, subject-based curriculum was the hegemonic curriculum[31] Few doubted its worth. Publicly, politically, professionally, subject-based academic knowledge was the most highly prized form of educational knowledge in society.

Yet in a hierarchical society of continuing social and economic inequality in which educational credentials played an important selective role, subject-based academic knowledge was also the currency of educational and social selection and opportunity. To possess this kind of knowledge was also to possess a kind of cultural capital that could be cashed in for educational credentials which in turn could purchase social and occupational opportunities and advancement.[32]

So entrenched was this hegemonic understanding of curricular worth, that when social democratic aspirations brought about attempts at educational and social improvement through comprehensive school reform in the 1960s and 1970s, the intention was not to *redefine* cultural capital but to *redistribute* it; to make the fruits of the hegemonic, academic curriculum more easily available to everyone, middle class and working class children alike. Grammar schools for all! For many social democratic educational reformers, this *redistribution* position still indeed remains the key strategy for effecting improvement in working class opportunities through education.[33]

By the late 1970s, the widespread adoption of this redistribution strategy, through the extension of the academic curriculum and public examinations to most of the secondary school population right up to age sixteen, had created what many perceived as a fundamental crisis in the curriculum. In an influential review of practice in the upper years of secondary education, Her Majesty's Inspectorate commented on how public examinations seemed to be narrowing the curriculum and cramping teaching styles.[34] In 1984, the Conservative Secretary of State for Education and Science made a high profile public pronouncement on the inappropriateness of the conventional academic curriculum for many young people in school, and on the widespread sense of boredom and disaffection among the young which such a curriculum helped create.[35] And intellectuals like David Hargreaves described how the academic grammar school curriculum had destroyed the dignity of many working class children, creating opposition or indifference among them to the experience of schooling.[36]

As this hegemonic crisis intensified, the curriculum became a matter of political and professional contestation. Some promoted an agenda of educational entitlement – a way of *redefining* and not simply *redistributing* worthwhile educational knowledge. This drive towards and redefinition of cultural capital took many different forms. Her Majesty's Inspectorate, for instance, advocated and actively sought to implement a policy of providing *all* young people, as a matter of entitlement, with a broad and balanced range of educational experiences.[37] In the Inner London Education Authority, a committee headed by David Hargreaves which had been asked to report on working class underachievement in the authority's secondary schools, challenged existing definitions of achievement as being too restricted, too confined to the academic domain only, and as therefore discriminating against working class children.[38] A wider definition of achievement, the Committee argued, which embraced social and personal and practical achievements as well as cognitive-intellectual ones, would maximize opportunities for success among all young people, but especially among many working class ones who had traditionally not fared well in the narrowly interpreted academic domain.

The radical and professional end of curricular contestation therefore seemed to be embracing a redefinition of cultural capital as a way of improving educational achievement and increasing opportunity and responsiveness among working class pupils. Such a strategy, had it been implemented successfully, would also have led to fundamental redefinition of one major aspect of the culture of teaching: its division and fragmentation on academic subject lines. Part of the material base for a widespread review and reconstruction of whole school arrangements for curriculum provision would thereby have been created.

Against this agenda of entitlement for all that would create a new curricular hegemony where educational value and worth would extend beyond the academic domain, has been counterposed an alternative agenda, however. In this second agenda, educational differentiation has been dominant. Entitlement has been on the ebb. It has been an agenda promoted by Conservative politicians and educational civil servants within the Department of Education and Science, where the place of academic learning and subject specialization within the school curriculum has been significantly reconstructed and re-asserted. This modern reconstruction of the traditional academic curriculum has further buttressed those definitions of cultural capital which have long been the currency of educational selection; a currency in which the middle classes have held a substantial investment.

In 1988 the British Conservative Government committed itself to introducing a centrally presented National Curriculum into English and Welsh schools through its Education Reform Act. This curriculum is unambiguously subject-based. There is not even the mildest flirtation with broader conceptions of areas of educational experience which Her Majesty's Inspectorate had for many years attempted to place at the centre of curriculum planning. The core of this subject-based curriculum is to be mathematics, English and science. The majority of the remaining time is to be taken up with a set of foundation subjects which will comprise a modern language, history, geography, creative arts, physical education and technology (the one innovatory concession). Academic subjects are in the ascendant. Little time, status or importance is to be given to aesthetic, practical or social and personal subjects, still less to forms of learning that have no clear subject designation at all. In the small portion of the curriculum remaining after the core and foundation subjects have been accounted for, there will be little time or space for social and personal education, political education, environmental education, development education, integrated studies, social studies, peace studies and the like. As one Department of Education and Science official has been quoted, there will be little room left for 'clutter such as peace studies'.[39]

The British national curriculum will therefore be an unarguably academic curriculum. With an uncanny air of historical familiarity, it will echo and emphasize the collection of academic subjects decreed by Robert Morant in 1904 to constitute the legitimate secondary school curriculum – a definition which, it should be noted, was also constructed to ward off the challenge of working class success which was increasingly being realized through the more practically based curricula of the Higher Grade Schools.[40] In the place of a not dissimilar hegemonic challenge embodying extended entitlements to a broad range of educational experiences and achievements, the Conservative Government and the Department of Education and Science are subsituting-compulsory confinement to a narrow band of subject-based academic ones. Cultural capital and its place in educational and social selection is being neither redefined nor redistributed, but *reinforced*. With the support and stimulus of testing in the core subjects at 7, 11 and 14, whose results may well be made publicly available to parents, schools and local education authorities, this national curriculum will enhance the process of educational differentiation on academic, subject lines. Overt differentiation, the separation of success from failure with all the self-fulfilling prophecies that surround it, will take place earlier, according to a narrow set of stipulated academic criteria, which working class pupils in particular will find difficult to meet.

Only when the work of educational differentiation has been done, on the basis of narrowly defined academic criteria that favour middle class inclination and inheritance, will more imaginative curricular innovation beyond the bounds of the academic, subject-based curriculum then be permitted. From the age of fourteen, a wider optional range of curriculum experiences will be tolerated, including special lower-attainer initiatives for the bottom 30 per cent or 40 per cent of the ability range. Prototypes for such initiatives involving strong emphases on practical achievement, social and personal education, community service and residential experience have already been widely experimented with in the United Kingdom, within the Department of Education and Science's Lower Attaining Pupils Project. Such innovations suggest not a redefinition of cultural capital nor even a redistribution or reinforcement of it. In effect, they amount to a *resignation* of cultural capital; a writing off of its accessibility and relevance to those groups of pupils on whose futures the sad fate of educational and social differentiation will already have been firmly etched.

The confinement of such forms of curriculum experimentation to older, lower attaining pupils is significant. It represents an attempt to retrieve and rebuild some of the motivation among large numbers of working class pupils that years of repeated failure within an academically dominated national curriculum will have taken from them. Were such curriculum innovation to be located earlier in young people's education, and made available to a wider range of pupils, it would then be fulfilling a considerably more radical purpose of redefining cultural capital; of restructuring what is to count as educational achievement and worthwhile valid knowledge. But by confining such developments to lower ability groups and postponing them until age fourteen, government and civil servants have successfully averted any such possibility. The structural reinforcement of the school curriculum on academic subject lines before that point appears to be defeating those alternative definitions of comprehensive curricular entitlement, of which I spoke earlier.

If the structural reinforcement of the hegemonic curriculum is strengthening its role in the business of educational and social differentiation, it is also reinforcing the existing culture of teaching and its subject-divided character. The academic, subject-based emphasis of the national curriculum reasserts the priorities of that culture. The establishment of benchmark testing in the core subjects increases the likelihood that in order to protect images of their own competence, teachers will adhere to these priorities. Retention of public examinations at sixteen through the development of the General Certificate of Secondary Education (GCSE), along with required publication of the results of these examinations, adds to that likelihood. Proposals mounted by the Department of Education and Science to improve the 'match' or closeness of fit between the subjects in which teachers are specifically qualified and those which they are required to teach, along with the mandatory allocation of increased time to subject learning within initial teacher education will, as we shall see in the next chapter, almost certainly lead to further strengthening of the attachment and loyalty that teachers have to their subject.[11]

It is clear that much of Britain is therefore undergoing major structural

reinforcement of the academic subject-based curriculum through the development of a national curriculum, and a series of related initiatives. It is a
strategy which is simultaneously fostering earlier educational differentiation
on academic criteria and, by reinforcing the fragmented subject base of the
existing culture of teaching, also defusing potential sources of opposition to
that process.

Important as it is, though, national curriculum reform is not the only
means by which the existing culture of teaching is being structurally reinforced and reproduced. Mounting pressures and constraints on teachers'
work are further assisting that reproductive process by reducing still more
the opportunities which teachers have for sustained and systematic reflection
about wider curriculum developments. Teachers are being subject to escalating pressures and expectations at a time of only marginal improvements in
the teacher–pupil ratio. Many of the innovations to which teachers are being
asked to respond require time-intensive commitment to extended preparation, individualized learning and more personal counselling and reviews of
individual pupil progress. Yet the extra staffing and resources that would
make such time available have not been forthcoming.[42] More than this, in
Britain, a vast range of centrally generated innovations have been mounted
simultaneously. Teachers have been asked to cope with compound or
multiple innovations; to respond swiftly and coherently to multiple and
apparently disparate demands on their practice in connection with major
reforms of the public examination system, rapidly introduced systems of
vocational education, and pedagogically demanding initiatives for lower
attainers, for instance.[43]

The intensification of these pressures, expectations and constraints promises only to bind teachers ever more tightly to the non-reflective immediacy
of the classroom.[44] So too do newly favoured government strategies of
professional development among the teaching community. Tighter government control of expenditure on teachers' in-service development has virtually put an end to extended, award-bearing courses of in-service education
where careful and systematic reflection of a critical and questioning kind is
possible. In their place have been submitted short, pragmatic, school-based
programmes of in-service training related to particular government
initiatives.[45] Such programmes are usually too brief to allow rigorous and
extended reflection about the initiatives under consideration. Nor do the
favoured, experiential approaches to staff training facilitate intellectually
rigorous questioning and careful deliberation either. Even the vocabulary of
professional development has changed – from in-service *education* to in-
service *training*. Education is out. Coaching is in. This signals a shift in
emphasis from rational and critical deliberation designed to help teachers
mount developmental programmes of their own, to training in the skills
required for uncritical implementation and delivery of programmes and
purposes decided elsewhere.[46]

In Britain, then, politically generated changes in relation to curriculum
development, classroom constraints and in-service training have led and are

leading to structural reinforcement of the culture of teaching. Perhaps this is the political intention. Perhaps it is intended that teachers are denied the reflective resources and opportunities to criticize and contest government education policy. Perhaps it is intended that teachers be withdrawn from the process of curriculum development and review, or confined to discussion of only its most minor details. But even if this is the case, those who seek to reinforce the subject-segregated and classroom-centred character of the culture of teaching, perhaps ought to appreciate that in doing so, they are almost certainly also sowing seeds of failure and frustration in relation to some of their wider educational objectives. The culture of teaching can be as resistant to centrally imposed curricular initiatives as to any others. Where centrally initiated policies cohere with the existing culture of teaching, successful implementation is likely. In this sense, one can reasonably anticipate success for measures designed to strengthen subject specialization, for in doing so, they will reinforce, not challenge the existing culture of teaching. But measures designed to promote more active learning (open-ended pedagogies) are likely to encounter a rather different fate. Where central initiatives call for substantial changes in classroom approach, the culture of teaching can supply powerful sources of classroom resistance. Evidence from the first phase of implementation of the new GCSE examination in Britain certainly supports such a hypothesis. This examination calls for wider use of group work and active learning by the teacher, but it is being found that teachers are apparently adapting the new programmes to their existing styles of teaching in order to minimize the disruption to existing syllabuses and routines.[47] Despite massive investment in national educational reform, the gap between curriculum policy and curriculum practice appears to be persisting.

The British case is not an isolated case. In the United States, for instance, recent years have witnessed the spread of basic competency testing along with some redefinitions, following an influential report by the National Commission on Excellence in Education of a set of 'New Basics' for the curriculum – namely, mathematics, science, social studies, computer science and foreign languages.[48] These New Basics, it has been proposed, should receive a substantially increased time allocation in the school curriculum. Here again, we can see a reassertion and reconstruction of the hegemonic academic curriculum, with increased emphasis, given anxieties about national economic performance, being placed on its mathematical and scientific elements. Once more we can see reinforcement rather than redefinition of the academic basis of the culture of the teaching.[49]

Conclusion: the case for structural redefinition

In this chapter, I have focused on the apparent intractability of the culture of teaching, its effects upon the processes of teaching and learning, and the resistance it poses to school-wide innovation. Attempts to transform that culture and create opportunities or innovation through processes of *cultural interruption*. I have argued, are unlikely to succeed unless they are linked with policies directed towards changing the existing material *structures* of subject specialization, inservice training and the like to which the culture of teaching is a response and upon which it feeds. Accordingly, I have advocated some shift in academic emphasis and practical intervention from a concern with individual teachers in individual classrooms and their capacity to reflect upon their own teaching – towards giving greater consideration to the educational *structures* which support and help reproduce the language, thinking and action of teachers. This structural level is precisely the one at which much of the future of schooling is now being shaped. The development of centrally initiated policies of curriculum reform, I have suggested, will most certainly lead to a *structural reinforcement* of the existing culture of teaching and its preoccupation, amongst other things, with subject specialist concerns. It is important therefore that those who embrace a wider and bolder vision of curricular possibilities engage with those policies; that they make a serious attempt to redefine the structural base of the culture of teaching.

A possible content for such a structural redefinition should now have become clear through the course of this chapter.

A widening of educational experiences and achievements for all pupils beyond the predominantly subject-based academic domain, to include ones in the social and personal, aesthetic and practical domains also. Why should these not be included in the new basics? This redefinition of worthwhile knowledge and cultural capital for *all* pupils would not only enhance educational fairness and opportunity for pupils. It would also redefine the curricular basis of the culture of teaching, reducing its fragmentation on subject lines and making collective, whole school planning more feasible.

More generous staffing policies, not to facilitate marginal overall improvement in teacher-pupil ratios, but to release teachers for collective planning, deliberation and review in school time, and to allow greater pedagogical flexibility and experimentation in terms of small group work, individual counselling and so forth. Such policies would not only raise the status of teachers' work outside the classroom, and provide the necessary support for pedagogical innovation: by providing such support it would also breach that classroom isolation that is the very core of the culture of teaching.

A shift in patterns of professional development from an almost exclusive emphasis on training, to a balanced and coherent mix of training *and* education of a more reflective, critical and questioning sort.

The importance of that kind of structural redefinition relates not just to debates about the relative merits of school-centred innovation on the one hand and of a nationally imposed curriculum on the other; it also relates to a host of other officially prescribed and supported measures designed to improve the quality of teaching in general and of subject teaching in particular. Such policies concerning Teaching Quality and the conceptions of curriculum and teaching contained within them are discussed in the next chapter.

4 Teaching Quality and Educational Change

In England and Wales, as elsewhere, there has, of late, been a good deal of concern expressed about improving the quality of teaching in schools.[1] Such concerns have been outlined most fully in the White Paper *Teaching Quality*[2] and are reiterated and developed in *Better Schools*[3] In terms of government action, the concerns and implications of these documents have been taken up most directly through the setting-up of national criteria as a basis for controlling and accrediting programmes of initial teacher training.[4]

Three 'theories' or sets of assumptions concerning the determinants of teaching quality appear to inform the analyses and recommendations contained within these influential government reports. One concerns itself with the sorts of personal qualities that are suited to teaching. It calls for more careful selection procedures to ensure that the 'right' sort of personalities enter training for the profession. The other two explanations appear to rest on somewhat inchoate versions of learning theory in claiming that teaching quality results from learned knowledge, skill and other technical expertise acquired through initial training and further professional experience. The recommendation following from this diagnosis is that more attention should be directed to developing these kinds of competence in initial training, not least with regard to teachers spending more time on becoming more skilled and knowledgeable in their own subject specialisms.

These explanations are broadly psychologistic in nature. They appeal to the characteristics of individuals – to competence, skill and personal qualities – as determinants of teaching quality. And it is on these individuals and those who train them that responsibility for the identification of such qualities and the development of such competences is placed. Poor teaching quality, it is implied, results from an *absence* of the required competences and qualities. What is being proposed here, in effect, is a *deficit* model of teaching where poor quality results from deficiencies in personality, gaps in learning, or weak-matching of competences to task.[5]

By contrast, I want to argue that much of what we call teaching quality (or its absence) actually results from processes of a social nature, from teachers actively interpreting, making sense of, and adjusting to the demands and requirements their conditions of work place upon them. In this view, what some might judge to be 'poor' teaching quality often results from reasoned and reasonable responses to occupational demands – from interpretative presences, not cognitive absences; from strategic strength, not personal weakness. Aspects of this more sociological and humanistic interpretation of teaching quality will be developed within the chapter through a discussion of teacher cultures, careers and strategies, and their implications for the maintenance and persistence of those 'transmission' styles of classroom teaching which appear to be incurring official disapproval. But first we need to examine the official interpretation of teaching quality and quality deficits a little more closely.

Teaching quality and quality deficits: the official view

Official views on what makes good and poor-quality teaching have become increasingly apparent in Britain over recent years with the publication of a number of surveys and reports by Her Majesty's Inspectorate on various parts of the schooling system. In one of the first of these surveys (of the fourth and fifth year curriculum in secondary schools) in 1979, HMI noted that secondary teachers made wide use of 'heavily directed teaching, a preponderance of dictated or copied notes, and emphasis on the giving and recall of information, with little room or time for enquiry or explanation of applications'.[6] Later, in their survey of new teachers in school, they argued that teachers who were insecure in their subject material adopted

teaching approaches which maintained an often slavish adherence to the textbook, reliance on narrow questions often requiring monosyllabic answers, an inability to follow up and extend pupils' answers and an overprescriptive method whereby the teacher was able to remain within a constricted, safe pattern of work.[7]

Such poor quality teaching has been described in similar terms in a range of reports by HMI on different age sectors within the education service – on primary and middle schools, for instance – and continues to be a consistent feature of their ongoing commentary on the quality of the present teaching force.[8]

What HMI appear to be taking issue with here is something that other writers have variously called 'formal' traditional, 'product', 'production', 'transmission', 'class-enquiry, 'recitation' and 'discipline-based' teaching.[9] Similar views on such teaching have also been expressed in the USA where researchers have voiced concern about the preponderance of what they call 'frontal teaching'. From her survey of high school classrooms, Barbara Tye, for instance, concludes that 'all classrooms are discouragingly similar'.[10]

Their physical layout and time scheduling are similar. The pattern of teacher dominance is remarkably uniform: frontal presentation, closed questioning and deskwork being the most commonly recurring features. There is, she says, little intellectual challenge, hardly any praise, not even much blame. The high school environment, it would seem, is one with few peaks and troughs, undemanding and emotionally flat. Listening and writing predominate as the major pupil activities, there being little opportunity for pupils to contribute to, or take responsibility for their own learning, to develop self-confidence, independence and similar personal qualities. In a parallel study of thirteen junior high and middle schools, Kenneth Tye found that they too were dominated by listening, writing quizzes and frontal teaching. Opportunities for choice and exploration were restricted, and the emphasis on control and conformity at this vital stage of children's development was even greater than in the high schools. In their attachment to frontal teaching and related methods it would therefore seem that the junior highs outsinned the devil highs themselves.[11]

What is seen as determining these disapproved-of patterns of teaching? What explains these seeming deficits in teaching quality? In *Teaching Quality, Better Schools* and *Circular 3/84*, the Department of Education and Science appear to be advancing three broad arguments in relation to teaching quality.

First, they stress the importance of the teacher's personal qualities. Referring their readers to HMI's survey of teachers in their first year in the profession, they repeat the survey's 'finding' that 'the personal qualities of the teachers were in many cases the decisive factor in their effectiveness'.[12] 'Personality, character and commitment', the DES note, are as important as the specific knowledge and skills that are used in the day-to-day tasks of teaching.[13] The need for teachers to have 'appropriate personal qualities' is reiterated in *Better Schools*[14] since, it is argued, 'the personality of the teacher and his relationship with pupils'[15] promote high standards. Given the importance of such personal qualities, the government have called for improvements in the selection of students for initial teacher training and have urged that only students with the 'requisite personal qualities' should be awarded qualified-teacher status at the end of their studies.

While government has been firm in its insistence upon the importance of personal qualities as a determinant of teaching quality, it has, however, been much less clear about what these particular qualities might be – sense of responsibility, awareness, sensitivity, enthusiasm and ease of communication being the only ones they have specifically identified, and then only in passing.[16] In the main, exactly which personal qualities are likely to make a good teacher are not discussed; nor is there any discussion of whether those qualities might vary according to the age group being taught, the special requirements of a teacher's subject, or the ethos of the school, for instance. And no advice is forthcoming either on *how* these (largely unstated) qualities might be identified through the selection process. HMI certainly gave no indication of the measures and procedures they themselves used for identifying the relevant qualities. All that is recommended is that experienced, practising teachers be increasingly involved in the selection process. It seems, then, that in the absence of more objective procedures and criteria, government is here prepared to place its trust in the process described in a well-known British idiom as 'it takes one to know one'.

This kind of guidance places excessive faith in professional intuition. Not only is this kind of personality-screening process likely to be chancy and unreliable, but – if change and initiative is the goal – downright counterproductive. Qualities that might generate and recoup excellent work in the classroom (including, for instance, risk-taking, creativity, originality, the valuing of independence and initiative, a questioning and critical approach, etc., none of which appear on the DES's own list) might not most endear new teachers to their colleagues; and qualities like 'tidy appearance' that may be essential for staffroom acceptance may be relatively unimportant to children.[17]

Secondly, the government clearly places considerable weight on the technical skills of classroom pedagogy or teaching method as determinants of teaching quality. Good teachers, they say, need to have the appropriate professional skills to teach their subject 'to children of different ages, abilities, aptitudes and backgrounds'.[18] *Better Schools* is more emphatic in *its* statement that intending teachers should be given 'training and practice in classroom skills',[19] and devotes some space to these – the skills of selecting appropriate materials, varying teaching styles to match the nature of the work to the type of pupil, guiding individual pupils, handling written and oral work, cultivating independent learning, using open and closed questions when appropriate, managing diverse opinions on sensitive issues, setting clear objectives, and so on. This is a formidable (and by no means exhaustive) list of relevant professional skills.

Greater involvement of practising teachers in the professional preparation of new recruits, the stipulation that a high proportion of teacher trainers directly involved with pedagogy should themselves have recent and successful experience of teaching and should create opportunities to renew this experience, and the setting of minimum periods for teacher-training courses and the practical elements within them – all these things are seen as ways of providing new teachers with greater and more effective assistance in the development of the necessary practical classroom skills.

The formula for change and improvement in teaching quality being employed here is again both legalistic and psychologistic in nature: more teachers in training, more trainers in schools. Most of the vital questions as to how these skills are acquired, how they are to be selected and adjusted according to context, how easily or not different kinds of school environment can accommodate them and so on, are begged. The government position appears to be that if teacher trainers spend enough time in schools, and if student teachers spend enough time alongside experienced ones and their newly expert trainers, the requisite skills will hopefully be acquired by some kind of osmosis. Such an acquisition of skills from existing practitioners, were it proved to be effective, might *just* be a defensible strategy for *maintaining* present levels of teaching quality (assuming we would be satisfied with that). But it would certainly not be an effective strategy for *raising* those levels – for introducing new, improved and professionally challenging skills, techniques and approaches into the system.

Thirdly, and most centrally, the government draw a great deal of attention to the need to establish a close fit or match between secondary school teachers' specialist subject qualifications, and their teaching responsibilities in school. In their 1979 survey of secondary schools in England and Wales, HMI had first pointed to what they called 'evidence of insufficient match in many schools between the qualification and experience of teachers and the work they are undertaking'.[20] In their subsequent survey of probationary teachers, HMI claimed that 'one teacher in ten revealed insecurity in the subject they were teaching',[21] an insecurity that was reflected in their teaching method. And in their survey of 9–13 middle schools, HMI argued that work was of a higher standard where there was a greater use of subject teachers, and where those subjects had been studied in a major way in higher education by the teachers concerned.[22] In view of such associations, the authors of *Teaching Quality* go on to state that 'the Government attach high priority to improving the fit between teachers' qualifications and their task as one means of improving the quality of education'.[23] 'All specialist subject teaching during the secondary phase', they continue, 'requires teachers whose study of the subject concerned was at a level appropriate to higher education, represented a substantial part of the total higher education and training period and built on a suitable 'A' level base'.[24] Moreover, they go on, even areas of the curriculum outside the specialist mainstream, like careers education, remedial work or vocational preparation, should only be undertaken by teachers who already have experience of teaching a specialist subject.[25] The importance that government attach to this link between subject match and teaching quality is further emphasized by their announced intentions to take subject qualifications into account in the selection of student teachers, to consider the relevance of students' subject qualifications to school subject teaching in their procedures for approving or accrediting teacher-training courses, and to undertake five-yearly reviews of selected secondary schools to ensure that subject match is being improved within them and being reflected in the pattern of teacher appointments.

The commitments to improving the extent of subject match through the control of teacher education, and the exertion of influence over teacher appointments, is therefore clearly substantial. There are serious problems with this subject match thesis as we shall see, but the subject match initiative undoubtedly provides one of the major thrusts behind the intended improvement of teaching quality.

To sum up, official government policy on the improvement of teaching quality in England and Wales appears to have identified three areas of influence in which intervention would be worthwhile: personal qualities, pedagogical skills and subject expertise.

Explanation in the Tyes' studies of the reasons for quality deficits in the US teaching force are remarkable similar.[26] Though their studies provide very little direct evidence on *why* teachers teach the way they do (they were not really asked this), explanations are advanced all the same. Perhaps teachers teach badly out of habit, it is ventured, or because they have never learned the skills of mixed ability work in training. In this way, the personality of the teacher and the level of his or her skill is made central to the Tyes' proposed change strategy. In fairness, it must be said that they do point to other influential factors as well – to the need to raise the status and public worth of the teaching profession, to improve leadership skills among school principals, to restructure the curriculum, and so on. But much of their case rests on a proposed strategy of selecting new entrants to the profession more carefully and providing better initial and in-service training in classroom skills. These two easily (or too easily) targeted objectives of personality and performance are given much more extensive treatment than the more politically contentious issues of professional status and recognition, and the basic conditions of teachers' work. It is not, I suspect, the authors' intention, but in their argument much of the blame for the present stage of teaching appears to rest with the teachers themselves and those who train them.

All of these explanations are predominantly psychologistic in their understandings (or misunderstandings) of teaching quality: and they are particular kinds of psychologistic explanation that take very little account of how teachers themselves understand, interpret and deal with the demands that their work situation makes upon them. Without such understandings of why teachers do what they do, it is then possible for researchers' and policy-makers' own interpretations to flood into the vacuum. Teachers are seen not to display the observer's own preferred skills; so they are diagnosed as not being competent in their use. Teachers are seen to display personal qualities of which the observer disapproves; so it is assumed they lack more desirable ones. Thus, when preferred skills and qualities are not observed, it is assumed the teachers concerned simply do not have them and should therefore be supplied with them (training), prevented from entering teaching at all (screening), or restricted only to those 'safe' areas in which they are competent (matching).

Explanations of this kind have a certain political attractiveness – by making training, selection and deployment the target of reform, things can be done, they can be *seen* to be done, and they can be done relatively cheaply too. Indeed, one wonders sometimes whether the apparent simplicity of such political remedies has, in some peculiar way, affected the diagnosis of the supposed 'sickness' in the first place (undesirable qualities, low levels of skill, weak subject expertise) to which those remedies were presumably a response; whether the remedies have produced the sickness, rather than vice versa.

Of course, other interpretations of teaching quality which considered how far different techniques and approaches were chosen to match the circumstances in hand, and others rejected as inappropriate, or which respected teachers as active and rational interpreters of their task and the conditions in which it is carried out, might suggest policy implications that would be more troublesome to manage, more expensive to implement, less easy to evaluate in the short term. But I would urge that in this case, as in all others, the attractiveness (or otherwise) of the remedy should not be allowed to influence the validity or accuracy of the diagnosis. What, then, might this other diagnosis be? What alternative framework is there for analysing teaching quality?

An alternative framework

The framework I want to propose rests upon a regard for the importance of the active, interpreting self in social interaction; for the way it perceives, makes sense of and works upon the actions of others and the situation in which it finds itself; the way it pursues goals and tries to maximize its own (often competing) interests; the way it pursues these things by combining or competing with other selves; the way it adjusts to circumstances while still trying to fulfil or retrieve its own purposes – and so forth. In this view, teachers, like other people, are not just bundles of skill, competence and technique; they are creators of meaning, interpreters of the world and all it asks of them. They are people striving for purpose and meaning in circumstances that are usually much less than ideal and which call for constant adjustment, adaptation and redefinition. Once we adopt this view of teachers or of any other human being, our starting question is no longer why does he/she *fail* to do X, but why does he/she do Y? What purposes does doing Y fulfil for them? Our interest, then, is in how teachers manage to cope with, adapt to and reconstruct their circumstances; it is in what they achieve, not what they fail to achieve.

The sorts of interpretation of teaching quality this framework suggests can be illustrated by looking at explanations for the development and persistence of transmission teaching that have been presented within that framework. Six such explanations in particular will be discussed (these are not intended to be exhaustive): the exigencies of cohort control, situational constraints, examination pressures, subject-related pedagogies, status and career factors, and teacher isolation. It will be seen that these explanations of transmission teaching and its associated connection with teaching quality (or rather, its lack), suggest a very different set of policy implications than those currently in political fashion.

1. The exigencies of cohort control

Transmission teaching, or 'recitation teaching' as it is more commonly called in the United States, is so pervasive within the school system that it can easily be interpreted as the 'natural' or 'proper' way to teach, as a network of rules and procedures special to the teaching environment which must be learned, rehearsed and developed in a practical way by the new teacher in order to gain competent membership of the teaching community, and of the classroom order in particular. Indeed, it is interesting that a good deal of mainstream American research on teacher thinking and the improvement of teaching quality treats this particular version of transmission teaching by and large as representative of teaching itself. 'Novice' teachers are regarded as different from 'expert' ones only in terms of their abilities to handle transmission-type skills – for instance, in selecting examples, illustrations and analogies that will best 'tell the story' in relation to some part of the curriculum.[27] Within such studies there is a tendency also to concentrate on those 'academic' components of the curriculum which more easily lend themselves to didactic modes of exposition and question-and-answer teaching. It is as if teaching quality is only an issue in subjects like mathematics and science.[28] What teaching quality might look like in drama, physical education, music and art, for instance, scarcely gets a mention. This serves only to reinforce our existing stereotypes of what 'teaching' and 'good teaching' really is. Thus, in trying to change teaching, ironically it is likely that the recommendations arising from this kind of research, like much of the research on teacher effectiveness that preceded it,[29] will help keep teaching the same by failing to look outside the parameters of the transmission model.

Teaching is certainly a matter of competence. But it is competence of a particular kind.[30] It is the competence to recognize and enact the rules, procedures and forms of understanding of a particular cultural environment. What is involved is not *technical* competence to operate in a pre-given, professionally correct and educationally worthwhile way, but *cultural* competence to 'read' and 'pass' in a system with its own specific history, a system once devised and developed to meet a very particular set of social purposes.

For Hoetker and Ahlbrand[31] and Westbury,[32] these purposes have their roots in the nineteenth-century American elementary school. Grace,[33] writing in the British context, fixes those purposes in the urban elementary context of that country, too. For writers such as these, the quick-fire, question-and-answer strategy of the recitation simultaneously solved the problem of mobilizing attention and sustaining control among large numbers of potentially recalcitrant working-class children, while getting information and material across in an environment where resources were in short supply.[34]

The features and functions of this recitation style of teaching have since been identified in greater detail. The funnelling of classroom talk through the teacher effectively reduces a potentially chaotic 'babble' to the carefully structured, question-and-answer pattern of two-party talk[35] where selected pupils act as proxy representatives for the whole class, where the teacher initiates lines of inquiry and the pupils merely respond, and where the teacher evaluates the accuracy, quality and appopriateness of pupil contributions, but not *vice versa*.[36] The 'hands up' pattern of pupil participation is carefully orchestrated by the teacher – competition is encouraged, attention sustained, some semblance of involvement secured – in the process of getting the pre-decided point across.[37] To lecture the material would bring only boredom and rebellion, which is why outright dictation is usually only practised with the most self-selected, high ability groups.[38] The organization of competitive pupil participation thus avoids excesses of boredom and inattention – especially where false questioning trails can be set in the early stages and the 'answer' or 'point' of the lesson delayed so that pupils have to work hard to discover it.[39]

Within lesson structures of this kind, teachers do not, in fact, orientate themselves so much to the needs of individual students, but tend to treat the whole class as a kind of 'collective student'.[40] The progress of groups of students in the higher (but not the highest) parts of the class achievement range is often monitored particularly closely by the transmission teacher and used to 'steer' his or her judgements about the management and development of the lesson for the class as a whole.[41] In these sorts of circumstances, the teacher's predominant practical concern is not with the learning experiences of individual students, but with the overall 'instructional flow' of the lesson – with how well it is proceeding to its intended conclusion and maintaining order as it does so.[42]

There are more or less coercive versions of this long-standing pedagogical strategy. Webb describes the drill sergeant approach of the secondary modern teacher, with his inflexible regime of parade ground regimentation and uncompromising obedience.[43] Hargreaves discusses 'policing' strategies in an urban middle school, with their detailed control over the talk, bodily movement and gestures of working-class children.[44] Woods reviews the extensive use of 'domination' style survival strategies among secondary modern teachers where control, especially over older and larger pupils, was a salient problem.[45] And Hargreaves has also identified strong traces of these styles and traditions among former secondary modern teachers working in middle schools with younger children, even in middle-class environments.[46]

These, then, are the techniques, rules and procedures which are widely adopted as part of the practical management of large cohorts of pupils.[47] Such patterns of classroom management are, perhaps, more common in secondary modern schools,[48] in the lower bands of comprehensives,[49] or in working-class elementary schools[50] – the most direct and obvious inheritors of the old elementary tradition.[51] As I have already suggested, transmission styles are much more widespread than this, though: so familiar a part of teachers' experience, in fact, that their practice quickly becomes a matter of habit and routine, of taken-for-granted competence, not strategic choice.

But it should be remembered that, historically, within the system as a whole, and biographically, within the unfolding careers of individual teachers, these familiar patterns do arise from, and are adopted through, conscious strategic choice. It is only when they have been thus adopted that conscious strategy turns into habitual rule; coping into culture. It is at this point, where the routines become more closely aligned with the self and where they appear to be dealing reasonably successfully with the ever-present problem of control, that the habit becomes hard to break and that threats to it will be resisted. This is especially so where 'recitation' or transmission patterns of teaching are strongly approved of and supported by other members of the school community, not least the pupils themselves. Where domination strategies are a pervasive feature of the culture of teaching in a school, pupils can be remorseless in their expectations that teachers conform to the 'normal' pattern and can exercise powerful sanctions of disobedience and disruption against those who allow reason or consideration of personal concern to show through; against those who seem to show manifest signs of weakness or softness, that is.[52]

Transmission teaching is indeed sustained through habit, then, but the habit is by no means irrational. It is a habit that has historically enjoyed a measure of success in maintaining control over and transmitting limited knowledge to young people in large numbers in the physically restricted space of the school classroom. If policy-makers wish to kick this habit out of the classroom, it is clear that training in new skills is not itself the answer. This lies, rather, in formulation and acceptance by teachers themselves of new, less control-centred educational purposes, along with easement of the constraints and conditions in which these purposes are to be fulfilled. This brings me to a second set of determinants of transmission teaching – those rooted in the situational constraints of the classroom.

2. *Situational constraints*

All teaching takes place in a context of opportunity and constraint. Teaching strategies involve attempts at realizing educational goals by taking advantage of appropriate opportunities and coping with, adjusting to, or redefining the constraints. Often, the coping strategies that teachers adopt to deal with contextual contingencies can beome so habitual, so routinized, that they seem like coping no more, but worthwhile and valid teaching. In this way, provisional adaptations turn into routine commitments.[53] When constraints are particularly heavy and pressing, though, teaching may become not just a matter of coping, which in some senses all teaching is, but of sheer survival. Woods[54] has outlined some of the constraints that appear to induce survival-based patterns of teaching in the secondary school system – the raising of the school-leaving age (to which we would now add growing youth unemployment), which encourages staying-on among those not otherwise especially enamoured of their school experience; the persistence and extension of 16 + examinations against which teachers' own success will be judged (more of this later); continuing high levels of class size and teacher-pupil ratios that make individualized treatment and small-group work difficult; and declining levels of resources, which make experimentation and adjustment of learning tasks to individual needs problematic and leave teachers in the position of having to rely on their own *personal* resources for managing the class.[55] To these things, we might also add the inappropriateness of and deterioration of standards in school buildings: the inconvenience of stairs and galleries for those wishing to use overhead projectors and other cumbersome audio-visual aids; the unsuitability of compartmentalized classrooms for team-teaching, resource-based learning, etc.; and the general discouragement that dilapidated walls and leaking roofs present to those who might otherwise take pride in improving the display and all-round aesthetic environment of their classrooms.

Material circumstances, then, do affect the standard and quality of teaching, as HMI have themselves noted in surveys of the effects of public expenditure policies on teaching and learning.[56] Low resources and poor material support encourage teachers to adopt a 'survival' or 'make-do' orientation to their work and incline them towards more control-centred, transmission-style patterns of teaching which revolve around the imposition of their own personal authority within the public setting of the classroom. Teachers, that is, do not just decide to deploy particular skills because of their recognized professional worth and value, or because of their own confidence and competence in operating them. Rather, they make judgements about the fit between particular skills and the constraints, demands and opportunities of the material environment of the classroom; about the appropriateness of particular styles or techniques for present circumstances. Although, in historical and biographical terms, these judgements rapidly become in-grained and routinized as normal practice, their roots in environmental circumstances, and therefore the importance of the character of those cir-cumstances, should not be forgotten.

The implication here for policy-makers who would wish to promote movement away from transmission patterns of teaching is that there is a need to ease and improve those conditions that currently incline teachers towards survival more than mere coping, and towards the control-centred transmission-style pedagogies that follow from it. This suggests not policies of improved training or selection, but of more generous and thoughtful resource allocation to the system to improve the material environment of teaching.

3. *Examinations*

The work attempted in the classroom was often constrained by exclu-sive emphasis placed on the examination syllabus, on topics thought to be favoured by the examiners and on the acquisition of examination techniques.

So wrote Her Majesty's Inspectorate in their survey of the curriculum for fourth and fifth years in secondary schools.[57] Their evidence for this judge-ment, as with those presented in most of their surveys, was loosely stated and difficult to verify, but the argument has been echoed many times in recent years in Britain by academics and policy-makers alike. In a polemical critique of modern comprehensive school practice, for instance, David Hargreaves has expressed concern about the ways in which public examinations can come to dominate the process of teaching and learning in secondary schools.[58] And a study of a large group of Scottish secondary school leavers, surveyed after taking their 'Highers', found that 'the most common single method of study was "exercises, worked examples, proses, translations" (73 per cent), followed by "having notes dictated to you in class" (60 per cent)'.[59] The researchers concluded that 'one may infer that many felt there had been a conflict between studying for interest's sake and studying for examination success'.[60]

Perhaps this inference, given its grounding in pupil, not teacher data, is a tendentious one. Perhaps David Hargreaves's remarks are also somewhat speculative since they rest on no other evidence than that presented by Her Majesty's Inspectorate (doubts about which have already been raised). Moreover, evidence from recent research by Hammersley and Scarth suggests that patterns of whole-class teacher-pupil talk do not differ significantly between courses that are assessed by terminal examinations, ones that are continuously assessed, and ones that are not assessed at all – even when these differently assessed courses are taught by the same teacher and within the same subject.[61] In claiming that terminal examinations have little effect on patterns of teaching and learning, Hammersley and Scarth's research does, however, focus on only one tightly defined area of classroom learning (overall patterns of public whole-class talk). It does not consider other features of classroom learning that might be more strongly affected by the presence or absence of examinations. These would include differences in the amount and type of group work and group discussions, the open or closed nature of classroom tasks, and the kinds of homework set.[62] Until the findings of such research become available, the weight of argument and evidence would appear to fall in the opposite direction. Both Weston and Olson, for instance, found that teachers involved in the Schools Council Integrated Science Project (SCISP) breached the project's guidelines by teaching from the board and encouraging pupils to revise – and that these teachers referred to the presence of examinations as the reason for their continuing use of these transmission-like styles of teaching.[63]

For some teachers, then, the presence of examinations seems to constrain them in their approach to classroom teaching; it limits innovation and inhibits their willingness to explore new teaching strategies. Achievement-conscious pupils may conspire with their teachers in this process of limitation too, drawing them back to safer pedagogical ground when exploration threatens to divert them from their examination destination.[64] Not all teachers are closet radicals, though, waiting for the moment when the unbolting of the examination doors will allow them to open up their pedagogical style. As Sikes, Measor and Woods have found in their life history interviews with secondary teachers, many teachers regard examinations not as a constraint but as a resource for motivating pupils at an age when their enthusiasm for school might otherwise be waning.[65] Many teachers, it must be said, though, are not aware of examinations as either a constraint or a resource. For them, examinations are just a 'fact of life' –an assumed and taken-for-granted part of the secondary school system to which their practice is routinely directed.[66]

Constraint, resource, excuse and fact of life: there are clearly a number of ways in which public examinations have a bearing on the maintenance of transmission styles of teaching. Their importance for the teacher is substantial: in a work environment where few other adults directly witness the quality of the teacher's work, examination results provide one of the few public and apparently objective indicators of a teacher's competence.[67] Teachers ignore the importance of these results at their peril. Indeed, since the 1980 Education Act's requirement that all schools publish their examination results, it is not unreasonable to surmise that the influence of examinations upon teaching quality (or its lack) it likely to grow in years to come.

Even so, it should not be assumed that the abolition of public examinations would necessarily put an end to transmission styles of teaching. Such styles are apparently as pervasive a feature of US high school teaching as of life in British secondary schools. The grade point average and the development of educational testing may in this sense have as much of a backwash effect on the teaching and learning process in the United States as does the public examination system in Britain. So, too, might the mandated curriculum, be it set at national or provincial level, in its fixing of external curriculum objectives and its restriction of teachers' room for manoeuvre. Clearly, examinations, the way they are perceived, oriented to and drawn upon as a source of professional justification by teachers, are but one source of influence on the continuing pervasiveness of transmission styles of teaching in the school system. Their removal or reform will bring no automatic pedagogical shifts, only the creation of opportunity for alternatives to be explored more thoroughly. I will say more about such measures in the second part of the book.

4. *Subject specialism*

For the DES, teaching quality at secondary level is enhanced by the possession of specialist subject expertise among those with responsibility for teaching the particular subjects in question. The DES's case for insisting upon more attention to be paid to subject competence in the training and deployment of teachers rests on two kinds of evidence. Both of these are somewhat insubstantial.

Firstly, in *The New Teacher in School*, HMI identified one secondary teacher in ten as revealing insecurity in the subject they were teaching (an encouragingly small proportion, one might have thought).[68] Moreover, as the National Union of Teachers argues in response to the White Paper *Teaching Quality*, the basis of and variation between different HMI ratings (formed on the basis of only two observations per teacher), are less generous than those provided by the teachers' heads.[69]

Secondly, in their 9–13 middle school survey, HMI looked at 'associations between particular modes of staff deployment and overall standards'.[70] They concluded that in schools where a high proportion of teachers spent over half their week teaching one specific subject, and in schools where a high proportion of the teaching was undertaken by teachers who had studied the relevant subject as a major element in their initial training – in other words where there was a strong degree of subject match – standards of work were better (to a statistically significant degree). This argument, too, as the National Union of Teachers again point out, is empirically weak, however.[71] For one thing, HMI leave implicit what they mean by and measure as standards. For another, statistically significant associations between standards of work on the one hand and resource levels and the strength of a head-teacher's influence on the other, which are even *stronger* than those involving subject match, are not developed through discussion or connected to policy suggestions. Once again, it appears that the nature of the available remedies is having some effect on the character of the diagnosis.

But let us assume, for one moment, that HMI's case is stronger than this; that subject match *is*, in fact, related to teaching quality. Is HMI's interpretation, resting as it does on the claim that teachers' possession of knowledge and expertise provides the basis for their classroom confidence, the only possible one? Have they been rigorous, robust and balanced in examining alternative possible theoretical interpretations of the evidence to hand? I want to suggest that they have not and that there are equally plausible (though less politically attractive) explanations for the associations they claim to identify. These explanations – ones which recognize and respect the meanings that teachers take from and give to their work – are concerned, in turn, with the effects of subject-based pedagogies, subject commitment and subject fragmentation.

(i) *Subject-based pedagogies.* When teachers are trained and develop expertise in paticular subjects, they do more than merely master appropriate content and gather relevant bodies of technical expertise. Induction into a subject is also induction into a subject culture or community – into a set of assumptions about how children learn, how they are best taught, how one should relate to them, and so on.[72] Though definitions of what is the appropriate methodology for a subject tend to shift over time,[73] at present, teachers of certain subjects – modern languages in particular – seem strongly inclined to a transmission approach to teaching.[74] The adoption of this approach within certain subjects is based on what Ball calls an academic perspective, where teachers tend to be strongly subject-centred, to view their own subject as setting special intellectual demands because of its allegedly 'linear' quality, to favour homogeneous ability grouping, and to prefer whole-class teaching methods.[75] In the case of certain subjects, then, it woud seem that the dominant assumption about teaching, learning and knowledge held *within* that subject community actually support the spread of those very transmission pedagogies of which government appears to disapprove.

(ii) *Subject commitment.* Subject membership is a hard-won achievement, a result of many years of studying and exploring that subject through school, through university and through teacher training. Almost inevitably, then, induction into a subject brings with it the development of commitment and loyalty to that subject too (and, by implication, weakened loyalty and commitment to others). Subject induction, that is, bestows subject identity.[76] Subject mastery is therefore not only a cognitive process – a matter of acquiring knowledge and skill – but a social one also, in which feelings of attachment, loyalty and identification are built up. So strong can these commitments become that teachers not only come to feel diffident about teaching and reluctant to teach subjects very different from their own, like religious education or personal and social education, which would be likely to form but a minor part of their timetable commitment,[77] but some teachers may even feel reluctant to teach subjects that would appear to have a fairly close cognate intellectual relationship to their own – as when physicists are asked to teach chemistry or integrated sciences, for instance.[78] In these circumstances, poor-quality teaching that arises from working outside one's own subject is not so much, or exclusively, due to lack of knowledge and expertise, but to weakened commitment too. And this weakened commitment may in turn be a by-product of the intensity of the subject commitments that have been built up elsewhere in the school curriculum. By this interpretation, the problem that appears as subject mismatch may not be due to too little specialism, but to too much.

(iii) *Subject fragmentation.*   These first two interpretations of the relationship between subject membership and pedagogical preference suggest that weakness in out-of-subject duties may well be caused not simply by unfamiliarity with content but by deep-seated divisions within secondary teaching as a whole brought about by strongly institutionalized systems of subject separation which inhibit the development of transferable pedagogic skills, restrict teachers' adaptability and responsiveness to educational challenge and innovation, and limit their commitment to children and to learning in general as against enthusiasm for particular bodies of content.

My own work on middle school teachers provides some support for this view. Teachers with interests in and commitments to humanities, English and creative and expressive arts felt ill-at-ease with teaching science and mathematics, not just because of their lack of confidence with the subject (though this was important), but also because of their discomfort with the very different pedagogies, very different ways of relating to children they felt were associated with those other subjects. As one expressive arts teacher put it:

> I think anybody who teaches in the creative arts has this (rapport) with kids, because it is emotionally based . . . whereas if you're dealing with a factual subject, a scientific subject, you're dealing more with things and objects and reactions. Actually, how you *feel* about SO_2 (sulphur-dioxide) coming out of a bottle doesn't come into it, you know.[79]

Similarly, in their life history studies of secondary teachers, Sikes, Measor and Woods came across some subject teachers who felt distinctly uncomfortable with the approaches they were required to adopt in other subject areas:

> Last year, I took some English. I couldn't teach it. I was nervous, and besides not being able to do it as well, you need a different approach to what you take in art. You couldn't treat the kids as individuals, like you do in art. You had to be a teacher in front of a class and tell everybody what to do.

> Well, I've got two styles of teaching. I've got the one that I deal with in the art room and the other that's formal because I teach part of my timetable in humanities . . . in art. I can relax and go round and talk to them individually . . . with the humanities, it's a case of come in silence and sit down . . . definitely teaching from the board.[80]

Other writers have pointed to the pedagogical anxieties art teachers feel when they move from the security of their practical areas into a more conventional classroom environment – even when they are teaching art appreciation.[81] Nor is the phenomenon confined to art. Ball and Lacey, for instance, have pointed to the tendency of non-specialist English teachers to be more attracted to transmission pedagogies than their specialist counterparts are.[82] What matters here is not so much this association between qualification and quality, but how it is explained. The evidence I have reviewed points to the possibility that poor-quality or transmission-style teaching arises in some subject teaching, not because that subject is being taught by poorly qualified generalists, but by *other* specialists whose commitments lie elsewhere and whose preferred pedagogical approaches are seen as incompatible with those required in subject areas other than their own.

Falling rolls and rapid technological and social change are bringing about constant adjustments and shifts in the secondary school curriculum, demanding in turn a degree of flexibility and adaptability on the part of the teaching force. Where subject fragmentation remains strong, where the firm boundaries and pedagogical dissimilarities between different subjects continue to be emphasized (no emotions in science, no hypotheses in history), where the subject specialist pattern of teacher training is maintained and strengthened, the chances of creating such flexibility, of developing the necessary degree of transferable pedagogic skills, will not be great. On the basis of this kind of evidence and interpretation, which recognizes the essentially *social* nature of teachers' developing curricular identities, commitments and pedagogical preferences, the improvement of teaching quality would seem better met by training and deployment policies which are less rather than more specialized in nature. Such improvement would also be better met by policies of counter-specialisation than by the introduction of an academic, subject-based national curriculum. On the basis of the explanation presented, such a national curriculum will, if anything, support the persistence of transmission pedagogies and undermine parallel attempts to develop pedagogies organized around the principle of 'active learning'. A subject-based national curriculum will inhibit teaching quality, not enhance it.

5. *Status and career factors*

> I think this year I have suffered from what they call teacher burnout.
> There is very, very little recognition here. Even a dog needs to be patted
> on the head, but you don't get that here. It makes you question whether
> it's worth it.[83]

Competence and efficiency are closely tied to personal senses of worth and
value. Much of that worth depends, as it does for the teacher cited above, on
recognition and status given to one's work by others. The importance of this
association is most evident when it is broken, when careers are truncated or
'spoilt', status is withdrawn and recognition seemingly denied. Such denials
of worth, whether they occur within the career structure of a particular
school, or whether through such things as pay erosion, they are seen to
emanate more diffusely from society at large, lead some teachers to seek an
exit from the profession. Where such options are not possible, though, status
denial begins to have adverse implications for professional motivation and
classroom performance. One teacher I interviewed in my middle school
study, for instance, felt she had not been well treated in the reorganization to a
middle school set-up and had resisted the head's attempts at change – 'We
don't, some of us don't change so easily!' She went on:

> I've considered doing part-time work . . . but it's almost impossible
> now with things as they are in this area. So I settled for the fact that you
> can't devote the time which I feel you would need to give to the job. So
> I'm settled now. I've abandoned all hopes. I'm just watching and letting
> things go.[84]

This process of role retreatism that follows from status denial has been
described particularly graphically by Riseborough in his study of a group of
middle-aged, male secondary modern teachers who had been reorganized
into an academically dominated comprehensive.[85] As these teachers realized
they were not to get the major posts of responsibility, that their objective
career progression had come to an end, that their own subject expertise was
being compared unfavourably with that of their colleagues from former
grammar schools, and that they were to be allocated the 'dirty work' of
teaching the lower-ability groups in the lower streams – they formed a staff
counterculture which set about resisting the initiatives of the head, and they
withdrew that commitment and enthusiasm in the classroom that previously
had been a major part of their secondary modern identity:

> What's happened must affect the teaching. You can't go into the
> classroom and forget about what's happening to you. I don't work as
> hard as I used to. I just make sure I'm not snowed under by kids. I've
> become quite mechanical. They took away what was important, the job
> I could do.

Put it this way, if I had children of my own at school, I would be very, very worried if they had a teacher like me. I'm purely a timefiller, a babysitter. You know, I sit in my stockroom half the day with my electric kettle and a fag and cup of coffee. And I don't care now that everyone else knows.

In this way, we can see how intimately connected teachers' classroom strategies are to teachers' cultures and careers; how what happens in the staffroom has implications for performance in the classroom also. This is a much more subtle (though politically more contentious) diagnosis than those which rest on notions of teacher burnout or personality deficiency and which individualize professional failure and blame individual teachers for it (or those who train and employ them)[86]

Once we recognize how far classroom competence has its roots in status and recognition, how closely the different elements of teachers' lives are tied together in a coherent structure of meaning and motivation, then the policy implications lead us not to personality-based initiatives or more careful selection, compulsory redundancy to remove 'incompetents' from the profession, or redeployment and the encouraging of taking of early retirement, but to strategies which will improve the levels of reward and recognition in the system in terms of pay, planning time, in-service opportunity and the like, and in terms of positive (not punitive) systems of staff support and development. Much of that kind of support, though, will obviously depend on greater opportunities being created for teachers to share and witness the success of what their colleagues do. This leads me to the last determinant of transmission teaching I want to explore here: that of teacher isolation.

6. *Teacher isolation*

One of the most pervasive characteristics of teaching is that of classroom isolation – the separation of teachers with their classes into a series of egg crate-like compartments, isolated and insulated from one another's work.[87] This creates an often welcome measure of protection from inspection and intrusion. It gives teachers a kind of autonomy which they will guard jealously if pressed. But isolation from colleagues also creates uncertainty. It removes opportunities for praise and support and therefore serves to undermine confidence about the success or otherwise of one's efforts. In circumstances such as these, colleagues are led to rely on the crude, more tangible and visible indicators of classroom performance to evaluate one another's success, like examination results and noise levels.[88]

This rather crude form of collegial evaluation tends to induce a certain kind of conservatism in teachers,[89] an attachment to existing classroom methods which appear to be reasonably successful in keeping results high and noise levels low. Team-teaching, exploration of new methods, collaborative approaches to improved teaching, constructive collegial criticism of classroom performance – none of these things are fostered by the isolation and individualism of the existing culture of teaching.[90]

Where teachers are isolated in this way, working under the weightening press of material constraints, and immersed in the practical immediacy of the classroom environment, personal classroom experience becomes increasingly attracted to itself. What has been done supplies the framework of justification for what is to be done. And as existing experience, unchecked by alternative views of collective reflection, becomes sedimented into teachers' consciousness as valued and successful procedure, so pedagogy undergoes petrification. Once that process of petrification is complete, little new pedagogical blood can then be squeezed from it. Classroom isolation, therefore, and the culture of teacher individualism which it generates, operates to support the persistence of transmission pedagogies. Such pedagogies appear to meet the crude, externally visible criteria for professional success, and the lack of collegial reflection or criticism provides no impetus for change in them either. If teachers' allegiances to transmission pedagogies are to be loosened, then, ways of encouraging their collaboration with colleagues must be found, along with the resources to do this.

Conclusion

In this chapter, I have examined the nature and validity of current 'official' explanations of teaching quality. These, it was found, rested much of their case on the importance of teachers' personal qualities, their technical expertise and their specialist subject competence. I argued that there was a lack of clarity (or clear research evidence) concerning what these appropriate qualities might be, an unfortunate tendency to abstract approved-of skills from consideration of the contextual circumstances in which they might need to be employed, and an inclination to present a one-sided interpretation of the implications of specialist subject expertise for teaching quality. Most of all, it was suggested, these explanations have placed most of the blame for quality deficits onto teachers themselves or those who train them, instead of examining the characteristics of the environment in which teachers operate and trying to understand and interpret the ways in which teachers make sense of, and adjust to, that environment.

Official explanations of deficiencies in teaching quality have tended to equate such deficiencies with tendencies to adopt transmission patterns of teaching. The paper has also explored possible reasons why teachers adopt transmission patterns of teaching, but has looked at this not in terms of why teachers fail to do something else, but in terms of what purposes transmission teaching serves for them. This more sociological approach to the study of transmission teaching points to the importance not of personality, skill or expertise as such, but to factors such as the following:

1. The control purposes that transmission teaching serves in managing large cohorts of pupils in restricted physical surroundings.

2. Its appropriateness for circumstances of low resource levels and severe material constraints.
3. Its compatibility with a mandated curriculum, whether this is govern-mentally set or determined by a public examination system.
4. Its association with particular subject specialisms and, elsewhere, its availability as a fall-back strategy for those teaching outside the secure boundaries of their own specialism.
5. The minimal effort demands it makes upon teachers who have lowered their investment in teaching due to career blockage and status denial.
6. Its suitability for, and protection by, the conditions of teacher isolation, where external criteria of professional competence are ostensibly met and inducements to change are absent.

For those who wish to weaken the hold that transmission teaching has within the educational system, this more sociological approach to understanding the conditions of teaching quality suggests not a tightening-up of selection procedures, an improvement of training, and an emphasis in training and staff deployment on the strengthening of subject expertise, but policies such as the following:

1. Re-examination of the control purposes of schooling and the extent to which they pervade the system to the exclusion of other personal and social ends like collaboration, independence and initiative.
2. Allocation of improved resources to the system and the alleviation of material constraints in a way that will enhance the development of new pedagogical approaches.
3. Weakening of the public examinations and grading systems and atten-uation of their influence on the school curriculum, possibly in favour of more continuous and pupil-centred forms of assessment, recording and review.
4. Weakening of teachers' attachment to particular subject specialisms, dev-elopment of subject competence across a wider range of the curriculum, and development and dissemination of awareness of the similarities in learning objectives and pedagogical approach between different subjects: in short, the easement of subject loyalties and demystification of subject differences.
5. Devising, extending and improving systems of staff development and collegial support (not hierarchical and possibly punitive appraisal) for teachers.
6. Creating opportunities and providing conditions in which teachers can spend more time working together, sharing problems, commenting on each others' performance, and collaborating in curriculum planning.

Reforms of this kind point to the importance of attending to the purposes and social context of teaching, if teaching itself is to be changed. In that sense, their political attractiveness is not likely to be as great as that of present policies which emphasize training, selecting and matching, and which address themselves to the individual qualities and characteristics of the teachers themselves. It would be sad, though, would it not, if the analysis of teaching quality were to be prejudged by the availability or attractiveness of particular solutions for dealing with it? One can only hope that, in coming years, politicians, bureaucrats and the teaching profession itself will be able to evade that particular trap.

Summary

Reformation within the curriculum cannot be achieved without reformations beyond it. This is the most important message of the first four chapters. Among these other reformations, the key one, perhaps, is the reformation of teachers themselves. After all, it is teachers who are ultimately responsible for delivering and defining the curriculum at classroom level. It is they who will decide what the curriculum-in-use is to be. For those who wish to secure substantial and effective curriculum reform, a grasp of the relationship of teachers to the curriculum and to curriculum reform is therefore vital.

When I speak of reforming teachers, I do not mean what educational policy makers usually mean by this, however. I am not concerned with improving their skills, altering their personal qualities, or getting them up to scratch in subject knowledge – or indeed with remedying any other alleged personal deficiencies on their part. Although educational reform proposals designed to improve teaching quality often suggest otherwise, teachers are neither foolish nor dumb. In the main, they are intelligent skilled professionals and diligent workers. But what teachers say and think and do is seldom shaped by what, ideally, might be viewed as the best way to learn or the best way to teach. Their thoughts and deeds, rather, are nested in, moulded by and mediated through a particular work environment: the work context of teaching.[1] When teachers fail to match up to ideal ways of teaching and learning, therefore, this is more usually due not to weakness of personality, skill and subject knowledge, but to the daily pressures, constraints and expectations of their work environment. What teachers think and do – the culture which they share and which binds them together – is a meaningful and rational response to the pressures and priorities of their environment.

One overwhelmingly influential feature of the work context of teaching is the way that, in most schools, it isolates teachers from one another within their own classrooms, making collaboration and collegiality difficult. This gives the culture of teaching a highly individualistic quality. Most teachers centre their working lives on the affairs of their own classrooms. From the point of view of curriculum development, one of the most important consequences of this classroom-centredness is that teachers place almost exclusive emphasis on personal classroom experience not only for thinking about their own teaching but as a basis for reaching and justifying collective decisions concerning curriculum change too. Whatever the preferred mode of innovation – be it top-down or bottom-up – this classroom isolation of teachers and the reliance it leads them to place on classroom experience as a result, presents serious problems for curriculum development.

In the case of bottom-up strategies of curriculum development, the problems are ones of inconclusiveness and limitation of curricular debate. Bottom-up strategies certainly help foster a sense of ownership of innovations among teachers, by involving teachers in their development. But the existing evidence suggests that school-centred innovation does not just appreciate and gear into teachers' existing knowledge, experience and understandings, but restricts itself to the knowledge and experience which teachers already value. In this way, school-centred innovation has been highly vulnerable to entrapment within the existing culture of teaching. Teachers' decisions and judgements relating to curriculum development have tended to become based almost entirely on the classroom experience that is overwhelmingly valued and deemed legitimate within that culture. Powerful, difficult and complex social and philosophical judgements of purpose and value in the curriculum have therefore been founded upon experiences which are very often simply inappropriate or insufficient for the scope of the task in hand. The culture of teaching credits the experience and knowledge of others, of those who have worked in, observed, studied, or read about schools elsewhere, with little importance. As a result, even the most profound curriculum discussions have tended to be based on contributions bound by what teachers have already experienced and known in their own classrooms.

These cultural limitations on curricular debate and development at school level have brought with them two important sets of consequences. On the one hand, discussions between teachers and their colleagues have often been unfocused, non-rigorous and inconclusive. This in turn has created pretexts for management's imposition of its own curricular wishes. On the other, decisions reached by teachers working in collaboration have often lacked boldness and imagination. They have rarely challenged the boundaries of existing, known practice. Indeed, by omitting non-classroom experience and knowledge from broad questions of curriculum planning, teachers have opened themselves up to control and influence by their more senior colleagues; colleagues who do have access to and are willing to draw upon such knowledge and experience during the course of debate.

The major implication of the culture of teaching for school-centred innovation, then, is that while SCI might foster a sense of ownership among teachers of the development with which they have been involved, what they own may not be all that different from what they have already experienced. Teachers may only own what they have known. In the absence of broad, sustained and rigorous debate, this severely limits the scope of what it is that gets developed.

Within the context of the culture of teaching, top-down strategies of curriculum change fare little better. The imposition of a National Curriculum might in part be read as an attempt to counter the limitations of reform through school-centred strategies of curriculum innovation. But as it has been conceived in Britain and elsewhere, the development of centralized curriculum reform appears to contain features that will, if anything, *reinforce* rather than transform the existing culture of teaching. This is especially so in the case of the academic subject-based emphasis being given to the new National Curriculum in Britain, which will almost certainly strengthen teachers' subject identities and deepen the divisions between them. But if mandated National Curriculum reform of a top-down nature will tend to strengthen the existing culture of teaching in important respects, other parts of the programme designed to bring about fundamental changes in teachers' approach, towards more open-ended pedagogies, active-learning styles, the use of higher-order questioning strategies, etc., will likely prove much less effective. For one thing, the subject identities strengthened through National Curriculum reform will, in the main, decrease teacher flexibility, and in many subjects, tie teachers even more firmly to the conventional pedagogies which are accepted there. For another, given the persistence of the culture of teaching, teachers will, within the protected isolation of their own class-rooms, continue to be able to resist the requirements of externally imposed innovation when threatening changes in pedagogy are called for.

Here is the fundamental dilemma of curriculum development. School-centred innovation increases teacher ownership and involvement and with it the likelihood that teachers will accept change. But because of the classroom-based character of the culture of teaching, the scope of that change will usually not be great. Moreover, the inconclusiveness of classroom-based discussions will incline senior management to usurp the contributions of ordinary teachers, undermine their participation and thereby prejudice their continuing commitment. Yet top-down curriculum reform, while it may sometimes be far-reaching in scope, will itself have little impact at classroom level where teachers, protected by classroom isolation, will be able to resist its implementation.

Bottom-up or top-down: one of the greatest obstacles to curriculum reform is therefore undoubtedly the culture of teaching and the work context in which it is embedded. Substantial change in the curriculum consequently requires parallel or preceding changes in the culture of teaching through which teachers relate to that curriculum. This, in turn, means changes in teachers' work, in the ecological conditions of teaching. If substantial curri-culum reform is to be developed and implemented effectively, teachers, as a routine and scheduled part of their work, must therefore be allowed, encouraged, indeed required to move beyond their own classrooms into other classrooms, into regular scheduled meetings with their colleagues, into other schools, and into contexts where they consider and discuss educational theory. In this way, educational theory and comparative experience outside the classroom will become a routine and accepted feature of teachers' work, as routine and accepted as classroom teaching itself. With such a reconstruction of teachers' experience, the curriculum development that teachers come to own will likely be of a bolder, more imaginative nature, created from a wider agenda of possibilities, and developed through a more intellectually rigorous and searching process of discussion and review.

Of course, whatever the process of curriculum development, not any old curriculum reform will do. Some patterns of reform like the subject specialist one embodied within the National Curriculum will reinforce the culture of teaching and thereby undermine other objectives concerning the fostering of active learning, for instance, that are contained elsewhere within the reform programme. In this sense, a broad and balanced whole curriculum, moving across and beyond existing subject loyalties is most likely to destabilize the subject-divided character of curricular loyalties. Such measures are not politically uncontentious among many teachers, of course. They threaten existing identities, loyalties and vested interests. Difficulties of this sort alert us to the fact that effective and imaginative curriculum development will therefore require both pressure from without (to destabilize existing loyalties) and support from within (to foster the exploration, development and ownership of new ones). And that combination of pressure and support will be most effective where non-classroom work receives high status and priority within the culture and work context of teaching.

A broad and balanced curriculum extending across and beyond the conventional academic subject range will also fulfil another important educational purpose. It will foster enhanced educational equality. In Chapter 3, I examined ways in which the hegemonic curriculum of an academic, subject-based kind prejudices the opportunities of working-class and many ethnic minority children. With growing resistance among many young people to the subject-based academic curriculum – a redefinition of cultural capital – which had little connection with their own lives and needs and which could no longer even purchase the guarantee of employment, a crisis of curricular hegemony swept through British educational policy from the mid 1970s. Growing support for a broad and balanced curriculum which would potentially threaten existing subject interests and which would be the right of all pupils as a matter of entitlement, marked the emergence of a serious counter-hegemonic thrust within curriculum development. Moreover, this was a thrust which cherished, protected and valued comprehensive ideals of common experience and entitlement among the generations of the future.

The resolution of that crisis in favour of increased support for the academic, subject-specialist curriculum marks a significant retreat by the state from such comprehensive ideals in favour of a movement towards increased differentiation and deepened inequalities of opportunity within the educational and social system. The hegemonic curriculum has been reasserted through national control. Conventional definitions of cultural capital have been reinforced. The one place in which comprehensive ideals and commitments still linger (though in a way which is still heavily contested) is in the area of assessment reform. The nature and consequences of profound and sweeping changes in educational assessment over recent years and their relationship to the curriculum reform process are the subject of Part II. We will see, however, that assessment reform and curriculum reform cannot be considered in isolation. Their fates are inextricably interlinked. And both are even more deeply embedded within the changing social, political and economic context of society as a whole.

PART 2

Assessment Reform

5 The Crisis of Curriculum and Assessment

Introduction

The 1980s has been a period of intense, rapid and far-reaching change in educational policy and practice. One of the main areas in which reforms have been concentrated has been educational assessment. Until proposals for a National Curriculum, assessment, more than curriculum or pedagogy, was the prime focal point for educational change. Indeed it would be no exaggeration to say that the 1980s has been the era of assessment-led education reform.

Interest among policy-makers in educational assessment is not at all new, of course.[1] But no previous developments in this sphere match up to the breadth and intensity of activity on the assessment front that we have witnessed during the 1980s. The implementation of the GCSE with almost indecent haste; the rapid proliferation of schemes of subject-based graded assessments beyond their early confines in a small number of subjects only, like music and modern languages; the development of the new Certificate of Prevocational Education (CPVE) along with other attempts to rationalize the system of prevocational qualifications; and the widespread adoption of pupil profiles and records of achievement – these are just some of the major assessment initiatives that have been launched in recent years.[2]

In the case of pupil profiles and records of achievement alone, it is interesting that as recently as 1980, fewer than 1 per cent of all secondary schools offered anything more than a structured testimonial, and scarcely twenty-five schools had a profile that was non-confidential, available to *all* pupils, included some reference to cross-curricular skills and personal qualities and was in a structured format.[3] Yet, by 1984, the DES had issued a clear policy statement on Records of Achievement; had earmarked some ten million pounds of its budget to fund nine pilot schemes in the area; and has since declared its intention that every secondary school issue its pupils with a record of achievement by the 1990s.

This is expansion and innovation on a scale and at a pace of remarkable proportions. What explains it? What accounts for the intense political and professional interest in changing patterns of educational assessment? Explanations for these developments have not been wanting. Some have attributed the changes to growing impatience, especially among the Inspectorate, with the adverse effects of public examinations on teaching and learning processes, and on the secondary curriculum as a whole.[4] Others have pointed to a sense of growing disillusionment amongst employers with the value of examination results as an effective screening device and predictor of job performance.[5] A number of politicians and educationalists with views ranging right across the political spectrum, have voiced concern about the plight of low attaining pupils in circumstances of growing youth unemployment – and about the need, therefore, to recognize and reward alternative kinds of achievement among the young.[6] Some see new patterns of assessment as devices that can unlock curriculum innovation where other strategies of whole-school curriculum change have failed.[7] And it has also been noted that the diversification of assessment activity and support for new initiatives by examination boards may have less to do with a new found liberal conscience on their part than with their entrepreneurial search for new sources of income as their existing ones are being eroded by falling rolls.[8]

These factors and others too, have undoubtedly been influential in the emergence of new patterns of assessment.[9] They have often been treated as if they were separate, though; as if they were only accidentally related to one another, just happening to coincide at the same point in time.[10] Picking off causes, influences and precedents individually in this way, however, does not allow us to get to grips with the interrelationship between them; to recognize the social patterns that bind them together. In this sense, I want to suggest, we would do well to heed the advice of the French sociologist, Emile Durkheim, that in educational changes of considerable scale, one can usually find reflections (and refractions) of much broader transformations within society as a whole.[11]

What social transformations have led to recent changes in assessment policy and practice, then – to assessment being an issue at all, in fact? If we are to understand the emergence of assessment as a major educational issue, we clearly need to locate it in some more general *social* theory of educational change in post-war years. We need to understand why assessment, and not something else, has emerged as a dominant strategy of educational change. And we need to understand what strategies of educational change have preceded assessment-based ones and why they have now been put aside.

In order to explain the emergence of educational assessment, we must go beyond it, therefore. We must address ourselves to major shifts in strategies of educational reform as a whole in Britain over the past three decades or so. In analysing such shifts, I want, in particular, to examine how well each of these strategies, assessment-led ones included, has addressed itself to two important social purposes: creating some measure of social consent amongst the young on the one hand, and meeting some definition of comprehensiveness, of equal access, common entitlement, or shared experience on the other. My purpose, that is, is to examine the relationship of assessment-led reform to patterns of reform that preceded it; and to evaluate the contribution of these different reform strategies to the comprehensive experience. When assessment is itself assessed, our questions should not end with matters of mere technical efficiency, with whether the new patterns of assessment improve motivation or not, for instance. They should surely extend to the whole purpose and direction of comprehensive education and the contribution of changing patterns of assessment to it. This is my purpose in this chapter.

Explaining educational change

What kind of social theory might best explain the changes in educational policy focus and reform strategy in post-war years? There is no shortage of theories purporting to explain the relationship between education and society. Most of these theories, however, have difficulty explaining major shifts of direction in educational policy. They tend to be stated at such a high level of generality that reproduction, resistance, relative autonomy, bureaucratization and so forth, become general *qualities* of education under Western capitalism, not variables that might help us understand shifts in policy strategy from one period to another.

At the same time, research which is focused more directly on policy issues – whether as a pragmatic response to the current exigencies of research funding, or as a way of providing a more solid foundation of evidence for theoretical claims – has sometimes made it difficult to see the wood for the trees. In developing detailed understandings of the workings of TVEI, Lower Attaining Pupils projects and the like, they have often lost sight of the social trends and requirements that give these disparate initiatives a more general coherence and logic. Critical overviews of the social context of different educational policy initiatives have been rare. Indeed, the decline of 'basic', independently funded educational research and the emergence, in its place, of more cursory and politically tied evaluations of particular initiatives actively discourages such overarching critiques (which might reflect poorly on the sponsors).

What we require, then, is a social theory that can begin to explain how and in what ways the dominant focus of educational reform has shifted over the past three decades or so, since the commencement of comprehensive school reform. My starting point for such an explanation is loosely derived from two general theories of social change that have an evolutionary quality about them – a capacity to identify phases of social development and to explain why there are shifts from one phase to the next. One of the theories is Jürgen Habermas's explanation of crisis developments in the modern capitalist state.[12] The other is Michel Foucault's interpretation of changing approaches to punishment, discipline and surveillance in Western societies.[13]

Both theories focus on social change in Western society. Both are developmental or evolutionary in character. Both identify three major phases of social development. Together, they have a significant capacity to illuminate the major patterns of social and educational change in recent times; to show them in a new light. But the theories also have their limitations. The periods to which they refer are very different – Foucault's model spans several centuries, Habermas' restricts itself to modern capitalism only. And neither of these periods coincides exactly with the period of educational change I am reviewing here. Nor are either of the theorists predominantly concerned with education – Habermas makes only passing reference to education in his writings on crisis development while Foucault confines most of his remarks on the subject to his final phase of development, where education and examinations in particular are said to play a major part in maintaining discipline and social surveillance.

I am not therefore claiming to offer a 'correct' or 'literal' interpretation of the theories. Neither am I suggesting that they are applicable or generalizable to educational policy developments in other societies. Nor do I want to claim that there is any evolutionary 'necessity' about the phases of educational reform that I identify – for as Habermas himself argued in the case of his own more general theory, such evolutionary claims have to be decided by empirical research, they cannot be theoretically assumed beforehand.

All I *am* suggesting is that the work of these two theorists has generated a set of ideas, concepts and interpretations and a broad evolutionary model, which seem to me to resonate particularly well with what I take to be some of the most significant aspects of educational change in post-war times. They help bring together and give coherence to an otherwise disparate and disconnected range of educational initiatives and developments.

Social crises and educational crises

In explaining the social context of educational change, it is important to recognize, with Habermas and Foucault, that most organized education is part of the state. The fortunes of education are therefore closely bound up with the fortunes of the state as a whole. The state has the task, amongst other things, of managing, intervening in, creating appropriate conditions for and compensating for the unwanted effects of, economic activity. Its management of specific spheres like education is therefore powerfully affected by the fortunes of the economy, and by the strategies deemed appropriate for dealing with the problems the economy throws up.

Notwithstanding partial 'boom' in the late 1950s and early 1960s, post-war Britain has witnessed an underlying trend of economic decline and therefore an experience of intensifying economic crisis – some would call this a capital accumulation crisis. As this overall crisis has intensified, the state has developed different strategies for dealing with it, so that, in many respects, the economic crisis has come to be displaced into the state. This in turn has

Table 1   Crises in education

Period	Type of social crisis	Type of educational crisis	Point of application	Locus of change	Policy focus
Late 1950s – mid 1970s	Rationality	Administration and re-organization	Body	Access and opportunity	Comprehensive education
Mid 1970s – early 1980s	Legitimation	Curriculum	Mind	Consciousness and belief	Common curricular entitlement
Early 1980s –?	Motivation	Assessment (and appraisal)	Mind	Disposition and discipline	Records of achievement

generated different kinds of crisis and patterns of adaptation within the state as the state tries to manage the wider economic problem and all its destabilizing effects. These crises in the state reverberate throughout its different parts, not least within educational policy, which experiences its own particular crises. These take the form of a succession of critical points where a significant gap is perceived between educational policy and practice on the one hand and society's needs on the other; where existing solutions are seen to be exhausted or to have failed, or where new needs are felt to have emerged. It is under such conditions that support grows for new styles of state management, different patterns of initiatives; for a new overall strategy which promises to produce a closer match between schooling and society's needs.

Following the work of Habermas and to a lesser extent Foucault, I want to propose that British education has, in fact, passed through *three* such phases since the 1950s, that it has responded to *three* sets of perceived crises as attempts have been made to restructure education to society's purpose. These are phases of reorganization by *administrative, curricular* and *assessment-led means*. Each of these phases has been precipitated by a particular kind of social and educational crisis – a crisis of administration and reorganization, a crisis of curriculum and belief, and a crisis of motivation and assessment, respectively. I shall now review each of these critical phases in turn, paying particular attention to the contribution each has made to the development of the comprehensive experience. For the advent of the crisis of assessment and motivation and all the problems accompanying it, can only be fully grasped if we also understand why previous reform strategies have been rejected. As a point of early reference, a summary of my overall argument here is presented in diagrammatic form in Table 1.

The crisis of administration and reorganization[14]

In the 1950s and 1960s, the dominant strategies of educational policy reform were administrative. The educational system responded to the problems with which it was presented in administrative terms, through forms of institutional reorganization and expansion. Throughout this period, state intervention in education extended as a way of generating a technically equipped, socially productive workforce, and an expanding economy, during an era of post-war reconstruction. Investment in education increasingly came to be seen not as a burden on the social purse, as a claim on state expenditure, but as an investment in human capital, in Britain's economic future.

These public attitudes were reflected in and reinforced through some of the major education reports of the period. The thrust of these reports was that the existing selective arrangements and restricted range of opportunities in secondary and higher education were leading to a 'wastage of ability' among pupils of high measured intelligence, especially working-class ones, who left school early, did not proceed to higher education, gained modest qualifications and secured only low-grade jobs.[15] There was, allegedly, a 'hidden pool of talent' among the young people of Britain which the educational system needed to tap, not only to maximize individual opportunities but to secure economic regeneration also.[16] Even the Plowden Report on primary education which has often been read as a testament to the importance of individual creativity and personal development in children's education, nevertheless justified child-centred education in terms of its capacity to produce flexible, adaptable citizens, able to switch jobs many times in their lifetime, as technological change required.[17]

Such reports, together with a mounting body of educational research which showed that many able working-class children were not fulfilling their intellectual potential within the existing selective secondary system, furnished a case for institutional reorganization and expansion in education on *economic* grounds. But commitments to reorganization and expansion also appealed to lingering post-war sentiments of fairness and social justice. In a sense, these policies 'bought' social loyalty by opening access, widening opportunities and meeting rising aspirations. They offered one way of responding to and accommodating the welfare demands of a socially aspirant post-war population. Policies like comprehensive reorganization were therefore designed to boost economic performance, enhance social consent, and respond to rising social aspirations, through processes of *administrative* change. The worth of the kind of education on offer (the traditional, academic, grammar school curriculum) was not in question. What mattered at this time of relative prosperity was increasing access to the demonstrably worthwhile social and educational opportunities that were available. Reform at this stage was therefore very much concerned with the movement of bodies into buildings; with investment, expansion and administrative reorganization in a broad context of optimism about expanding opportunity and social improvement. The new policies of comprehensive reorganization were therefore underpinned by a strong degree of social and political consensus and optimism. Existing education offered a demonstrably beneficial route to individual improvement and economic growth. All that was needed was more of it, for more of the people.

By the mid 1970s, however, this faith in the social and economic benefits of administrative expansion and reorganization had collapsed. There were two reasons for this. Firstly, by that time, the bulk of comprehensive reorganization, the main administrative reform, was already under way. The strategy of educational reform through comprehensive reorganization had begun to exhaust itself.[18] This exhaustion of existing policies provided one of the preconditions for new initiatives to flourish. As time ran out for the reorganization strategy, a second precondition for change, already rooted in the economic logic of state intervention and educational expansion itself, began to make itself felt more keenly. A fundamental paradox was built into the very heart of this pattern of reform. While the state, during this period, was expanding its involvement in and expenditure on social and economic life in order to provide support for economic development, the financing of this itself entailed deduction of expenditure from the very thing (profits and revenue) the intervention was designed to enhance. What this meant for educational policy was that while there was investment in comprehensive education for economic development and to secure social loyalty, the investment could not be too costly, the price not too high. Despite broad rhetorics of expansion, therefore, actual educational expenditure, even at a time of relative prosperity, was somewhat limited. This means that comprehensive reorganization, like many other educational reforms, was carried out very much 'on the cheap', by principles of administrative convenience, using existing buildings, wherever possible. Indeed, Ministry of Education and DES regulations insisted on this.[19]

Junior high schools, middle schools, split-site schools – all these major new developments in educational provision were the result of this basic paradox working its way through educational policy decisions.[20] Such policies revealed a certain *irrationality* in the administrative pattern of educational intervention – that education was taking place in buildings ill-equipped for the purposes that were intended. Middle schools in inflexible, old secondary modern premises; large comprehensive schools of Kafkaesque proportions which subjected eleven and twelve year olds to the experience of vast, impersonal bureaucracies for the sake of retaining a large sixth form of academically able youngsters; split-site schools with their chaotic trudging of pupils, staff, or both between premises; open-plan schools, often established more to cut costs on use of space than to realize the principles of child-centred learning – these were some of the irrationalities that administrative convenience introduced into the comprehensive system.

However, as long as the economy remained relatively buoyant, as long as jobs were available, opportunities appeared to persist and aspirations had a chance of being met, these irrationalities scarcely surfaced as a public issue – or if they did, as among the Black Paper writers in the late 1960s, for instance, they were given little serious attention. But with the waning of growth and the deepening of recession by the early-to-mid 1970s, the 'irrationalities' became more noticeable and overt. Education, and comprehensive education in particular, like many other state institutions, became subject to what has been called the 'onset of doubt', and now found itself in the midst of a *crisis of rationality*, a crisis in which the administrative system was patently failing to fulfil the economic requirements demanded of it. From being a much needed investment, educational spending quickly came to be regarded as a non-productive luxury the nation could no longer afford.[21] Expansion and reorganization, it seemed, were not just too expensive in the new climate of severely curtailed public spending, but they had not worked either – and they quickly fell out of political fashion.

This period of educational reform therefore culminated in a crisis of rationality. Administrative reorganizations continued, of course – school amalgamations, tertiary reorganizations and, most ironically, unscrambling of many middle school systems which expediency had brought into being as recently as the late 1960s and early 1970s. But these new administratively expedient changes were no longer part of a major strategy of intervention and unification, but simply an exercise in pragmatic cost-cutting with scarcely any educational justification added.[22] It was in other strategies of educational change that the language of educational justification began to prosper.

The crisis of curriculum and belief

With educational institutions no longer apparently meeting the ideals and aspirations of openness, opportunity and improvement that had come to be expected of them during the period of post-war reconstruction, doubts began to emerge and questions began to be asked about the value of what these institutions had to offer, about the character and quality of the processes that went on within them. The crisis of administrative rationality was therefore quickly compounded by a crisis of belief in the very legitimacy of society's basic institutions. In education, this crisis of legitimation led to questioning of the quality of schooling itself and set in motion a re-examination of its basic purposes and processes.

There were accusations by the now more seriously regarded Black Paper writers of the New Right that comprehensive education and educational progressivism more generally were undermining Britain's industrial competitiveness.[23] Events at the William Tyndale junior school in London were given wide publicity which pointed to the dangers posed by extreme progressivism which prospered when the curriculum was not subject to public accountability and control.[24] And there was media-hyped treatment of research findings claiming to show that 'informal' teaching methods produced lower standards of attainment in reading and mathematics than more formal ones.[25] All these things both reflected and reinforced a deepening moral panic about the failure of the educational system, in the absence of political and public control, to sustain economic growth and political stability.

The wider crisis of legitimation and belief therefore created, in schools, a crisis of curriculum.[26] This crisis of curriculum not only reflected the diffuse dissatisfaction with education's capacity to deliver the economic goods, however. It was not just that the curriculum, cast adrift from public control, was apparently failing to meet existing economic requirements. The curriculum was also invested with a positive social role. It was a basis for hope as well as a source of despair. As confidence in the institutions of state and government more generally came under threat, the school and its curriculum came to be identified as having a major ideological role in creating a new set of social beliefs, a new basis for social consent and cohesion.

The curriculum may have become the target for increased political control on the one hand – as Prime Minister Callaghan's Ruskin College speech on education and the Great Debate that followed it indicated. The contents of the curriculum garden were no longer to be kept a professional secret – as became evident in a whole series of HMI and DES pronouncements on the curriculum in the late 1970s. But political incursions into the curriculum also opened up a new and important phase in the development of the comprehensive experience – where the essential nature of that experience came to be seen not as a matter of common institutional *access* (with curriculum decisions left to the professionals), but of *common curricular entitlement*: entitlement by right of all pupils, whatever their abilities, to the same breadth and balance of educational experience.

Potentially, this could have been a radical departure for the development of comprehensive education. The existing subject specialist basis of the secondary school system, geared towards public examinations and slanted towards the academic interests of 'grammar school' pupils, could have been overturned in favour of new curriculum categories, designed to foster useful and rigorous education for all in the furtherance of the common good. A new common entitlement curriculum might, for instance, have embraced Raymond Williams' recommendations that all young people up to sixteen should learn the language *and culture* of at least one other country, that they should be familiar with the workings of national, local and community politics, and so on.[27] It might have offered support for innovative categories like integrated studies or community studies as the basis for a common curriculum in the way that David Hargreaves suggested in the early 1980s.[28] It might even, just as controversially, have followed the lead of the new educational right and, like Rhodes Boyson, have proposed specific curriculum contents such as key book titles and named figures in political history as required elements of study.[29]

But the new proposed common curriculum did none of these things. Instead, HMI avoided controversial value questions of this kind, and the social and political choices and commitments that necessarily accompany them, by defining the curriculum in terms of eight (now nine) broad areas of educational experience to which all pupils had an entitlement.[30] These categories and the way HMI suggested they be applied in the school did not challenge the continuing academic, specialist base of the secondary curriculum and the purposes of social selection and elite recruitment that it served. HMI advised that the 'areas of experience' be used as a kind of checklist, against which current curriculum coverage, including that taking place within existing subjects, could be monitored, to try and ensure balance and breadth. The categories were added to the curriculum. They did not imply or recommend that anything be taken away. They were a complement to, not a substitute for existing coverage. The vague way in which the areas were defined, the fact that they were purely an advisory basis for curriculum planning and included no statutory requirements for minimum coverage on a cross-curriculum basis, along with their additive, complementary character, may all have helped secure a measure of professional consensus, but they did nothing to foster a radical and practical re-examination of existing curricular arrangements.[31]

As a result, at this broad level of policy formation, continuous choices between subject contents were avoided, allocations of timetable priority not established, and implications for the status and importance of existing subjects not spelt out. It was left to teachers and schools to make their own decisions about these matters. And as HMI themselves discovered when they worked with teachers and schools in five LEAs using the areas of experience as a basis for whole school curricular appraisal, teachers did indeed make such practical curriculum judgements but in a way which served only to reinforce existing subject specialist interests.[32] In a critical commentary on the fate of this exercise, HMI candidly recorded that 'since the major commitments and loyalties of most teachers are within subject departments, it has often been more difficult for them to identify and explain those aspects of their specialisms which contribute to cross-curricular concerns'.[33] Similarly, they noted that 'it has proved extremely difficult to avoid aligning (the areas of experience) with subjects when considering issues of balance within the curriculum. It has also been too easy to justify each subject in terms of the eight areas'.

Just as importantly, HMI drew attention to the problems posed by formal examinations, by 'society's requirement that young people should possess qualifications at the end of their formal education in the subjects of the conventional curriculum'.[34] This pressure, they noted, has if anything been heightened in recent years. They did not go on to say that, in part, this is actually a direct consequence of government policy, through the 1980 Education Act's requirement that schools make their examination results public. But they implied as much when they said that

> The schools see themselves increasingly at the mercy of the market force of parental choice in a time of falling rolls, and they judge their examination results to be among the major factors which determine the exercise of parental choice. This has led them to be understandably cautious in making decisions about the acceptability of change in the

current curriculum even where there has been considerable agreement about the desirability of such modification.[35]

The GCSE, developed subsequently to these observations of HMI, offers little hope of modifying these pressures and patterns. Indeed, by fixing broad subject criteria at national level through cumbersome procedures of discussion and development, it looks likely to inhibit the creation of new and innovative curriculum titles.[36] And there is evidence to suggest that in the early phases of GCSE implementation at least, teachers have been teaching syllabuses as close as possible to ones with which they are familiar.[37]

By the early 1980s, then, the curriculum as a whole was no longer seen as a dominant strategy for securing social consent, restoring common belief, re-establishing broad legitimation for society's purposes and institutions at a time when opportunities remained sparse, jobs scarce and rewards thin. The reluctance to decide upon competing political values, to attack high status subject specialist interests in the school system and the position of those who benefit from them, and to devote expenditure to the time, staffing and resources that effective whole-school curriculum change requires has put paid to broad and common curriculum reform as a dominant strategy of state management, within the context of widely held ambitions for comprehensive education.

Lip service of a muted kind continues to be paid to common curricular entitlement within HMI documents.[38] But the recommendations are, if anything, made in an even more tepid and advisory form than in previous documents. They are given neither the force of statutory requirement, nor the stimulus of financial incentive. Such requirements and incentives can, however, be found in the new curricular policies of the 1980s – policies which emphasize and reinforce subject specialization, and support broad principles of educational differentiation. Here, it would seem that having been unable to break the academic subject-based hegemony of the secondary school curriculum, the DES and HMI have decided to strengthen it still further. 'If you can't beat them, join them' so to speak. The relevant measures here relating to the development of a National Curriculum and the awarding of higher priority to subject specialist studies in teacher education have already been reviewed in Chapters 3 and 4.

This swing to specialization in curriculum policy has been further reinforced by Government's increasing commitment to educational differentiation. Within the 14–16 curriculum in particular, one can already detect the trial of prototypes for the reintroduction and refinement of selective, tripartite principles within the existing comprehensive structure. At the apex of this pyramid of provision is the existing and now strengthened academic, 'grammar school' curriculum, supported by the new policies on subject specialization and reinforced by the introduction of a GCSE with a differentiated entry structure, and with a virtually complete absence of reference to vocational interests and criteria.[39] In the centre is a broad vocational and technical band, the principles of which have been piloted through schemes which tend to exclude the most and least able groups of pupils (who 'choose' not to opt in to TVEI).[40] And at the base of the pyramid are the types of programme currently being experimented with under Sir Keith Joseph's Lower Attaining Pupils' Project, which, notwithstanding the detailed variations between particular schemes, tend to stress practicality, community links, residential experience, and social and lifeskills.[41]

In the 1980s, then, the secondary curriculum is no longer a basis for social consensus or comprehensive entitlement, but a mechanism of social and educational differentiation. In the proposals for a National Curriculum, there are no positive signs that these trends will be reversed either. As we have already seen, the proposed National Curriculum seems geared to setting standards of attainment of a traditional kind within conventional high status subject specialisms – the 'basic' subjects as the Secretary of State calls them – such as English, mathematics, science, modern languages, history and geography. This kind of National Curriculum will serve only to reinforce existing academic specialist interests within the secondary curriculum, and to perpetuate the process of educational differentiation which specialization fosters. Admittedly, it also proposes to give some coverage to areas like health education and education in personal and social qualities, attitudes and values too, but by not being tested, and by not being designated 'core' or 'foundation', it is likely these will be given lower priority than the 'old', 'traditional' grammar school subjects dressed up as the 'new' basics. Moreover, some areas of the curriculum, vital to the forging of common purpose and the development of the social good – such as political education, development education, social studies, environmental education and integrated studies – look at present as if they will be excluded from the National Curriculum and will therefore be consigned to lesser, optional status in the school curriculum or omitted altogether. Given such developments in National Curriculum policy towards increased specialization and differentiation it is in assessment that the last vestiges of comprehensive ambition and the continuing attempts to secure some kind of common social cohesion are being invested.

The crisis of motivation and assessment

As what the state has to offer looks increasingly ill-coordinated and ineffective, as belief in the value and legitimacy of society's basic institutions subsides, as aspirations are eroded and hopes are dashed, society then begins to experience what Habermas calls a crisis of motivation – a generalized response of 'Why should I conform?' 'Why should I bother?', 'Why should I care?' There are, Habermas argues, two reasons for such deficits of motivation.

Firstly, the reasons for conforming to established norms are taken away. In British secondary education, for instance, while public examinations have long been recognized as having a stultifying effect on the process of teaching and learning, many young people were prepared to endure this experience because of the qualifications they might attain at the end, and because of the social opportunities these qualifications could purchase. Like the CSE 'ear 'oles' interviewed by Paul Willis, many young people were, until recently, prepared to trade their obedience for qualifications.[42] But once there are very few or no jobs at all available for school leavers, and once a few qualifications can no longer guarantee employment, therefore, then the existence of these qualifications can no longer be relied upon to secure classroom consent or effort. As John Gray and his colleagues have remarked, 'pupils on a course in which success is either assured or virtually unattainable will . . . tend to lose motivation'.[43]

A second cause of motivation deficits, Habermas argues, arises from the erosion of existing cultural supports as the state intrudes more and more into community and family life, and existing bonds of loyalty and association are weakened. Frustrated aspirations no longer have their compensations in the solidarity of working class community life, as in the 1930s. Unemployment, lack of opportunity, absence of hope, increasingly becomes an individual, solitary experience. Without the support of friends and community, without an alternative basis for the development of a meaningful identity and sense of worth or purpose, the experience of unemployment or frustrated aspiration can become a lonely one and have serious consequences for motivation.

It seems likely that, together, the impact of economic recession on the wage economy and the decline of traditional forms of emotional or cultural support will have profound implications for the motivation of the young. This thesis still awaits firm scientific proof, of course, and indeed, it has been contested on the basis of Scottish truancy statistics which appear to show a *fall* in rates of truancy (as an indicator of motivation) at a time of rising youth unemployment.[44] In the end, however, the actual levels of decline in motivation among young people, even if they could be measured accurately, are not important from the point of view of educational policy. It is the political and public perception of the threat that matters. This public and political reading of trends in employment and pupil behaviour is the vital lever for policy change.

The importance of motivational factors in stimulating educational policy change can be seen very clearly in the development of pupil profiles and Records of Achievement. In HMI's review of ten secondary schools experimenting with early profile schemes, one of the two major reasons that schools put forward for their development was their capacity to increase motivation among the less able.[45] In her survey for the Schools Council of profile provision in nine secondary schools, Balogh found that the 'desire to improve pupil motivation by involving students in their assessment process or by making it clear that their behaviour and attitude could affect their leaving statement' was a very important factor in their development.[46] Goacher, following up Balogh's research with a programme of action-research to develop records of achievement in other schools, found that many of the schools participated because the 'pupils would benefit from improved motivation due to a better indication of what was expected'.[47] And Harrison, in his review of over sixty Graded Objectives in Modern Languages (GOML) schemes, found that the advocates of these schemes pointed to their capacity to increase pupil motivation and, as evidence for this, cited increases in the proportions of third year pupils opting for modern languages since the introduction of GOML.[48] By the time of the publication of the DES Policy Statement on records of achievement in 1984, the improvement of pupil motivation was listed as one of the four major justifications for their introduction into secondary education.[49] And pupil motivation is persistently mentioned as a justification for records of achievement in the many documents and newsletters accompanying the numerous local and regional schemes being piloted around the country.

Improved motivation, it is claimed, is secured in several ways within records of achievement. Firstly, the recording of personal and social experiences and achievements broadens the definition of achievement valued by the school beyond the academic domain, stimulates the school to give more emphasis to these other achievements, and thereby increases the amount of success experienced by pupils, particularly the non-academic ones most susceptible to motivation deficits. Secondly, where pupils record their own personal achievements on a regular basis, this gives them the opportunity to define and declare their own identity as a way of increasing their self-awareness and independence. Thirdly, the negotiation of records of progress on a continuous, periodic basis between teacher and pupil, involves pupils more in their own assessment and encourages them to take more responsibility for their own learning once they can see they have some positive and influential stake in it. Fourthly, the assessment of subject learning on a continuous step-by-step basis, through a series of graded, hierarchical levels with certificates to be gained at each level, provides pupils with a clear structure of rewards and incentives. Fifthly, the breaking up of the curriculum into a series of separate levels, or discretely assessed modules of a few weeks each in length with a 'course credit' to be collected at the end of each module, replaces the dispiriting trudge for public examinations over two years between fourteen and sixteen, with a set of more immediate, achievable targets.

In the next chapter, I shall discuss some of the difficulties of achieving these motivational purposes in an educational context which, as we have seen, still values and promotes educational selection. Here I want to raise an even more fundamental point about pupil motivation. Is motivation, I want to ask, always unarguably a good thing, a thing of unquestioned educational value, worthy of positive support and encouragement?

Motivation or manipulation?

One of the major educational justifications for profiles and records of achievement is that they are not just a 'bolt-on' addition to the existing curriculum in the sense of a more extended leaving statement or a separate set of tutorial discussions, but that they are integral to the curriculum itself, central to the learning partnership and the process of curriculum review. In this sense, the new patterns of assessment are seen as being intimately tied up with curriculum change. This indeed is why people speak of assessment-led curriculum reform.

However, the association between assessment reform and curriculum change applies in only two respects, and not in an important third one. Assessment reform is certainly intended to serve as a device for changing the *process* of curriculum development – involving pupils in self-assessment necessarily involves them in negotiating their teaching and curriculum too, which leads to a re-negotiation of the curriculum, where possible, to meet their individual needs.[50] Assessment reform is also intended to help change the *structure* of the curriculum, by encouraging the development of modular or accumulated credit schemes.[51] What is absent, however, is any discussion of the relationship between the new patterns of assessment and the *content or focus* of the curriculum. There is virtually no discussion within the new assessment initiatives of the social purposes of the curriculum; of the essential knowledge and experiences to which all pupils are entitled. The profound implication of this is that in records of achievement, we have a system designed to enhance pupil motivation but without any broadly based political or professional discussion and agreement about what pupils are being motivated *towards*; about what sorts of things we are committing young people *to*, and whether these have any educational or social legitimacy. We run the risk, that is, of taking on the characteristics of objectives-based educational developments in the United States as described by Popkewitz where 'learning, motivation or satisfaction become ends in themselves', where 'what is to be learned, motivated, counselled or satisfied is left vague and unimportant'.[52] Under such circumstances, the enhancement of pupil motivation shifts from being an *educational* process of positive disposition to learning worthwhile knowledge; to a *socio-political*, state-managed process of accommodation to the realities of economic crisis; of adjustment to diminishing prospects of employment and economic reward and to an educational experience that, for many pupils, can no longer promise social and economic benefits in adulthood. Motivation, that is, becomes transformed from a process of educational encouragement to a strategy of social crisis management.

Consequently, where assessment strategy is developed in isolation from discussions of curricular purpose and entitlement, the development of pupil motivation can even, with the best intentions, become equivalent to a manipulation of generalized dispositions, habits and inclinations – the adjustment of young people to whatever the social, economic and political system requires of them, especially, as even the relatively radical ILEA review of secondary education acknowledged, adjustment to the experience of failure.[53]

There are, then, serious objections to assessment-led reform *unless* it is developed in conjunction with a clear sense of curricular purpose. Otherwise, motivation-inspired changes in assessment will be but vehicles to undermine the principle of comprehensivism. For people will no longer be given access to common and socially valuable experiences. They will only be furnished with a common and diffuse disposition to adjust them to any purpose within the social system in present or later life – however suspect or iniquitous it might be. In present government policy, then, assessment initiatives have been unhooked from important earlier discussions about common curricular purposes and entitlement. The development of common, diffuse human dispositions has been divorced from any intention to forge common social and technological knowledge and belief.

More than this, if we reflect back on the fate of common curriculum reform, we can see that the new assessment-led system of dispositional adjustment, of generalized inclinations towards institutional and social loyalty through negotiation, discussion, establishment of contracts and the like, has been grafted on to an increasingly differentiated and divided curricular system. In this sense, the development of common motivational dispositions within a differentiated curriculum works to adjust young people to their social fate and, through complicated systems of credit accumulation and modular study, denies them access to an overall grasp of the processes, structures and mechanisms by which such differentiated adjustment is achieved.

Through the use of graded assessments and stepped levels of achievement, horizons are not just shortened, but limited too (a modular step-by-step curriculum, for a modular scheme-by-scheme life, perhaps?). Through the use of pupil profiles, processes of negotiation and target setting, institutional loyalty and adjustment are secured. Through the development of elaborate, modular, credit-based structures, the system is bureaucratically mystified and made non-accountable to those who use it and whose opportunities are affected by it.

When we view assessment reform strategies in this light, it is clear that *common* motivation and disposition developed through profiling and related assessment strategies on the one hand, and the new forms of curricular *differentiation* on the other, are not at all unlikely bedfellows. Their interrelationship is exceedingly intimate. Indeed it is incestuous. They are both very much part of the same political family. Assessment-led strategies of curriculum reform, that is, look as if they might well be adjusting many pupils to their failure, underwriting this adjustment through the establishment of agreed contracts and other consent-gaining processes and through the development of modular structures, obscuring the means by which all this is achieved. To many, the patterns of common assessment in the form of records of achievement for all appear to be the successors of curriculum reform in trying to meet the principles of comprehensiveness. In fact, they may well turn out to be the opposite – a method of gaining and reinforcing pupil consent to newly developed structures of curricular differentiation.

Once this fundamental problem is recognized, it seems to me important for those who wish to retain some vestige of comprehensive ideals that discussions about and strategies relating to assessment reform must be conducted in tandem with those sorts of discussions about curriculum content and entitlement which we failed to resolve, and therefore quietly dropped, in the 1970s. It seems to me vital, therefore, that if assessment reform is to make a positive contribution to the restoration or further development of the comprehensive experience, then the development of common motivation and loyalty must be linked to the development of common experience, belief and purpose also. Motivation, we should remember, is but a *means*. It is the *ends* of learning that are ultimately most central to the comprehensive experience. In this sense, we could do no better than heed and act on the words that are tucked away in a broadsheet jointly produced by the Centre for the Study of Comprehensive Schools, the National Profiling Network, and the School Curriculum Development Committee, which urge that 'records of achievement should reflect a curriculum of entitlement for all young people'.[54] This entitlement, I would add, should be a common one. With the clear harnessing of records of achievement to the establishment of such common and broad entitlement, there would be a real possibility that the new patterns of assessment would advance the socially progressive interests of comprehensive development, and not undermine them with a manipulative bag of motivational trickery designed to adjust young people to the experience of government-sponsored educational and social differentiation. The choice is between developing records of achievement as servants of social differentiation, or as forces for comprehensive educational improvement. It is important that teachers and schools make this choice by careful deliberation and not by hasty default.

6 Assessment, Motivation and Selection: the Case of Records of Achievement

Introduction

On 28 November 1983, the then Secretary of State for Education and Science, Sir Keith Joseph, pledged ten million pounds of government money to support the development of Records of Achievement for all school leavers. The purpose of these records, he stated, was the assessment of skills, personal qualities and achievements beyond the usual subject attainments. The two reasons for this initiative to which the Secretary of State drew particular attention and which appear to be of pressing concern to both schools and employers were the need:

1. To acknowledge 'the totality of what pupils have done in order to improve their motivation and help schools identify their needs more closely.'
2. To provide 'a testimonial respected and valued by employers and colleges.'

In the draft policy statement, 'Record of Achievement for School Leavers', these aims were stressed yet again and with even greater emphasis. The Secretaries of State (for England and Wales), the draft policy statement said, wanted the Records of Achievement:

> to improve pupils' motivation. There is evidence that some pupils who are at present poorly motivated would aspire to higher standards of attainment if they knew that their achievements and efforts would be formally recognized.[1]

> to offer pupils a certificate which is recognised and valued by employers and institutions of further education when the pupils seek work or admission to a course. The intention is that most potential users . . . should gain from records of achievement a more rounded picture of

candidates under consideration for jobs or courses; and that many should make direct use of this information in deciding how the applicant could best be employed, or for which jobs, training schemes or courses he should be advised to apply.[2]

In its completed pamphlet – *Records of Achievement: a Statement of Policy* – the Department of Education and Science stated that the Secretaries of State believed there to be four main purposes which records of achievement should serve. Among these, they listed:

Motivation and personal development: they [the records – AH] should contribute to pupils' personal development and progress by *improving their motivation*, providing encouragement and increasing their awareness of strengths, weaknesses and opportunities.

A document of record. Young people leaving school or college should take with them a short summary document of record which is recognised and valued by employers and institutes of further education. This should provide a more rounded picture of candidates for jobs or courses than can be provided by a list of examination results, thus *helping potential users to decide how candidates could best be employed, or for which jobs, training schemes or courses they are likely to be suitable.*[3]

As we saw in the previous chapter, one of the dominant reasons for developing records of achievement, not just for the DES but also for many of those schools which had already produced their own home-grown schemes, was and continues to be the enhancement of pupils' motivation. The Department of Education and Science, agencies like Her Majesty's Inspectorate and the (late) Schools Council who advise them, and (not least) a number of individual schools themselves, saw in records of personal achievement an important opportunity for boosting the motivation of those pupils who had so far had little else to gain from the secondary school system.

The school's capacity to realize these motivational goals is, of course, significantly limited by the discouraging press of economic realities on the hopes and aspirations of young people. That is to say, the problem of motivation, while encountered widely within schools, is not at all confined to them. Weakened motivation to work, to aspire, to conform is an increasingly pervasive feature of social life in modern Britain. With few prospects of work for many young people, depressingly little promise of any substantial improvement in overall living standards, and growing doubt as to whether hard-earned academic achievement will reap the once customary financial rewards, it is little wonder that bonds of mass loyalty to the present social and economic order should weaken, that indifference and dissent should increasingly prevail. It is not just problems of motivation in school that have to be faced therefore, but a deep-seated and far-reaching crisis of motivation, of loyalty and commitment to the present social order in society as a whole.[4]

Only economic and social policies which offer young people realistic prospects of opportunity and improvement at least at the levels their parents had
come to expect as usual, can ultimately deal adequately with a crisis on this
sort of scale.

But if the economic context of educational reform is not particularly
conducive to the very changes it requires, a second factor poses an even more
immediate and direct threat to the motivational aims of records of achievement: the use of such records in the process of occupational selection, as a
document that will be 'recognized and valued by employers'.[5] I want to
propose that these two purposes, motivational and selective, are fundamentally incompatible in important respects.

It is commonly assumed that employers will normally be among the major
'users' of a student's final (i.e. summative) record of achievement and of its
personal record component in particular. As the Records of Achievement
initiative has gathered momentum and gained a national impetus, the practice
of including employers in the design of such records has therefore become
increasingly widespread, if not ubiquitous. Within a political and educational
climate where industrial values are attaining increasing force and respect-
ability and where they make up an important part of the context of educational reform, it is easy to understand why educators are considerably more eager
than they once were to encourage employer involvement in this and other
innovations for the secondary age range, and why they are keen to design
those innovations in such a way as to be 'user friendly'.

The move to involve employers and be mindful of their needs and interests
concerning records of achievement is a politically astute one, then. Yet there
is more to that move than sheer political opportunism. Employers have
themselves grown increasingly dissatisfied with the present system of examinations results supplemented by confidential references as a basis for
selecting new employees. For a long time, successful performance in examinations has had to be interpreted by employers as an admittedly crude
indicator of qualities of perseverance, commitment, motivation and so forth,
when more direct information on such personal qualities would often have
been preferred. Employers have thus begun to express cautious interest in a
more extensive system of documenting pupils' personal achievements than
most current forms of assessment allow.[6]

Though there are clear arguments in favour of such a shift of attitude and
orientation among employers towards a recognition of young people's
personal as well as academic qualities, in practice such a move creates serious
points of difficulty too. These are to be found at both the summative and
formative stages of the recording process.

The summative statement

Schools and employers often have different views on the format that the final,
summative record of achievement should take. The effectiveness of systems

of recording in meeting motivation and selection needs respectively has varied very much with the type of system adopted. I will now review the potential of different recording formats for meeting motivational and selection requirements. This classification of types of summative statement closely follows that developed by Hitchcock, and includes four broad types: personal recording, grids, comment banks, and open-ended prose summaries.[7]

1. *Personal recording*

Most systems of pupil self-recording derive from a model developed by Don Stansbury in the Swindon area in the late 1960s: the Record of Personal Achievement (RPA). Variants and derivatives of this model include Stansbury's own later version, the Record of Personal Experience (RPE) and the Schools Council's funded development of this scheme, the Pupils' Personal Record (PPR). Though there are differences between these schemes, they all revolve around entries made by pupils on a variety of headed cards – Hobbies, Family, etc. – which are then stored in a file. The file is controlled by the pupil and access to it can only be gained with the pupil's permission. This 'wodge' of material can later be made available to employers and other potential users if pupils so wish.

Personal recording systems seem to have met with some success in improving pupil motivation, particularly among the less able for whom, incidentally, most of the schemes were initially and primarily designed.[8] The privacy and control afforded to less able, sometimes deviant and potentially disaffected pupils, and the possibilities this has created for them to record experiences and activities which would probably otherwise be at best neglected and at worst frowned upon elsewhere in the schooling system, has almost certainly been helpful in this respect.

Against the success of the schemes in *motivating* many of the less able, must be matched their virtual worthlessness to employers as aids to *selection*. The sheer bulk of the final 'wodge' of materials and the difficulty of knowing just what sense to make of its voluminous contents has seriously undermined the credibility of personal recording systems with employers.[9] Moreover, as Swales points out in his evaluation of RPA, when schemes of personal recordings were extended to include the more able, this group of pupils held serious doubts about the schemes' value, and their parents, indeed, were often anxious that the schemes presented a serious and damaging distraction from 'real learning'.[10] In the case of more able pupils, it seems, for whom future occupational success is a very real possibility, success through *formal* selection via the conventional external examination route at 16 plus, is motivation enough. To sum up: where success in conventional exam-based selection is unlikely, schemes of personal recording make a strong, compensatory contribution to the development of pupil motivation, but they scarcely improve the process of non-exam based selection at all. Schemes of pupil self-recording, that is, apparently score high on motivation but close to zero on selection.

2. *Grid profiles*

In the case of grid-type profile summaries of pupil qualities, skills and achievements, the tendency is precisely in the opposite direction: towards efficient non-exam-based selection, and away from the development of pupil motivation, even though motivation (albeit the extrinsic motivation of meeting short-range targets and objectives) has ranked highly among the aims and intentions of those developing and adopting profile systems. The Scottish Council for Research in Education led the way in developing profile systems with its own *Pupils in Profile* scheme,[11] but elsewhere, profile grids have perhaps been most widely used with the 16–19 age range; the major initiatives being made by the Further Education Curriculum Review and Development Unit (FEU), the City and Guilds 365 scheme and the Manpower Services Commission.

As with forms of pupil self-recording, the exact nature of the grids and checklists vary, but most include a list of qualities (leadership, initiative, punctuality, etc.) or skills (talking and listening, use of powered machinery, etc.) and an assessment of whether and how far pupils/students possess those qualities or have mastered those skills. Such systems of evaluation are usually teacher-dominated or even entirely teacher-controlled, but there are a number of important exceptions (e.g. FEU) where pupils or students participate in and negotiate the construction of their profile with their teachers or tutors.

Of all the systems of recording personal achievements, employers seem to respond best to these.[12] They are brief and easily scanned; they are standardized across all pupils participating in a single institution and in some cases across many institutions; and the skills and qualities listed have at least a superficial resemblance to those in which employers appear to have an interest. From the employers' viewpoint, grid-type profiles are simple and relevant: they can be significant aids to the process of *selection*.

However, as the work of Goacher and others suggests, an assessment and recording system neatly tailored to the needs of employers may be less than beneficial in boosting pupil motivation.[13] Aside from all the criticisms that can be made of the terseness of the categories on the profiles and checklists and of the misunderstandings that can therefore commonly occur about their meaning, and apart from any worries one might have that the 'gaps' between different grades of skill mastery often appear inconsistent and uneven, one of the most distressing features of the operation of grid-like profiles is that in many cases they seem not to increase pupil motivation at all but if anything to depress it still further. It is not difficult to predict the effect upon a pupil of ticks being consistently placed in boxes which attest only to the most elementary level of skill mastery, especially where he or she is witness to and at least nominally involved in the production of this authoritative statement of his or her apparent incompetence. As Goacher points out in his work with schools developing some form or other of recording personal achievements, the very descriptions of elementary skill mastery in some of the grid-type schemes he reviewed – 'can handle *simple* tools with safety', 'understands *simple* scientific language', etc. (my italics) – only served to undermine pupils' sense of worth and to instil deep resentment among them.[14] Equally, after examining the grades used in profile schemes used by the Manpower Services Commission and the Further Education Unit, a group of Scottish evaluators concluded that:

> The grades are . . . vague, uneven, and far too widely spaced to register progress . . . We feel that they work against the central MSC principles of progression, motivation and catering for young people's needs. The grades look as if they belong to a labelling strategy rather than to a learning strategy.[15]

Perhaps it is because of these threats to motivation implied by grid-like schemes that the DES in its draft policy statement directed that:

> One feature of some existing schemes which the Secretaries of State would not wish to see imitated is the practice of grading personal qualities in the form of ticks or letters whose significance is not clear, however conscientious the attempt to define the grade descriptions. Such gradings contain unsupported and often negative judgements and are open to misinterpretation.[16]

To sum up: although developers and adopters of grid-type schemes of profile assessment have been at least as interested in improving the motivation of pupils unlikely to succeed in conventional CSE and 'O' level assessment at sixteen, as they have been in providing information of use to employers, in practice it seems that once more, motivation needs and selection needs are in conflict with one another. Goacher may be right when he remarks that this system of recording pupils' personal achievements (and the lack of them!) should not 'be expected to perform a motivating function except in a very general way by encouraging, for example, attendance'.[17] Getting pupils to underwrite their inability (or unwillingness) to succeed in employer-desired skills and competences will do little to improve their motivation or their sense of worth. Grid-type profiles that is, seem likely to score high on selection but largely at the expense of pupil motivation.

3. *Comment banks*

Proposals which promise to circumvent these difficulties of contributing to occupational selection without prejudice to pupil motivation involve a final document which takes the form of a succinct prose summary involving 'sentences written for each pupil'. This, the DES argue, is 'fairer to pupils' and 'less open to misinterpretation'.[18] Prose summaries can be open or closed, however. In the case of the closed summary there is less student input than in the more open counterpart. Here the consequences for motivation are questionable. Such systems of relatively closed prose recordings are known as *comment banks*. For reasons of cheapness and efficiency to which I shall return shortly, comment banks have been widely discussed and developed as a serious optional form of records for personal achievement.

Comment banks consist of pre-selected statements which identify before-hand the significant areas in which recordings are to be made, and the precise ways in which (indeed, the precise words through which) this is to be done. Thus, to take an example from the draft personal record sheet considered by one LEA, the tutor (in some cases with the student) circles or ticks an appropriate category under headings like 'attitude to people', 'attitude to activities' etc.[19] Under two sub-sections of 'attitude to people' for instance, the tutor must ring at least one of the following, adding any descriptive evidence as appropriate.

P3A   He/she has a cheerful personality

P3B   Considerable concern for others has been shown

P3C   His/Her confidence and assurance enable him/her to relate to other people well

P3D   The openness of his/her relationships enable him/her to solve conflict situations sensibly

P3E   He/she has shown himself/herself to be a responsible person

P3F   He/she is well mannered and courteous

P3G   He/she has a lively sense of humour

PD1   corresponds to a pupil who finds it very difficult to maintain relationships with (a) adults (b) pupils

PD2   corresponds to a pupil who refuses/is unable to relate to others despite encouragement

PD3   corresponds to a pupil who has formed no lasting relationships

PD4   corresponds to a pupil who is aggressive or lacking in self control

PD5   corresponds to a pupil who has shown neither an inclination, nor a capacity, for leadership.

What eventually appears as an open, continuous summative statement is in fact compiled from an assemblage of encircled, numbered categories. It is a disguised grid, no less. It is sometimes argued that systems of this kind have advantages for rapid systems of employer selection (though this assumes that the employers have access to the hidden 'codes' the comment banks contain), and for savings on teacher time by enabling them simply to encircle categor-ies or punch them into a computer, rather than compile elaborate prose statements of their own. But these things are achieved at some cost; the cost of taking away the student's voice, his/her authorship, the stamp of his/her personal identity from the records of personal achievement and experience. In comment banks, student involvement is in effect reduced to making selections from lists of statements which, while they contain options, are not themselves negotiable and are not of the student's own making. While such sacrifices of personal involvement and authorship, such confiscations of the students' own voices and declarations of identity, might bring about certain short-term gains in organizational efficiency and employer relevance, the sacrifices made are probably quite damaging to the motivational purposes that records of achievement are intended to fulfil.

This is not to deny the need that schools may often have for some kind of guide, assistance or additional support for students and tutors involved in personal recording, especially where unskilled tutors and shy or inarticulate students are involved. Indeed, this argument is often put forward in defence of comment banks. But if it is starting points that are needed, or a list of possible areas to probe when discussion flags, then what is required is a supportive and suggestive 'prompt sheet', an optional tool to *stimulate* and *extend* the open-ended and two-sided process of recording students' positive achievements and experiences.[20] The comment bank, however, constrains, contracts and closes down discussion rather than extending and enabling it.

4. *The open-ended prose summary*

Where the final statement is more open-ended, where the choice of mentioned activities and experiences, the qualities they imply and the very words in which all these things are expressed are heavily influenced by the pupil, motivational ends could well be fostered more effectively. The voice, the authorship of the documents can be more the students' own; a matter which is as important for the longer term formative process, if not more so. As the contributors to a newsletter of the Oxford Certificate of Educational Achievement indicated, the personal development and recording process should, in this respect, be very much 'about the student, by the student, for the student'.[21]

As a way of trying to achieve a more equitable balance between motivation needs and selection needs, and in a way that will optimize the fulfilment of each, a number of schools and consortia of Examination Boards and LEAs have run serious trials of more open-ended yet succinct prose summaries of pupil achievements in and out of school. Some of the early advice of the DES was certainly inclined in this direction too. They said:

> There are strong arguments in favour of designing records in such a way that personal qualities and skills are mainly inferred from accounts of actual achievements in activities in which the pupil has participated – or from the absence of such information.[22]

In the succinct, open-ended prose summary, there is at least some possibility that a record of achievement could meet motivation needs by affording a more rounded and positive picture of a pupil than seems feasible in grid-type schemes, and by involving pupils themselves in the long and continuous formative process of self assessment and reappraisal which many see as essential to the construction of the final document. Moreover, it is also possible that employers *might* be persuaded to see the selection implications of a document of no greater length than, say, one side of A4 paper – if only for the purposes of interviewing applicants.

In the succinct prose summary of pupil achievements, then, we may have a form of summative statement which does not pose too many threats to the enhancement of pupil motivation and which does not appear to be unduly prejudicial to the interests of employer selection.

The formative process

However, notwithstanding the importance of the form that the final document takes, it would be unwise to assume that the construction of an appropriate summative document will, of itself, resolve the motivation/ selection dilemma. All that the construction of a concise yet open summative document may do, in fact, is to displace that dilemma into the detailed process of interaction between teachers and pupils through which the final document is ultimately constructed. It is in this process, in the perspectives held by teachers and pupils respectively, in the meanings that pass between them, and in the capacity of one party to impose its meanings upon the other, that pupil motivation needs or perceived employer selection needs are likely to make themselves felt most powerfully and decisively.

There are, Balogh argues, 'good reasons for involving pupils in their own assessment: improved motivation, the fact that they may have the best knowledge of their own strengths and weaknesses and that there are few areas where they could be considered not to have the right to make a judgement'.[23] Some writers, like Burgess and Adams, have gone further than this still, and proposed that the negotiation of assessment between a teacher and a pupil can provide the basis for and be a constitutive part of a new learning, curriculum and assessment contract, negotiated between them on open, democratic terms.[24] Indeed, in a commentary on the Secretary of State's initiative, Burgess and Adams took issue with the draft policy statement's suggestion that the record of achievement should be the responsibility of the school and proposed instead that it should be the responsibility of the pupil. The benefits to the student of the record of achievement, Burgess and Adams suggested

> are better served if students themselves are offered initiative in their own learning and responsibility in compiling their records. In particular, motivation is greatly enhanced where students exercise such initiative and responsibility.[25]

Nor, they continued, will the benefits of democratic involvement accrue solely to the student, for

> the motivation of students and the perception of teachers would alike be enhanced by being expected to discuss together the programmes of work under consideration for school groups and individual students.[26]

Whatever the worth or feasibility of this democratic ideal, it has to be said that the actual practice of negotiated assessment all too often tends to fall well short of it. Negotiating a pupil's assessment with him or her can too easily be discharged in a swift, perfunctory manner and, as Goacher has observed, may even involve the teacher putting pressure on a pupil to alter that assessment.[27] 'Authority', remarked Willard Waller in his classic text *The Sociology of Teaching* 'is on the side of the teacher. The teacher nearly always wins. In fact he must win or he cannot remain a teacher'.[28] It is because of this insight, perhaps, that Waller felt drawn earlier in his book to advancing the following view of the self-governing school.

> Self government is rarely real. Usually it is but a mask for the rule of the teacher oligarchy . . . The experimental school which wishes to do away with authority continually finds that in order to maintain requisite standards of achievement in imparting certain basic skills, it has to introduce some variant of the authority principle, or it finds that it must select and employ teachers who can in fact be despotic without seeming to be so.[29]

Negotiation, however open and fair teachers and heads may declare it and perhaps believe it to be in principle, is nonetheless usually and perhaps inevitably very much one-sided in character. This may or may not be a good thing: but whatever one's beliefs and preferences, its existence has to be conceded.

Roy Hattersley, MP, gives us a salutary insight into this fact in his recollections of life as a second year pupil at Sheffield City Grammar School. He recalls receiving his end of year report and remembers being delighted with the immense improvement in his test results and class position. Yet he was also incensed that:

> the comments alongside the figures bore no relationship to my achievements. They were just the same as the year before when I had been near to the bottom of almost anything. The judgements lacked originality as well as relevance – 'could do better if tried' . . . 'must work harder' . . . 'greater effort needed'![30]

The admirably impetuous Hattersley stormed off to the staffroom in protest and after a brief unsatisfactory encounter with his form-teacher, marched towards the study of the man who 'instead of striking out the libels of my year's industrious progress . . . had lamely added his name in confirmation of the calumny' – the headmaster. Fortunately for Hattersley, he was intercepted outside the head's study by A. W. Goodfellow 'senior master, head of the history department, sometime Commandant of the Sheffield Air Training Corps, President of the Local History Association and man of general cultivation and refinement!'

I looked at him – gleaming shoes, pinstripe suit into which no crease would ever dare to intrude, stiff white collar and clipped moustache – and I explained. I think that the phrase 'not fair' was repeated half a dozen times in a single spoken paragraph. 'These', he said, 'are extremely good results', pausing to allow his emollient message to sink in. 'But you can hardly expect the comments simply to make the same point. If the results and the comment columns said the same thing, the comment column would be wholly unnecessary. Take the two things together – top in English and History but could do better still'. He emphasised the 'still' as if the word actually appeared on the offending report card. 'I would', he concluded, 'be proud to take that report card home'.

'To this day', Hattersley concludes, 'I do not know if I walked out of the school office a more rational human being or the victim of a confidence trick'.

Now readers of Hattersley's autobiographical account might reasonably argue that the stuffy days of pupil deference to gentlemanly authority that characterized life in boys' grammar schools in the 1940s have long since passed. They might equally object to the candid if somewhat vitriolic remarks which Waller passed upon many of his apparently authoritarian colleagues in teaching, on the grounds that these were made more than half a century ago and no longer apply to the more open and democratic educational institutions in which pupils participate today.

Would such criticisms and their implicit optimism about current educational practice be justified, though? Research studies of attempts to democratize and widen choice in other parts of the state education system are not encouraging. At the level of primary schooling, for instance, the trend towards individual choice and self-direction in pupil learning in the 1960s and 1970s was largely restricted to the level of educational rhetoric and seemed to impinge little on the daily realities of classroom practice.[31] Teachers did not abrogate their control over the curriculum. Nor did they hand over learning decisions and choices to pupils in any fundamental way. They simply disguised their control and interventions by exercising them in a more subtle, less overt manner: 'leading from behind' as it was commonly called. At the secondary level, similar processes could be discerned in the broadening of option-choice systems at fourteen to pupils participating in the expanding comprehensive sector. Yet, while in principle this offered many pupils a far greater latitude of choice, in practice it simply placed more of an onus of guidance and selection on to the individual teacher's shoulders – a duty which often involved 'persuading' pupils who had made 'wrong' choices to choose again.[32]

In both cases, it seems – progressive primary teaching and subject option choice – the more that the business of choice and negotiation is conducted through the details of teacher-pupil interaction, the more the outcomes of those choices and negotiations become subject to teachers' judgements and stereotypes of what is appropriate for particular pupils given their perceived ability, their behaviour, their sex and so on.[33] The more informal the process of guidance and choice, that is, the more likely it is that pupils will be channelled along routes which conform to teacher stereotypes of their potential.

Is there any reason to believe that things will be any different in the case of informal, negotiated processes of pupil assessment? Is it likely that secondary school teachers who will continue to be bound to their subject specialisms (perhaps even more in the wake of the initiatives discussed in earlier chapters) and who will continue to spend much if not more of their time teaching for the 16+ examinations (for few advocates of Records of Achievement, least of all the DES, have seriously proposed the abolition or even substantial reduction in scope of such examinations), will be any more sensitive, open and democratic in responding to their pupils' personal and educational needs than their 'progressive' primary colleagues? Under these kinds of continuing pressures – the pressures of dealing with records of achievement alongside existing and perhaps mounting commitments to examinations and subject specialist teaching – it is difficult to see how secondary teachers can, even if they would wish to be, *that* responsive. Certainly, Broadfoot's anxiety that informal processes of pupil assessment 'will be subject to the well-known disadvantages of . . . the halo effect, social class bias and personal antipathy' seems worthy of serious consideration.[34]

What meanings will teachers bring to their encounters with pupils when assessments are negotiated with them? The difficulty for pupils and tutors here, in knowing just what to record, is that the qualities employers value and wish to see schools record are often not altogether the ones that schools themselves promote, or that some of their pupils deem to be important.

As long as the activities and experiences which pupils record and wish to record have the ring of such qualities as leadership, loyalty and obedience that employers value – they do not, contrary to popular belief, place much weight on initiative[35] – as long as their forte is with the piano, with scouting and guiding, or with the fishing club, then there is likely to be little conflict of interest or purpose between the pupil's own needs to declare and define his/her identity, and the interests of employers in identifying young people with qualities they regard as appropriate for employment. But how will teachers react to activities that do not chime so sweetly in the ears of the employers; to activities that suggest dissent (such as feminism or peace-campaigning) or to ones that imply deviance or nonconformity (such as Rastafarianism or breakdancing)? Here, pupils and their tutors are placed in a real quandary: whether to define and declare interests and identities, however unconventional, even at the risk of prejudicing employment; or whether to edit, select, or even distort personal records a little so as to present a good impression to employers, but at the cost of concealing, suppressing or falsifying important aspects of pupils' own identities.

In the case of teachers and pupils alike, the choice of either option has a 'Catch 22'-like quality about it. Declare pupil activities and involvements, however unconventional and you will probably enhance pupils' motivation, but only at the cost of their job prospects. Stick to recording only clearly 'reputable' activities and achievements and you will communicate a more positive sense of a pupil's employability, but only at the expense of failing to declare and therefore implicitly denying vast chunks of the more unconventional pupil's experience and identity. The consequences of such a denial for a pupil's identity and motivation are potentially very serious; for whereas poor performance in conventional subject examinations possibly labels a pupil as an academic and intellectual failure, the public excision of large parts of his or her identity entails failing that pupil utterly as a person. Thus, the more all-encompassing the assessment, the more total and damaging will be the consequences for the identities of those more unconventional pupils who are subject to it, even more so if they actively participate in the construction of that assessment, if they actually underwrite this public statement of apparent personal failure. Clearly, when pupils and teachers are playing for stakes as high as these, for declarations or denials of personal worth, no less, the task of identifying the means which different types of pupils and teachers attach to the recording and assessment process, and the ways in which these meanings are negotiated between them is an urgent priority.

Conclusion

In their incisive account of the reorganization and reconstruction of secondary education in Scotland since the war, John Gray and his colleagues point to three problems which have accompanied educational expansion: problems of difficulty, selection and motivation.[36] One combined effect of these problems, they argue, is that in the interests of fair, meritocratic *selection*, the examination system has been extended to encompass a wider and wider section of the ability range. But, they go on, this has only served to subject many pupils of moderate or low ability to forms of assessment of very great *difficulty* and to exam-directed courses of little intrinsic interest. This, in turn, has affected pupil *motivation*, particularly among the less able as they experience courses in which their prospect of failure or of only the most limited kinds of success, are very great.

In the conventional examination system, it seems that with less able pupils, selection needs and motivation needs are very much at odds with one another. Whether restructuring of the examination system through the new GCSE will alleviate these difficulties still remains to be seen. But how sad and ironic it would be if more open forms of assessment, one of whose central purposes is to provide alternative ways of generating pupil motivation *despite* the exams, actually turned out only to depress motivation still further among many pupils, particularly the unconventional and 'unclubbable'. If we are to stand any chance of avoiding these difficulties, a number of policy priorities seem worthy of further exploration.

Most controversially, perhaps, the most satisfactory solution to the dilemma I have outlined would be to remove one of the parties engaged in this conflict of interest: i.e. to exclude the employers. It is customary, indeed it seems to be almost obligatory to involve employer representatives in the construction of records of achievement, and to regard them as one of the major users of such records. Yet, while one can understand the fearful keenness with which educators court employer involvement in an educational and social system which is becoming increasingly directed towards industrial values, one cannot help wondering whether the extent of employers' involvement might be far outweighing their practical importance. I have already pointed to some of the negative backwash effects that employer values can have on the assessment process. The fact that employers are simply there, as potential users, is probably enough to guarantee this. Their involvement in the actual design of records just makes such effects more certain still. But with so few students now going direct into employment at sixteen, and so many going on to further education or training, employers are scarcely *users* of records of personal achievement at all. Other than for reasons of political appeasement, then, there would appear to be few other grounds for their continued inclusion. Certainly, schools and exam boards and the like would do well to ponder the importance they attach to employer involvement, and the possibly negative implications of such involvement for the recording process and the motivational goals it is designed to achieve. In this case, the use of records of achievement as a selection device for employment could reasonably be deferred until post-compulsory education, thereby releasing Records of Personal Achievement in the compulsory stage to concentrate more exclusively on the satisfaction of motivation and personal development needs alone.

Short of strategies of exclusion of employers, however, the resolution of these difficult dilemmas, of these important value questions, will come to rest (as is so often the case) on the professional judgement of the individual classroom teacher as he/she participates with pupils in the process of negotiated assessment. Here, in making and having to make complicated philosophical and social judgements about what are acceptable and unacceptable activities for pupils to declare and record, teachers will need to be very much aware of the value questions that are involved to be able to reappraise their own values, to be aware of the dangers of stereotyping and to be able to monitor the effects of their own value assumptions on the recording process. For teachers – indeed for any human being – these are very challenging tasks to have to undertake, and if they are to be properly discharged they will demand the highest level of skill, awareness and sensitivity on the teachers' part.

It scarcely needs saying that a judgemental task of this magnitude and seriousness will require strong and continued in-service support, and sufficient time to treat it with the care and sensitivity it patently requires. Such in-service training and the research basis on which it could be mounted should be designed not only to alert teachers to the dangers of stereotyping nor even to coach them in the difficult skills of negotiation, but also to stimulate rigorous collegial discussions of the values that are involved in the assessment process; not least so that teachers can come to recognize and appreciate the value of certain pupil activities and achievements not normally recognized as worthwhile by schools and employers.

The initiatives, both local and national, to develop Records of Personal Achievement for secondary school pupils have the potential to realize a number of long-hoped for and worthwhile human ideals in education concerning the development and personal growth of young people, and the encouragement of their own active involvement in that development. Few people would argue that, in principle, this is a bad thing. Yet amid a movement whose passionate educational optimism has sometimes reached proportions not far short of religious fervour, it would be a pity if we could not turn to dispassionate evaluations of this initiative. This would help us to identify different forms that records of achievement might take and assess their consequences in each case; it would help us pinpoint difficulties and obstacles regarding their implementation and suggest practical guidance for overcoming them; and, not least because of the intensity of almost religious conviction behind this innovation, it would help keep a few sobering heretical thoughts (not least the exclusion of employers) on the policy agenda.

In the meantime, the issues of time and of staff support are critical. Both these things have implications for the school context of purpose and constraint in which records of achievement are implemented. This context is the concern of the next chapter.

7 Assessment and Surveillance

Introduction

A second major dilemma for Records of Personal Achievement concerns whether, intentionally or unintentionally, schools use them to increase pupils' independence and capacity for self-determination on the one hand, or to expand and refine schools' own capacities for maintaining surveillance, for instilling an unobtrusive but pervasive kind of discipline, on the other. Both these tendencies – the development of independence and the suppression of it – are contained within the Records of Achievement initiative. Either of them can follow as a widespread consequence of that initiative becoming established.

Assessment and personal development

For many people who have been involved with records of personal achievement, such records hold out the hope of a radical departure from conventional secondary school practice. They offer – as many of the advocates of 'progressive' primary education in the 1960s did – the hope, the possibility of placing young people at the centre of their own learning, giving them increased responsibility for their own development and assessment, empowering them with the capacity for self-determination. Such principles were, for instance, central to the personal recording movement instigated by Stansbury.[1]

This was a movement which emphasized the student's autonomy, his/her ownership of and control over the process and product of recording. Here the role of teacher intervention was reduced to a minimum; the teacher's opinion and evaluation of what the student was recording was only offered if the student specifically wanted it.

In a document produced by the Management Group of one of the best known successors of these early schemes, PPR (Pupils' Personal Recording), this process was described as being:

> owned and controlled by the pupil and is made without imposition of ranking, rating, marking and censure. It is not something which develops merely as a response to teacher intervention. It can provide a framework for confident personal development in young people.[2]

That kind of development, they went on to say, is 'the highest aim in education'. It amounts to nothing less than 'the promotion of personal autonomy which will allow each person to make free, informed decisions as responsible adults and to exercise 'a sense of personal power'.[3] Moreover, the group argued, successful PPR experience of this kind 'provides the bedrock for pupil participation in Records of Achievement'.[4]

Burgess and Adams have also advocated strong pupil involvement in schemes which record and assess their personal achievements, arguing that such involvement will help secure a basis for a whole new learning contract between teachers and pupils, based on principles of partnership rather than hierarchy. School-leaving statements which include records of personal experience and achievements that students have helped compile themselves, they say, would 'encourage young people to take charge of their own circumstances so that they leave school not only knowledgeable but also competent and independent'. This, they continue, 'will require teachers not to prepare for examinations by teaching to a syllabus, but to respond directly to what young people themselves need'.[5] As various practical examples in an earlier book of theirs indicate, the acceptance of pupils' rights to assess that sort of need carries with it an inescapable obligation to allow them opportunities to criticize the teaching and the curriculum they already receive, and to negotiate changes in it where appropriate.[6]

If the Department of Education and Science have not subsequently embraced these principles of 'pupil power' with quite that degree of enthusiasm, choosing instead to blur the issue of what form and extent pupil involvement should take – a strategy for which Burgess and Adams have criticized them heavily[7] – developers of particular schemes at more local levels have been less circumspect. In its draft handbook for pilot schools, for instance, the Oxford Certificate of Educational Achievement described the personal record component as aiming 'to involve students as active participants in their own development' and 'to open up possibilities for broader and deeper relationships between students and teachers'.[8] And a glance at some of the Certificate Committees' working notes and memoranda would reveal pupil-centred statements of an even more forthright character.

Much of the grass-roots impetus behind records of achievement, then, is to do with the recognition and realization of pupils' identities, with the development of their powers of independent judgement; with the enhancement of their identity and independence as a whole, that is. Nor are these things desired solely for their capacity to boost motivational ends. They are seen as something important and worthwhile in their own right, too.

Assessment and surveillance

Alongside these values, which place a premium on autonomy and independence, records of achievement also contain a set of possible purposes and consequences with different, indeed absolutely contrary, implications. The personal record component of records of achievement also has an extraordinary capacity to restrict young peoples' individuality, to discipline and control them through the power of a pervasive and intrusive pattern of personal assessment. I want to argue that this pattern, with its assessment and monitoring of affect as well as intellect, of personality as well as performance, according to a carefully graded schedule of systematized review, is in fact bound up with a more generalized trend towards the development and implementation of increasingly sophisticated techniques of social surveillance within society at large. In this respect, while records of personal achievement can certainly be used as part of a commitment to personal care, they can be employed equally well as part of a complicated apparatus of social and institutional control. What characterizes this swing to surveillance, and what particular part might records of personal achievement be playing in this particular social development?

According to the French philosopher and historian, Michel Foucault, attitudes to discipline and punishment have passed through three broad phases. At first, he says, punishment for serious crime was treated as a kind of vengeance where public torture provided a spectacle of retribution, in which the marks of that vengeance were applied to the body of the condemned person as a lesson in terror for all.[9]

In the second phase, punishment by vengeance was superseded by systems of correction designed to reintegrate offenders into society. Here, by opening prisons to the public and, through publicly visible signs of the convicts' dress, the chain gang, and such like, justice was *seen* to be done; a warning to others that it would be exercised on *them* if they should ever transgress in turn.

It is only quite recently, Foucault argues – mainly in this century – that the treatment of actual or potential offenders has entered a third and critical phase. Here, he says, punishment of whatever form has been gradually replaced or complemented by *discipline*. The purpose of this discipline is neither merely corrective nor even simply preventative, but is bound up with the very make-up of modern society and its concerns of control and efficiency.[10] Discipline, Foucault argues, is a finely graded, carefully regulated process of administrative control over both body and mind. As personification of this disciplinary process, Foucault cites Napoleon, a man who

> wished to arrange around him a mechanism of power that would enable him to see the smallest event that occurred in the state he governed; he intended, by means of the rigorous discipline that he imposed, to embrace the whole of this vast machine without the slightest detail escaping his attention.[11]

But this pattern of discipline is not merely exercised by particular individuals, by fascist dictators or even benevolent despots, but by and through entire adminstrative systems, where surveillance is perpetual and pervasive, intense and intrusive, continuous and remorseless in its application and effects.

At the heart of such systems of surveillance, Foucault argues, are two central principles: *normalization* and *hierarchy*. Normalization, or normalizing judgements, involves comparing, differentiating, homogenizing and excluding people in relation to assumed 'norms' or standards of what is proper, reasonable, desirable and efficient.[12] *Hierarchy* involves a process whereby power is exercised through 'a mechanism that controls by means of observation',[13] where the powerful observe but are not themselves observed, where they see without being seen, where they judge, rank and rate, but are not themselves evaluated.[14]

Few processes, Foucault suggests, represent and embody this convergence of the principles of normalization and hierarchy more clearly than the examination. For Foucault,

> the examination combines the techniques of an observing hierarchy with those of a normalizing judgement. It is a normalizing gaze, a surveillance that makes it possible to qualify, to classify and to punish.[15]

All this, Foucault claims, makes it possible to establish and reaffirm the norm, and place people in relation to it.

In response to this interpretation of the role and function of examinations as instruments of surveillance, of normalization and hierarchy, defenders of records of personal achievement might want to argue that they offer a pattern of assessment and a prospect for pupils' personal development which is quite different from and in many respects superior to the conventional examination system, with its principles of norm-referenced attainment. They would, I am sure, want to emphasize the non-hierarchical elements of partnership and negotiation involved in the personal recording process. They would want to stress the fact that pupils own and control the use of their final summative statement. And they would want to point to the distinctive contribution that self-assessment – assessment according to one's own set standards rather than to normative criteria established by others – makes to the recording of personal achievements and experience. A very good case indeed could therefore be made for saying that records of personal achievement are supremely equipped to mitigate and compensate for those very tendencies towards hierarchy and normalization that are built into the conventional system of formal examining at 16 plus: that they can actually increase independence and suppress surveillance.

It is instructive to note, however, that when Foucault discusses examinations and their contribution to social surveillance, he by no means confines himself to conventional formal examinations with written papers, time limits and the like. For Foucault, the psychiatric examination and the case record assessment as applied in the prison service and social work are very much part of the same system. Indeed, it is in the case recording process that normaliza-tion, hierarchy and all-embracing observation are at their most systematic.

Once upon a time, Foucault tells us, 'to be looked at, observed, described in detail, followed from day to day by an uninterrupted writing was a privilege',[16] it was to have chronicled a biography of greatness and distinc-tiveness, to be part of a process of heroization. But with the advent of disciplinary methods, he says, written description became 'a means of control and a method of domination . . . no longer a measurement for future memory, but a document for possible use'. In this particular kind of examination, Foucault goes on, each individual is simply made into a documented 'case'. It is a case which 'constitutes a hold for a branch of power', a case which describes, judges and compares the individual as someone who may now, or at some future unknown point need to be 'trained or corrected, classified, normalized, excluded, etc.'.

This building up of a dossier, of an extended case record, to be retrieved and referred to at any future point where the difficult work of institutional guidance and channelling, control and correction needs to be done, comes uncomfortably close to some aspects of the formative process of recording pupils' personal achievements. For instance, Broadfoot has noted how the system of continuous pupil assessment, of *orientation* in the French school system, already runs very much on these lines.[17] And in Britain, comment banks seem as if they will be particularly well suited to the purposes of surveillance and control; ranking and rating pupils in relation to pre-selected (if thinly disguised) hierarchies of presumed institutional importance – according to the institution's criteria, not pupils' own – and in a form appropriate for easy and rapid processing and retrieval.

Moreover, the hooking up of personal records, particularly of the forma-tive kind, to computer facilities in school, as a large number of schools have now done, presents a strong threat to pupils' independence by enabling schools to keep hi-tech tabs on their pupils' emotional and behavioural whereabouts; to subject young people to and process them through a sophisticated technological apparatus of institutional control. In this respect, while very serious questions have quite properly been raised about who will be the users of a student's final summative record of achievement, we have scarcely begun to discuss the equally important question of who will be the users of the *formative* records – pupils or teachers? – and for what purposes. Many of the decisions that schools and their teachers will make in relation to the purposes of either independence or surveillance will hinge upon how this sensitive issue is resolved.

If the conversion of developing persons into easily processable cases is one surveillance-related danger inherent in personal recording, another is the development of a principle of observation and monitoring whose sophistica-tion and comprehensiveness is virtually unsurpassed in the history of school-ing. Foucault, following a hypothetical architectural structure of a perfect social and disciplinary observatory devised by Jeremy Bentham, terms this principle *panopticism*.[18] Panopticism is a principle of discipline in which power is exercised through an all–seeing but unseen observer, i.e. one who is so positioned to observe all those arranged around him without himself being observed. More than this, the power of panopticism resides not just in observation *per se*, but in the observed never knowing whether they are being observed or not at any particular moment.[19] For Bentham, this design was not just an architectural structure but an ideal abstract principle, a vision of how disciplined social relations could be sustained in society as a whole. Perfect surveillance!

The great advantage of panopticism is not only that it allows those in power to intervene at any moment, but that 'the constant pressure acts even before the offences, mistakes or crimes have been committed . . . its strength is that it never intervenes, it is exercised spontaneously and without noise'.[20]

In education, there have been few places where panopticism was more palpably evident than in the otherwise innocuous environment of the 'progressive' primary school. Here, despite a public and professional rhetoric which often stressed the collaborative quality of teacher–pupil relationships, and despite the superficial appearance of openness and equality which the architecture and internal organization of 'progressive' primary schools tended to convey, teachers did not stop controlling pupils' learning behaviour, but simply changed the mode of its operation. Control was no longer explicit and overt but, to the 'outsider' at least, implicit and covert; quiet, detailed, unobtrusive in its operation.[21] In making this shift to the implicit mode, teacher control did not diminish. On the contrary it became more comprehensive and more intrusive. In this 'invisible pedagogy' of the primary school, as Basil Bernstein called it, more and more of the child's life became open and subject to assessment.[22] Not just performance, but emotions, behaviour, personal relationships – all were now subject to evaluation, appraisal and institutional intervention; to the teacher–judge's ever-watchful gaze. And if assessment now penetrated deeper into the child's personal and emotional being, it also extended across a wider range of his/her actions too. As the privacy of feeling became eroded, so too in principle did the realm of private space. Wherever children went, they were open to assessment. In the Wendy House they were watched. In the sand tray they were watched. In theory, no place was private. There was in the words of the old detective serial 'No Hiding Place' from the teacher's relentless, if benevolent, pursuit.

In practice, however, surveillance was much less perfect, much less efficient than this. For strategies of teacher control and direction which are implicit and individualized, personal rather than public, also make exhaustive demands on teachers' time and energy where large pupil groups are managed on an individual basis in an open-plan setting. Under these conditions, personalized observation (the observation of eye and ear) is insufficient, and pupils often find that they are able to exploit the classroom's physical fluidity to escape the teacher's gaze and to avoid working. As some pupils I interviewed in a study of a 'progressive' middle school remarked,

Teachers aren't often there to see you . . . With the teachers not being in the classroom all the time, they're all over the place looking after the other ones. All you have to do is stop dead and almost go to sleep.

If you don't want to do it, there's nobody sort of jumping down your neck asking for it.

Well you go into the toilets and you disappear and nobody really notices you until you're found later on.

You can skive. They never know where you are, really.[23]

The personalized, individualized observation of eye and ear in an open, large group setting is therefore necessarily limited in the degree to which it can realize the panopticist vision of perfect surveillance. Indeed, the recognition of those limits by teachers and heads in part explains why the use of written records has expanded in the primary sector in recent years as an aid to improving, monitoring and evaluating pupil progress.

But it is in the process of recording pupils' personal achievements and experiences that the combination of eye, ear and written word are potentially at their most powerful for fulfilling the task of social surveillance. Like 'progressive' primary teaching, records of personal achievement also review and regulate personal and emotional development, but they can do these things with far greater force and effectiveness. Firstly, they carry with them the force of compulsion, of required pupil attendance in one-to-one sessions with their tutors, where it is virtually mandatory for emotions, feelings and intentions to be exposed and subjected to scrutiny. Secondly, they bear the power of personalization that is inherent in the intimate but imbalanced relationship between tutor and student, a relationship both intense and intrusive in the extent to which it allows the tutor to delve into emotional and personal areas that the student might otherwise wish to keep private. Thirdly, they embody the continuous controls of periodic, regular reviews; a process which positions the pupil in relation to a document or computer-stored series of past reviews, marking his/her progress towards or deviation from 'normality'. This process, through the pupils' certain knowledge that there will be inescapable future reviews in an almost unending process of repeated and regulated assessment, suppresses 'deviant' conduct even before it arises.

The worst possible scenario for records of personal achievement, in which the principle of surveillance not independence is the dominant one, might be the 'ideal' system of modern penal treatment described by Foucault. Such a system, he argues,

Would be an indefinite discipline; an interrogation without end, an investigation that would be extended without limit to a particular and ever more analytical observation, a judgement that would at the same time be the constitution of a file that was never closed.[24]

This is a nightmarish Orwellian vision of records of personal achievement, a vision in which all private alcoves, all means of escape from the all-encompassing gaze of permanent observation and assessment have been removed, a vision from which only the terror but little of the discipline of Orwell's OCEANIA (a name with an uncomfortably close resemblance to OCEA – the acronym for the Oxford Certificate of Education Achievement) has been removed.

If this vision is a depressing and frightening one, thankfully it is not by any means inevitable. The positive potential of records of personal achievement is very real: potential for independence, collaboration, criticism and question-ing, for fostering genuine personal development and social awareness. But the dividing lines between care and control, independence and surveillance, are exceedingly thin ones. If I have devoted more attention to the possibilities for surveillance than for those of independence, that is because I regard the dangers and the imminent threat of increasing and intensifying surveillance in schools, as in society at large, as being very great: a threat to individual liberty, personal privacy and human diversity, no less.

Schools and teachers, then, must recognize the choices that they have to make when they develop systems of recording pupils' personal achievements and experiences: choices between independence and motivation on the one hand, or selection and surveillance on the other. These choices are not merely academic; not just matters of theoretical nicety. They carry with them very serious practical implications. Systems which embrace the former (and in my view, more positive) set of values will require teachers who have a clear and agreed collective commitment to them, who are aware of the practical difficulties they entail in dealing with the more unconventional student, and who have the skills, sensitivity and professional courage to be able to foster qualities of independence and assertiveness on the part of their pupils, when the temptation to use the process of negotiated assessment as a mechanism of censure and control might be understandably greater.

Assessment and constraint

If choice, commitment and awareness are essential to the business of im-plementing records of personal achievement in schools as a tool for enhanc-ing personal development and independence, then schools and those who finance them must also recognize that teachers need time and opportunity to make these choices, to develop their skills and awareness. In this respect, I want to argue that if records of personal achievement are to be treated with the sensitivity and seriousness they patently require, then a number of other constraints that operate on teachers, that restrict their time and affect their educational commitments, will need to be attended to. Goodwill and ex-hortation will not be enough. In this final section, I want to explore four areas of constraint and pressure, whose management will in my view have important implications for the way in which teachers interpret and manage the personal recording process. These areas of constraint are time, subject commitments, examinations and what I call compound innovation.

1. *Time*

In *Records of Achievement: A Statement of Policy*, the Department of Education and Science recognize that the process of recording and discussion will make demands on teachers' time.

> The amount of time involved will need to be investigated. It will be essential to work out cost-effective arrangements for accommodating the processes of recording and discussion within schools' regular routines and to identify the scope for savings in other reporting systems and elsewhere.[25]

The problem of finding teacher time for records of achievement has already been widely discussed in the literature on pupil profiles and is one that Her Majesty's Inspectorate have also identified as placing major constraints on teachers' involvement in innovation more generally.[26]

In *Curriculum 11–16: Towards a Statement of Entitlement*, for instance, HMI noted that teachers' existing time commitments severely restricted the extent to which they could become involved in processes of whole school curriculum reappraisal based on HMI's classification of the curriculum into eight areas of experience. They wrote:

> The work of the enquiry has demonstrated the difficulties of undertaking sustained evaluation and planning of the curriculum *and at the same time* meeting the pressures and demands of teaching and administration in a school . . . Problems of communication within the schools have been accentuated by the *limited time* which is available for this work in the normal context of school life.[27]

In other words, unless teacher-pupil ratios are substantially improved and non-teaching periods increased, one might expect, with DES and HMI, that shortage of time over and above that allocated to ordinary class demands will create major problems for teachers and schools in the administration of records of personal achievement. And if, as a result, the recording process comes to be handled within rather than outside of the conventional class or tutor group setting, one might then expect the distribution of teacher time *within* the class to be experienced as a major problem too, and to influence the kinds of teaching strategies that teachers adopt there; perhaps pushing the rest of the group into busy work while the more personalized business of one-to-one assessment is being done.

Furthermore, if cost effectiveness and the making of economies in reporting systems are allowed to dominate unduly the management and operation of the personal record component of records of achievement, then teachers, schools and LEAs may well find themselves drawn to systems which allow rapid and easy processing and which are quickly administered, easily stored and rapidly retrieved under these conditions. The comment bank and similar systems of pre-determined categories and criteria will look especially attractive, and teachers will be tempted and pressed into discharging the task of one-to-one negotiation in a swift and perfunctory manner, all at the cost of student involvement, of his/her own personal development and struggle towards assertive independence.

It is essential, therefore, that schools are provided with sufficient resources and teachers with sufficient time to administer personal recording with the sensitivity it requires; and that sufficient in-service opportunity is also made available on a continuous basis for teachers to recognize, clarify and confront the difficult social and moral value questions which are inextricably embedded in almost every moment of the recording process.

2. *Subject commitments*

> The pilot schemes will need to address the implications of records of achievement for in-service training of teachers . . . In-service training is likely to have an important role to play in helping to equip teachers with *the skills needed* to make a success of the recording system.[28]

Curriculum and assessment innovations often carry with them requirements for change in teachers' pedagogy – the neutral chairperson in Humanities' Curriculum Project,[29] the organizer of collaborative group work in Active Tutorial Work,[30] the non-interventionist teacher of PPR, and so on. As I have indicated in earlier chapters, one of the major areas of difficulty here is that the degree and kind of change needed in the development of new teaching skills often varies according to the teacher's subject.

For one thing, the segregation of the teaching community into competing factions defending territorial claims seriously inhibits collective agreement on cross-curricular change. For another, a teacher's subject membership also affects his or her approach to pedagogical issues, be these concerned with children's writing,[31] mixed ability teaching[32] or active tutorial work.[33] Here, one might expect teachers of certain subjects to experience rather more difficulty than others in acquiring the interpersonal skills necessary for recording pupils' personal achievements and experiences. Physical science, mathematics and modern languages are three of the subjects that come most readily to mind here, subjects which have conventionally attributed little importance to the exploration and discussion of pupils' emotions and personal development.[34]

The identification of such likely areas of difficulty are, of course, only loose predictions based on observation of how different subject teachers have responded to innovation elsewhere in the system. They are not hard and fast research findings – those are eagerly awaited. But they do suggest that schools might consider easing their teachers' long-standing subject loyalties a little by giving them a broader curricular role with younger pupils, encouraging them to offer unusual fourth and fifth year curricular modules outside their own subject in TVEI courses and the like, in order to widen their pedagogical experience and expertise. Such a policy would, of course, run directly counter to one major arm of government educational policy at the moment which, through the National Curriculum and related measures, is currently seeking to tighten up the relationship between teachers' subject qualifications and the areas of the curriculum they teach in school. It seems to me, however, that a policy of easing rather than strengthening teachers' subject loyalties may be extremely important for the successful implementation of Records of Personal Achievement.

3. *Examinations*

There has not been any serious proposition at the level of national policy that records of personal achievement should *replace* more conventional procedures of public examining at 16+. Many writers, including Her Majesty's Inspectorate, have been asserting for some time that examinations exert a constraining, cramping effect upon the secondary school curriculum and upon the processes of teaching and learning that go on within it.[35] Their restrictive effects on innovations within particular subject areas have been widely documented[36] and HMI have also noted how teachers' commitments to examination work make it difficult for them to embrace, or take seriously, proposed changes in their teaching which would seem to threaten their success in such work.[37] Evidence for these claims was reviewed in Chapter 4.

On the basis of these observations, we might predict that where examination-directed work and records of personal achievement make competing claims on a teacher's scarce time, then priority will be allocated to the former rather than the latter. Moreover, where most teachers' classes are geared to examination work we would expect those teachers to experience particular difficulty in conducting the processes of one-to-one discussion and negotiation with pupils in the spirit in which those processes were intended.

If public examinations at 16+ do indeed present a sizeable obstacle to the successful implementation of records of personal achievement – and it seems that these examination commitments are not only persisting, but actually increasing since the advent of GCSE (whose introduction occurred at the very same time that many schools were also taking their first steps in relation to records of achievement) – then schools might do well to consider ways of *easing* the weight that they attach to examinations and examination work.

Within the market system of parental choice, any school which *individually* decided to reduce its commitment to public examinations would, in effect, be putting itself into voluntary liquidation. But one strategy schools might consider as a reasonable and somewhat daring move, particularly where these schools are located in a coherent geographical area, would be to have a federation which agreed policy across a number of schools to lower examination entry ceilings at 16+ to no more than five or six subjects per pupil. This would bring about a *de facto* reduction in the competitive market influences of parental choice, reduce the prominence of examinations within the curriculum and create more space, time and alternative experience for the building up of other kinds of commitments. It is common to hear heads extol the virtues of co-operation and collaboration amongst their pupils and their staff. It would be interesting and, as an act of innovative leadership, instructive to see what heads could co-operatively achieve amongst themselves in this one important area at least. In the long run, the benefit to records of personal achievement and other curriculum and assessment initiatives might turn out to be considerable.

4. *Compound innovation*

The advent of the GCSE points to a more general problem for schools which have already committed themselves to or wish to commit themselves to records of personal achievement: how can they deal adequately with the requirement this innovation will make of them, when many schools are simultaneously being encouraged or (through the policy of 'earmarked' funding) enticed into taking on a number of other cross-curricular innovations too? How will schools respond to the records of achievement initiative when they have also committed themselves to, say, CPVE, TVEI or the Lower Attaining Pupils Project, for instance, not to mention the *de facto* commitment to GCSE itself? How will schools and teachers balance these competing commitments on their time, energy and educational loyalties? What will be the implications of this climate of escalating pressure and constraint on the management and success of any one innovation, like records of personal achievement? What are the implications for in-service training and staff development; for teachers' very capacity to cope? And what priority will teachers attach to records of achievement when there are many others enjoying higher status and stronger resource support in the compound package?

Conclusion

Few of these constraints are easily resolved. All are politically sensitive. Easing most of them could run directly counter to current government policy. Yet if the innovatory angels of curriculum development understandably fear to tread for too long in these earthly realms of politics and finance, of conflict and constraint, this may only mean that their high celestial principles achieve only the weakest degree of success when they are transported into the real world of schools. Schools and policy-makers may have to face the fact that the price of short-term 'realism' and 'pragmatism' is ultimate failure. Time, resources, the easement of other competing commitments – these ecological, contextual changes in teachers' work are almost certainly essential to a personal recording process which is undertaken with the sensitivity and seriousness it deserves.

At the end of the day, the way in which records of personal achievement are interpreted and implemented will depend on the views and visions of social purpose they are seen to realize: independence, motivation and self-realization on the one hand, or streamlined selection and intensified surveillance on the other. If it is the first set of values they are to realize and not the second, then teachers will also need the time, the space and the opportunity to develop and deploy the appropriate interpersonal skills and to deal with the difficult questions of social values. It is on these issues – the clarification of purpose and the conquering of constraint – that the success of a record of personal achievement which is personally liberating and not socially repressive will almost certainly depend.

8 Reforming Educational Assessment: a Test for Socialism

In British secondary schools, few matters concern and preoccupy those who teach and those who are taught more than educational assessment – especially in the form of public examinations. Pupils work hard to acquire them. Teachers measure their own and their colleagues' competence by them. Much of the curriculum is geared towards them. And parents and politicians judge the performance of schools in terms of them. As Patricia Broadfoot puts it, examinations therefore attest to *competence*; they organize curriculum *content*; they stimulate and regulate *competition*, and they maintain overall *control* over educational development and change (or its absence).[1] Clearly, secondary school examinations have a powerful and wide-ranging set of functions and effects within the modern educational system.

Why is it, then, that the Labour movement and the Left more generally have apparently taken such little interest in public examinations or indeed in assessment as a whole? Why has assessment been largely absent from the Left's policy agenda on education? Further, what might the consequences of such continuing neglect be for educational development under socialist or social-democratic leadership? And what positive steps towards bringing about change in educational assessment might usefully be adopted in the future that would be consistent with socialist policy and practice? This final chapter raises issues that might stimulate discussion about these questions.

The neglect of assessment

The Left and the Labour Party in particular never really seems to have grasped the nettle of examination or assessment reform. Proposals for reform formed part of but quickly subsided from the Great Debate in the mid 1970s. Discussions about common examining at 16+ also took place under Shirley Williams' ministership but these were drawn out and indecisive – first diverted to the Waddell Committee which reported in 1978, then overtaken by a General Election. In part, this indecision was almost certainly due to delaying tactics by the DES; to its attempts to defer decisions about this vital and influential area of educational policy until it (rather than the teacher-dominated Schools Council) could establish a firmer grip on the policy-making process.[2] But in some measure, the indecision was also due to Labour's lack of conviction about and commitment to examination reform of a radical nature.[3]

By contrast, Conservatives have accorded central importance to assessment in their policy agenda. Reforms like the GCSE, the CPVE, graded assessments, Records of Achievement, and the required publication of examination results have in their scope and in the speed of their implementation, signalled the Conservative Government's keen awareness of assessment as a dominant influence upon the curriculum; and as something over which Central Government is able to exert relatively direct control in the further-ance of its own educational and political ambitions.

The response of the Left and the Labour movement generally has been disappointing. They have, of course, complained about the under-resourcing and over-hasty implementation of the GCSE. Less strongly, they have also expressed reservations about the maintenance of differentiated levels of entry within the new examination. And, especially with the teacher unions, they have voiced anxieties about the financing and staffing of new assessment developments overall.[4] Such are the worries that underpin the most common objection to assessment reform – 'Where is all the time going to come from?' Aside from complaints about general levels of staffing and resourcing, though, the Left has had very little to say about the educational or social desirability of the newly emerging patterns of assessment – about profiles, graded assessments, the national criteria for GCSE, etc. Nor has it outlined in any detail what patterns of assessment would be compatible with a specifical-ly socialist approach to education. On these matters concerning the general purpose and character of educational assessment, the Left's voice has been disappointingly mute.

In a Fabian pamphlet outlining Labour policy in education for the 1987 General Election and in a key speech preceding it, by Labour's then shadow Education Minister, Giles Radice, the Party committed itself to an ambitious programme of reform and expansion – expansion of access to further and higher education, better remuneration for teachers, more resources for books and buildings, redirection of state resources and support from the private to the state sector and so forth.[5] All this was couched in an urgent but optimistic language of expansion, opportunity and investment in human potential.

After a long period of serious retrenchment in educational expenditure, it was reasonable to believe that the restoration of firm commitments to improved access, expansion and opportunity would be a popular move. At the same time, one cannot help feeling that socialist thinking should really have been moving further than this – into the no-longer-secret garden of the curriculum which the Conservatives have increasingly made their own, landscaping it to their own taste and design; and into the related areas of educational assessment too. In some respects, it was the failure of Labour and the Left more generally to develop a broad, popular and distinctively socialist set of policies on curriculum and assessment that helped remove it from government. As I argued in Chapter 5, its policies of access and expansion were no longer tenable in the midst of the 1970s recession. And the preference for reform by administrative means seemed less and less relevant as the bulk of comprehensive reorganization was completed.

The Conservatives had already seized the initiative on the issues of standards, quality and the curriculum. And for want of a clearly thought through and broadly agreed socialist view of the *process* of education, when Labour *did* reluctantly enter the debate about the content and process of education, most notably through James Callaghan's Ruskin College speech and the Great Debate that followed it, all that could be offered was a pale replica of Conservative thinking – the need to tighten up the relationship between school and working life, to give more attention to basic skills and so on.

To some extent, modern Labour educational policy proposals have repeated this error; seeking to meet the educational challenges of the 1980s with the solutions of the 1960s. Of course, the case for expanded resourcing of and equalizing opportunities in education has undoubted strength and popularity, and whatever policies are ultimately adopted relating to the content and process of education, they will require an adequate infrastructure of human and material resources if they are to be carried out effectively. But even if Labour found itself in a position to implement policies of this kind, what would happen when the brief expansionist honeymoon was over? What policies would the Left then have to offer on education?

So far, the limit of Labour's commitments in the area of assessment policy appears to have been a twin pledge to remove the differentiated levels of entry in the GCSE, and to couple this academic qualification with more vocationally orientated ones like the CPVE into a unified examination system. The Socialist Education Association has expressed its wish to encourage more emphasis on course work assessment and profile reporting, but these ideas have not really been elaborated upon.[6] Similarly, Giles Radice's Fabian Pamphlet contained only one paragraph on educational assessment up to sixteen. It argued:

> Existing public examinations, even the new GCSE exam, assess only some of the skills which pupils need to develop. They also place too little emphasis on continuous assessment and project work. The pursuit of higher standards will require more broadly based assessment systems, including pupil profiles and records of achievement.[7]

The pamphlet then went on to advocate modular approaches to study with pupils being assessed at the end of each six-to-eight week module so that they would 'have something to show for their efforts'.[8]

None of this, it should be said, is recognizably different from approaches to educational assessment that have been developed under and with the support of Conservative Government. Many of the Conservatives' new assessment initiatives have therefore been tacitly endorsed by Labour. Beyond all this, it has simply been suggested that assessment policy (and now a National Curriculum too) be left to be developed by a broadly constituted Educational Council and a newly defined inspectorate. Indeed, Giles Radice even said that the existing GCSE might provide a useful basis for further developments of this kind. On the one hand, this deferral and delegation of important educational policy decisions might be interpreted as a reinvestment of political faith in and respect for the professional judgement of teachers and others closely involved in education. It might, however, equally be interpreted as setting aside political judgement and guidance on the content and process of education in a socialist or social-democratic society, or as a concern to avoid arousing hostility among sensitive parts of the electorate. Which of these is the case? This in turn raises the more general question: Why neglect assessment?

Why neglect assessment?

There are, it seems to me, at least three possible reasons why assessment is currently downgraded as a feature of socialist education policy.

1. Assessment, at least in the shape of public examinations, has commonly been associated among wide sections of the public with standards, fairness and opportunity.[9] Radical policies of examination reform put these notions and political support for them at risk. Such policies can either threaten to downgrade allegedly rigorous forms of assessment with 'CSE-type' modes of examining; or if they involve abolition, they can threaten to replace public, objective and fair forms of selection with processes of selection that are private, subjective and unfair.
2. Clear government guidelines or even starting points for discussion on assessment and indeed on curriculum, smack of centralism and of those bureaucratic intrusions upon teacher professionalism and individual judgement which have occasioned such strong resentment among teachers and LEAs under modern Government.[10] The presentation of new policy guidelines on assessment therefore risks alienating not only parents with their concerns for standards and fairness, but the teacher unions too, concerned as they are to restore some dignity and public influence to the judgements and wishes of their profession.
3. In modern societies which continue to be characterized in some measure by economic and social inequalities, examinations and assessment more generally are closely intertwined with the business of educational and social selection. This places socialist educational reformers in a number of apparently awkward dilemmas. If they present proposals for abolition of examinations at 16+, say, this is not only likely to arouse hostility among ambitious parents keen to retain a public and fair contest in which their

children can compete; but it also begs the important question of what forms of assessment might be developed instead. This is perhaps why even some of the most ardent Left abolitionists as yet appear to have no clear policy proposals concerning alternatives to examinations.[11] On the other hand, if socialists propose more minor adjustments to or reforms in the assessment system, they can then be accused of merely tinkering with, adjusting, perhaps even making more efficient, the existing process of educational selection – a task and set of purposes that is very much out of tune with the Left's equality ethic. Pupil profiles and records of achievement have been particularly open to these sorts of charges.[12]

It may be, then, that the Left's and especially Labour's caution about setting out proposals for new patterns of educational assessment is as much to do with maintaining confidence among standards-conscious parents, respecting the professional sensitivities of the LEAs and the teacher unions, and reassuring its own supporters about its commitments to equality, as it is to do with any confidence in the future professional deliberations of the proposed Educational Council. At a time when Labour is doing its utmost to secure and maintain a broad base of popular electoral support in the lower and middle reaches of society, such cautions are understandable. But perhaps they are not entirely necessary! Why is this?

Firstly, parents' cause for concern that educational selection at sixteen remains open, objective and fair in the form of public examinations, retains its credibility only if many young people directly enter paid employment at sixteen. Once direct entry to employment is deferred beyond sixteen as it is in many Western European countries, the acute need for an objective and rapidly processable sorting device is removed. *De facto*, we are, in Britain, currently experiencing a situation where less and less young people move directly into work at sixteen, but continue with some kind of further education or training instead. Perhaps we might now usefully consider making what is increasingly a matter of fact into a matter of legal statute – extending the period of education and training for all up to seventeen in the first instance, and bringing it within a common framework where opportunities for course access and for movement between courses and programmes are maximized to the fullest possible extent.

Progress through this system might be managed through a process of continuous course review, where continuous records and statements of achievement and course completion are passed through different parts of the system. No doubt, a need will continue for some years for public certificates at seventeen or beyond, but by deferring selection beyond sixteen, useful space will be be afforded for curriculum change and the development of alternative forms of assessment before that point. This would give the secondary curriculum and the processes of teaching and learning that go on within it the kind of breathing space for development and innovation that primary schools enjoyed when the 11+ was abolished.

Secondly, sensitivity about heavy-handed intrusion upon teachers' professional judgement and autonomy might deter and perhaps should deter educational policy-makers from imposing new assessment policies by legal dictat without the benefits of broad consultation with those who share in the educational partnership. However, in its reluctance to pre-empt professional dialogue, there is no reason why the Labour Party and the Labour movement more generally should deliberately hide its political light under a consultative bushel. The political movement of socialism forms an important part of the educational partnership and it is proper that however open to modification and amendment its views on assessment might be later on, those views should be declared at the outset – in a discussion document perhaps – as part of a process of open, rigorous and vigorous debate. This means, of course, that the Left will need to have thought through its own views on assessment long before any new Education Council sets about its work.

Thirdly, while assessment is often turned to the purpose of educational selection, it needs to be recognized that it serves other valuable, indeed indispensable educational purposes also. At its best, assessment can aid diagnosis of learning difficulties, enable teachers to identify strengths and weaknesses in their own teaching; give pupils feedback on their own learning and help them improve it; and (in the form of self-assessment) help pupils become more aware of and responsible for their own learning, discussing and negotiating it with their teachers where appropriate. In these senses, assessment is not just a way of ranking and rating the products of learning, but an integral part of the learning process itself. Even the most ardent abolitionists, keen to eradicate all traces of selection from the educational system, must come to terms with these other purposes of assessment and consider their educational and social value.

A socialist assessment policy does not end with the abolition of public exams then. Nor should a policy on assessment reform be overlooked if the anti-selective goal of abolition turns out not to be immediately feasible. Assessment serves many other important social and educational purposes as well as selective ones, and the Left needs to think through its position in relation to them.

These, then, are the reasons why it is defensible, indeed vital for the Left to have a detailed and carefully worked out policy on educational assessment. I now want to outline some issues that might merit consideration as part of such a policy within three broad assessment areas: public examinations, graded tests and assessments, and pupil profiles and records of achievement.

Public examinations

Examinations are widely held to be responsible for a number of common ills in the teaching and learning process. It is said that they lead to didactic teaching, cramming, over-emphasis on dictation and written work and to a lack of group work and opportunities for the exercise of individual initiative. Interestingly, though, as we saw in Chapter 4, while the claim is a common

one and has reached the status of becoming virtually accepted 'fact', supportive evidence in educational research findings is not strong. In explaining
their preference for didactic methods, there is limited evidence that teachers
do sometimes invoke examinations as a constraint or an excuse,[13] though for
many teachers, exams are neither a welcome incentive nor an oppressive
constraint, but simply part of the assumed background or 'facts of life' of
teaching.[14] Observational evidence in research carried out by Hammersley
and Scarth, however, indicates that the proportions of time allocated to open
and closed questions do not appear to be associated with whether the courses
are examined, not examined or examined by different modes.[15] These
findings may not, however, reflect differences that are important to teachers.
To teachers, it may be no surprise at all that public classroom talk does not
differ greatly between exam and non-exam classes. Indeed, such talk may be
highly closed and teacher-dominated in classes using a lot of group work,
since the purpose of that talk is to deliver instructions and report back on
more open-ended tasks set on a small group basis. It could be, then, that
Hammersley and Scarth have chosen to measure differences that are of little
consequence for the exam debate. Even if it *could* be shown that differences
between individual teachers were not great, though, this would still not
demonstrate that exams had no effect on teaching. For what comparisons
between teachers cannot really show is the extent to which the culture of
examinations and examining exerts its influence upon the secondary school
system as a whole, the breadth of its curriculum and its dominant styles of
teaching.[16]

The force of the influence exerted by exams can be overstated, though.
Observational work on teaching styles in the United States – a nation with a
very different pattern of assessment than Britain – reveals strikingly similar
preferences for didactic, teacher-centred or 'frontal' patterns of teaching.[17] As
we saw in Chapter 4, there are many other factors responsible for didactic
teaching as well as the constraints of public examinations – a preoccupation
with the necessities of classroom control; a tendency for teachers to favour
whole class teaching within particular subjects such as modern languages; the
rooting of teachers by biographical habit to styles and patterns they have
developed earlier in their careers, or the way in which poor career prospects
or opportunities 'spoilt' by reorganization or amalgamation can lead teachers
to lower the effort and commitment they give to producing classroom
excellence. It should not be assumed, therefore (as the promoters of the
GCSE have done), that examination reform or abolition will automatically
reduce the amount of influence of didactic teaching within the secondary
school system. It will simply offer some opportunity for further reform
initiatives to be developed with some hope of success. That is all.

Indeed, reforming the style of examining may influence teaching styles less
than the persistence of public examinations as such, whatever their form.
Particularly relevant here are the findings of research into the effects of
examination reform before the advent of GCSE, on teaching and learning
processes in the classroom. Research on Schools Council History, for

instance, a project whose criteria and patterns of assessment are fairly close to those which have been embodied in the new GCSE, has suggested that teachers respond to the criteria very differently depending on how they themselves perceive the nature of teaching history, the patterns of teaching to which they have become accustomed through previous experience, the way in which they get pupils through large quantities of material in the short time available, etc.[18] As the research shows, this can lead to wide variations in teaching new curricula and managing new patterns of assessment, even in the same school.

One should not assume, therefore, that even when new, more pupil-centred learning criteria are built into a reshaped examination structure such as the GCSE, this will automatically produce the expected shifts in patterns of teaching and learning at classroom level. The continuing presence of public examinations, as such, whatever their form, and the persistence of all the other factors which encourage didactic teaching may together conspire to inhibit the widespread development of those new teaching styles which the GCSE is seeking to encourage. The hopes and the fears of those who have viewed GCSE as a way of manipulating teachers into new styles of approach may therefore be exaggerated.[19] Teachers are not manipulated that easily. Their isolation in the classroom still offers them considerable protection.

More important for socialist education policy, perhaps, is the criticism that public examinations lead to an over-emphasizing of intellectual-cognitive skills to the detriment of practical and social and personal ones; to the dominance of mainstream traditional subjects where written work pre-dominates and knowledge can easily be regurgitated.[20] The emphases that public examinations give to and reinforce within the secondary curriculum make it difficult for new subjects like environmental education to establish themselves without becoming examined.[21] They make it difficult for marginal subjects like personal and social education to gain status and recognition among teachers and pupils, equivalent to that of other secondary school subjects.[22] And they make it difficult for marginalized areas of the curriculum like development education and political education to retain their relevance and social importance, their emphases on discussion and decision-making, without being converted into just another area of academic study with written work and an examination at the end in order to enhance their reputation and status. In this respect, it is telling that within the context of the present public examination system, even the relatively radical ILEA Report on *Improving Secondary Schools* advises that personal and social education be formally examined so as to increase its credibility.

More important than the influence examinations have on teaching styles, then, is the restrictive effect they exert upon the school curriculum.[23] They inhibit breadth or range of educational study. Such breadth, such acquaint-ance with a wide range of subjects, and experience of different kinds of educational achievement, operates in the interests of socialism, as right wing advocates of the removal of peace education, world studies, political education and the like from the curriculum fully recognized.[24] A narrow and conventional subject-based curriculum like the National Curriculum with little relevance to issues of contemporary human importance where critical judgement and social awareness might otherwise be developed, serves conservative interests. In this sense, the appropriate response to a partisan, restricted, traditional, subject-based curriculum, is not an alternative, equally partisan one organized around specifically working class interests,[25] but a broad curriculum – one which widens the scope of social and environmental awareness, arouses emotions of human concern and deepens the powers of critical judgement. Anything which restricts genuine curricular breadth and balance is, in this sense, a threat to the development and realization of socialist education policy. It is for this reason that reduction of the impact and influence of public examinations on the curriculum ought perhaps to be a key feature of Left policy on education.

The GCSE has special importance here. Through its setting of national criteria, some of which have taken up to four years to devise, it inhibits the creation of new examination titles. It also discourages development in areas of the curriculum that do not conform easily to existing subjects and schemes; like integrated studies, for example, Lastly, by subjecting schools and departments to a list of national criteria, it gives little scope for the development of new curriculum-related assessment initiatives at school level. It undermines school-based curriculum development and school-based examining of the earlier Mode 3 type.[26]

In short, because of its employment of national criteria, the GCSE will restrict curricular breadth, undermine school-based development and change, and stifle individual teacher initiative. It will encourage narrowing and ossification of the curriculum in a way that will be prejudicial to socialist and social democratic interests. Nor will this necessarily be offset by changes in teaching style. For we have seen that while national criteria might limit the content that teachers can cover, their potential to reshape teachers' long-standing approaches to their teaching is not sufficiently great to penetrate the autonomy of the classroom. The persistence of public examinations at 16, the requirement that schools publish their results, and the consequent rating of schools and teachers by their examination record is not going to do much for encouraging more 'high risk', open-ended strategies of teaching either. Nor, given the independence, initiative and involvement that the national criteria have taken away from teachers, is it likely that teachers will have the motivation and commitment to change their styles in the way GCSE requires. Taking all these things together, it is therefore clear that an effective socialist educational policy must involve a revaluation of the GCSE and of the principle of public examinations at sixteen as a whole.

Graded tests and assessments

The development of graded tests and assessments from their experimental application in a limited number of school subjects like music and modern languages, to their incorporation, in one way or another, into broad schemes of Records of Achievement in the ILEA, in the West Midlands, among the 22 LEAs who are members of the 'Northern Partnership', and within the Oxford Certificate of Educational Achievement, for instance, constitutes one of the most significant developments in educational assessment in recent years.

The advantages of such schemes of graded assessment and testing, it is claimed, are that they set short, achievable targets which pupils can work towards with a realistic sense of purpose in a way that they find difficult during the conventional two-year haul of narrow examination-based courses; they enable virtually all students to have their achievements recognized (however modest); they encourage individualization of the learning process through their principle that pupils be tested and assessed not *en masse* but only when they are personally ready; and by setting new criteria of achievement (for instance in practical or oral work), they encourage changes in teaching method.[27]

A system of assessment geared to continuous work, in an individualized way, such that it is integrated closely into the fabric of the curriculum might, in principle, enhance and improve the learning process more than the one-off examination (although it should be remembered that graded assessments are a complement to the public examination system, not a substitute for it). There are, however, a number of key issues in this area about which the Left might have legitimate cause for concern.

1. Despite an elaborate rhetoric of justification, the essential impetus behind graded assessments may amount to little more than acceptance of the principle that 'pupils like to receive certificates', as HMI concluded in a survey of one LEA's use of graded tests in modern languages.[28] Initially, this may perhaps be true. But one wonders whether, over time, pupils will become aware that these graduated certificates are not spurring them on to higher levels of achievement, but, at the lower levels at least, simply acknowledging what they can already do. Within the development of graded assessment schemes, the lower levels of achievement are indeed specified on the basis of surveys of existing pupil competence which show that most pupils have, at the expected age, already mastered the relevant skills and concepts.[29] Of course, giving recognition to existing success may still be educationally worthwhile. But this is a very different matter from actually *raising* standards of achievement.

2. Many good things in education are effective because they are exceptions; a bit different from the mainstream. The danger is that sometimes onlookers can become so impressed by these new initiatives that they feel tempted to spread them across the rest of the curriculum. As soon as this happens, though, they lose their special value. They suffer from overkill and become as ordinary and routine as the systems they replaced. Awarding certificates for graded tests, one suspects, is prone to this danger.

Where they are rare, hard to earn, and only to be found in some parts of the curriculum, certificates are like gold sovereigns. Their currency value is high. When they are easily earned and can be collected anywhere, the certificates become more like Spanish pesetas. Their currency is devalued. People are no longer specially motivated to collect them. One suspects, then, that the motivating force of graded tests, when used across the curriculum, will turn out to be much more limited than enthusiasts in particular subjects have claimed.

3. The concentration on short-term targets, with its appeal to pupils' extrinsic motivation, may shorten the otherwise dauntingly distant horizons of educational success. But in shortening those horizons, might graded tests/assessments not also limit them – encouraging young people to run from one modular skyline to the next without ever having grasped the nature and purpose of the course as a whole. One of the dangers, in directing learning to such short-term targets, is that pupils and teachers may be wholly motivated towards acquiring the course certificate at the expense of being concerned about the intrinsic purpose and validity of what is being taught and learned. Another problem is that when graded assessments are linked to principles of credit accumulation for successful completion of short units or modules of study, pupils may become bewildered by the coherence of and interrelationship between the credits and modules as a whole, and may find it difficult to assess the implications of all this for their wider educational and social opportunities. In shortening horizons, that is, graded tests and assessments may contribute to a confusion and mystification about educational choice and its implications for life and work after school, which is far greater than the much criticized, more conventional system of option choice at fourteen. Pupils, that is, with their educational horizons now foreshortened, might be more easily open to 'guidance', manipulation and channelling – to covert selection by their teachers who have a greater and deeper but also more inaccessible and unchallengeable knowledge of the curriculum as a whole.

   Lastly, as with the GCSE, teachers and pupils involved in graded assessment schemes may become increasingly subject to what Apple calls the logic of technical control – the subservience of their curriculum and learning needs to closely specified criteria drawn up at national and regional level.[30] Witness all the professional effort expended in writing purportedly unambiguous/non-jargonized 'descriptors' at each level. Such systems of curriculum control might help bring about initial curriculum change. But once instituted, these descriptions and criteria run the risk of deskilling the teacher, of undermining his or her own professional judgement; in addition to inhibiting possibilities for further change and development.

4. A fourth concern is that graded assessments have predominantly been developed within existing, conventional subject areas – most usually the high status ones of mathematics, science, modern languages and English; though increasingly craft, design and technology as well. This develop-

ment of graded assessments within existing high status subject areas of the secondary curriculum is unfortunate and has been much criticized – in response to the Schools Council sponsored Manchester Assessment Project, for instance.[31] The development of graded assessments within certain subjects only, endorses and reinforces the untoward importance these subjects are already accorded in comparison with other areas of the curriculum. It endorses and reinforces the existing division of the curriculum on subject specialist lines. It inhibits the development of assessment policies on a cross-curricular basis (or by implication deems these to be of lower importance than the skills developed within 'real subjects'). And it makes it even harder for new, emergent and currently marginalized areas of the curriculum such as environmental education, world studies, political education and the like to gain coverage, status and recognition in the curriculum on a par with the more traditional specialisms.

5. As presently defined, then, subject-based graded assessments could well end up 'conning' pupils into believing they have gained special achievements (when they might well have done so anyway). They are prone to devaluation as their use spreads across the curriculum. They run the risk of reducing pupil's involvement in and grasp of the overall purpose and coherence of the parts of the curriculum they are studying and indeed the coherence of the modular or credit-based curriculum structure as a whole, with all the implications this has for their own educational and social opportunities. They run the risk of buttressing the already well-established priorities accorded to conventional subject specialisms in the secondary curriculum at the expense of emergent and currently marginalized areas whose purpose is to explore those areas of human concern and controversy whose consideration is or should be such a vital part of a socialist or social-democratic educational agenda. And, unless their relationship to the GCSE is clearly defined on a basis that recognizes equivalence of status between them, they are in danger of being outflanked by the preoccupations with public examinations.

The Left, it seems to me, therefore, needs to consider its position in relation to subject-based graded assessments and associated schemes of accumulated course credits very carefully indeed, since they can easily lead to narrowing of the curriculum, shortening of pupils' horizons, and to opening pupils up to covert, non-accountable processes of selection and differentiation through modular and credit-based systems – especially among those likely to be designated as 'less able'.

Pupil profiles and records of achievement

The expansion of pupil profiles and records of achievement from a point of relative obscurity in the early 1980s to an expected situation of near universal adoption in all state secondary schools by the end of the decade is a remarkably rapid educational development, even by modern standards. Many reasons have been put forward in support of their development, not least by the DES itself. Profiles and records of achievement, it has been argued, recognize alternative kinds of educational achievement (especially social and personal achievement) among the young, in addition to those normally rewarded through public examinations. Because of this recognition, they give increasing prominence to these alternative forms of achievement within the curriculum. They enhance pupil motivation (especially in circumstances of growing youth unemployment) as non-academic achievements and experiences are then given greater emphasis. They involve pupils in their own assessment (self-assessment) and thus develop in them a greater sense of responsibility for their own learning. They stimulate the development of more effective procedures for diagnosing learning needs and difficulties. Through the processes of negotiation and discussion that are involved in profile assessment, they democratize the teacher-pupil relationship. They foster and facilitate curriculum change, as pupils are increasingly involved in negotiations about curriculum, and teachers are given systematic and repeated feedback on the impact and effectiveness of what they teach and how they teach it. And they meet the criteria of comprehensiveness by being available as a matter of entitlement to secondary pupils of all ages and abilities, not just the less able.

From a socialist and social-democratic point of view, profiles and records of achievement have the potential to give status to achievements outside the academic domain, to increase pupils' independence, assertiveness and critical judgement; to involve young people more in their own education; to humanize the teacher-pupil relationship; and to give pupils a greater say in the curriculum they receive. In this latter sense, by involving pupils in curriculum change, they add a completely new meaning to our existing understandings of bottom-up innovation, which we usually assume begins with the teacher. Through profiles and records of achievement, we can start to grasp the important principle that bottom-up innovation should perhaps begin with the child.

For socialists and social democrats, there remain, of course, all the usual important questions about the need to provide adequate time, staffing and resources to enable this pattern of personalized assessment to be carried out effectively. But there are more fundamental questions to be resolved also concerning the overall purposes of profiling, the very different uses to which profiles and records of personal achievement can be put, and the threat this can pose to the purposes of independence and collaboration that many have invested in the profile innovation. Not everyone sees profiles as vehicles for radical change and personal liberation, as the Junior Education Minister, Bob Dunn has himself hinted by issuing the following warning:

> If we are to achieve consensus we must be realistic. Pilot work on existing new initiatives naturally attracts enthusiasts [that classically understated term of bureaucratic abuse! – AH]. This is exactly as it should be. Some

even see records of achievement as the herald of an educational revolution in the classroom. Perhaps this may prove to be so in the long term. But *we must not allow ourselves to be carried away* [my italics].[32]

I have discussed the conflicts of purpose and difficulties involved in records of achievement in some detail earlier and so shall review them only briefly here from the particular vantage point of their implications for socialist and social democratic educational policy.

1. One of the major aims behind the development of profiles and records of achievement, we have seen, is that they should ultimately lead to a document which can be presented to employers or other 'users'. In other words, many of those involved in profiles still hope that they will contribute to occupational *selection*. In Chapter 6, I argued that one of the difficulties of profiles being used for these purposes and not just for the pupils alone, is that the ultimate knowledge that profiles will be used for selection purposes (even if only with the young person's permission) may have a backwash effect on the continuing formative process of discussion and negotiation between teacher and pupil.

    There are various ways of managing these resulting dilemmas between motivation and selection, not least by making a strict separation between the long formative process of discussion and negotiation over a young person's educational career, and the calculated construction of a final document (with an eye on the likely perceptions of employers and other external users). But, in the present context of widespread youth unemployment, it is arguable whether employers need to be involved in the design, development and use of records of personal achievement at all. In many respects, employers have often been involved in the business of profile development less for reasons of their own practical need, than out of schools' educational deference (under implied political pressure) to dominant industrial values. Under a socialist government, there is no reason why this kind of gratuitous vocationalism need continue.

2. As we saw in Chapter 7, while profiles can be used to enhance independence, they can also be used as instruments of social control; as ways of securing conformity to the system, of heading off deviance before it starts, of prying into and keeping track on emotions and feelings that might have disruptive consequences for the school. In this respect, one needs to ask whether the agenda for any one-to-one discussion is framed to serve the pupil's interests or the school's. Questions like the one that appears in the profile used by one LEA (Warwickshire), for instance – 'I believe it is important to keep up the reputation of the school – YES/NO' – clearly serve the interests of the latter. Overemphasis on matters of appearance, timekeeping, remembering homework, etc. is also a sign that teachers and schools are trying to serve their own control interests instead of the personal needs of their pupils. The establishment of learning contracts, of agreed targets for the future, which show statements of intended be-

havioural change on the part of the pupils, but few similar such undertakings on the part of the teacher, also indicates that profiling is being used
as a one-sided mechanism for imposing control, and not a two sided,
open–ended process of discussion and negotiation in a learning
partnership.

3. Where profiles and personal recording are open to these kinds of abuse,
    procedures for storing and gaining access to recorded information which
    the pupil might regard as private and confidential, or personally sensitive,
    will need to be carefully drawn up and scrupulously checked – especially
    where such storage is computerized. Who will have access to pupils'
    personally compiled records? Will the pastoral care system be able to plug
    into it anytime it has a problem to solve? Or will pupils be able to exercise
    veto over access to all or parts of their continuous statements? Socialists
    and social democrats alike will need to think carefully about the ways in
    which such personal freedoms can be protected, and the storage of
    sensitive personal data regulated. This is important not only to protect
    human dignity, but also in order to make the process meaningful. For
    there is evidence to suggest that where pupils do feel evidence may be used
    against them, where they feel that other adults have too easy access to
    what they record, where they feel that their records can become the
    subject of gossip among teachers and their colleagues – where, in other
    words, they feel they cannot trust their teachers to keep confidences –
    then they will not record anything of value in the first place.[33] In
    these circumstances, the profiling process can rapidly degenerate into a
    dreary, time–consuming and irrelevant routine for teachers and pupils
    alike.

4. One vital issue for those concerned about the need to protect personal
    privacy is the extent to which records of achievement encompass home
    and family life, as well as achievements at school. It is probably right that
    young people be given the opportunity to bring their achievements out of
    school to the attention of their teachers, so that they might develop more
    positive conceptions of those young people's capabilities. It is probably
    also advisable to draw parents into the learning partnership with teachers
    and pupils, discussing and contributing to what their children have
    achieved and can achieve.[34] But when, as in the Warwickshire profile,
    parents are asked to comment on and indeed *assess* their children's
    performance in the family – to assess how well they keep their bike in
    repair, if they can be trusted on it, how often they do the vacuuming, how
    they handle their pocket money, and how good they are at getting up in
    the morning – something else is happening as well as involving parents in
    the learning partnership. The state is, in fact, extending its influence and
    surveillance into areas of people's private lives over which it should have
    no proper jurisidiction – asking parents to spy on their childrens' personal
    habits and, by implication, assessing those parents and the quality of their
    home lives too, according to a yardstick of middle class manners and
    morality. Socialists and social democrats ought to address themselves to

such unwarranted extensions of state influence into the private and domestic spheres.

To sum up: profiles and records of achievement can be particularly helpful in advancing personal development, equality of opportunity and curriculum change – by deepening pupils' involvement in the curriculum, heightening their critical awareness, widening existing definition of achievement, and so on. But profiles and records of achievement can be used as techniques of surveillance and selection as well. Socialists and social democrats need to think through how they might usefully be turned to the first set of purposes, and prevented from encompassing and being dominated by the second. Commitment and clarification of purpose will be important priorities here. So too will the provision of adequate time and resources to allow profiles to develop in a more flexible, pupil-centred way. And the shadow that the GCSE casts over parallel developments like records of achievement, putting them in the shadow of its own high profile, will warrant attention too.

Conclusion

Clearly, assessment involves much more than selection. It is a central part and determinant of the learning process, not just its culmination. Conservatives have shrewdly grasped the educational importance of assessment and made it a central and compelling feature of their policy. Socialists and social democrats concerned with educational policy-making would do well to do likewise, by placing assessment high on its list of policy priorities now, and not simply deferring its discussion to a future and distant Educational Council. Much of the important professional detail would, of course, be left to such a Council, but its work might best to conducted within a confidently stated set of broad political guidelines. Principles that such guidelines might reasonably affirm, could well include the following:

- minimizing the role of assessment in relation to educational selection.
- delaying the use of educational assessment in relation to selection until as late a point as possible in a young person's career – and certainly beyond sixteen.
- giving very serious consideration to the abolition of the GCSE.
- extending the process of education and training for all beyond sixteen to seventeen and then eighteen, with possible retention of public examining at these later stages for those considering entry to higher education (though that principle too might be reviewed in due course).
- reintegrating policies on assessment with ones on an agreed, broad and balanced range of curriculum content, so that assessment is made a firm and integral part of socialist education policy on comprehensive curricular entitlement.
- allowing any common curriculum to be divided into easily digestible

chunks or modular components where appropriate, but guarding against modular systems being used as disguised and non-accountable forms of option choice, with all its selective implications.

- assessing performance until sixteen on a continuous, not a one-off basis, through graded assessments and pupil profiles.
- allowing high local flexibility in the development of graded assessments and profiles within broad guidelines, to increase teachers' ownership of and therefore commitment to them. Regional consortia of assessment boards, LEAs and teachers might well take on this kind of work.
- checking that graded assessments do not degenerate into the large-scale production of certificates, but that certificates are awarded judiciously, where real and hard-won achievements have been made.
- ensuring that graded assessment schemes maintain an emphasis on improving the quality of the learning process and the forms of intrinsic motivation that come with that, more than on merely awarding certificates in order to stimulate extrinsic motivation.
- removing employers from involvement in records of achievement in order to eradicate the gratuitous vocationalism that creeps into the recording process.
- establishing clear procedures for access to pupil data compiled through the recording process in order to protect privacy and confidentiality. This might include 'coding' data (by the pupil, and under his or her control) at different levels of confidentiality, each of which entails progressively wider access.
- setting up a National Accrediting Body for records of achievement whose principles would include ensuring that such records protect the privacy and personal liberty of the pupil, that they do not involve employers unless they would be direct users of any such records, and that they are designed as tools of personal development, not as mechanisms of behavioural control.

A reconstruction of the curriculum and assessment system of secondary education on these sorts of lines might help us recapture and redefine those images of entitlement and opportunity that formed much of the spirit of comprehensive educational improvement over the years. They might help give that spirit some much-needed practical substance. And in doing so, they might begin to release the educational system, its teachers and its children, from the darkening forces of differentiation and decomprehensivization that are now sweeping the land.

PART 3

Conclusion

9 Curriculum and Assessment Reform

The first four chapters of this book explored different models of curriculum development – school based and centrally imposed – and found them both wanting in the absence of parallel changes being made in the culture and work of teaching. Curriculum development and teacher development, I argued, were closely interdependent processes. Each entailed the other.

Practical curriculum change at classroom level could not be effected without substantial changes in the culture and work of teaching. Behind the closed doors of their classrooms, most teachers did not find it hard to resist the imperatives of centrally imposed curriculum change. Where teachers were involved in more school-based patterns of curriculum development, their continuing commitment to that centrality of classroom experience, which lay at the heart of their work and culture, restricted them in the scope of their shared curricular ambitions and in the courage of their curricular convictions.

If the culture and work of teaching has hampered the process of curriculum development, the broad international trend towards more centralized patterns of curriculum development is in turn placing profound restrictions on the possibilities for teacher development. The connection of teacher development to curriculum development requires that there be something of sufficient scope and importance to develop in the first place; that teachers are given real and wide-ranging discretion to exercise their professional judgement. If the possibilities for local curriculum development and teacher involvement are pre-empted by central curriculum prescription; and if teacher collaboration and collegiality is confined to the technical details of what the North Americans call programme implementation, it is unlikely that much development will take place, be it development of the curriculum, or development of the teacher.

Here is the central dilemma of curriculum reform and its relationship to the culture and work of teaching. In decentralized models of curriculum development, the persistence of the individualistic, classroom-centred culture of teaching inhibits and renders inconclusive any discussion of the ends, the ethics and the alternatives to be explored within the curriculum. It undermines the effectiveness with which teachers can address the very foundations of curricular judgement – judgement about the very purpose, value and consequences of what it is that young people should learn. This interaction between school-based curriculum development or school-centred innovation, and the individualistic culture of teaching leads, and has led, by default to the persistence of the academically dominated curriculum, the hegemonic curriculum, whose boundaries and assumptions have, in the main, not been seriously questioned by teachers themselves on a local basis.

The other side of the dilemma is that whatever changes are brought about in the culture and work of teaching to weaken its classroom-centred preoccupations, the impact of those changes on curriculum development is obviously going to be minimal if the authority for curriculum decision-making is arrogated to the centre. Interestingly, there are signs that in many Western nations, teachers' work is indeed beginning to undergo profound changes, particularly in terms of scheduled time spent away from the classroom. In British schools, in-service funds have been channelled away from traditional, providing institutions like university education departments, towards the schools themselves, so they can provide their own on-site professional development for their teachers, including release time from classroom work. The terms of the new nationally legislated teachers' contract, drawn up in 1987, also include categorizations of teacher time spent outside the classroom, some of the time being 'directed' by school management. In Norway, elementary teachers have been released from lessons for one period per week, to work with colleagues on the implementation of the new national curriculum. The United States has seen a proliferation of developments in peer coaching, mentor systems and collaborative planning in order to foster greater collegiality among teachers. And in Ontario, Canada, most elementary teachers have been granted a guaranteed minimum of 100 minutes per week planning and preparation time outside the classroom. Such developments might suggest that at last significant shifts may be occurring in the culture of teaching, weakening its traditional, individualistic, classroom-centred preoccupations. Yet paralleling these movements towards greater collaboration among teachers have been hastening trends towards the centralization of curriculum control; leading in turn to strengthening, to structural reinforcement of the hegemonic, academic curriculum. Among the community of newly collaborative teachers, this centrally defined hegemonic curriculum is not itself negotiable. Teachers can collaborate to implement it; not to change it. In this sense, while teachers certainly collaborate with each other, they also unwittingly collaborate with government in its structural reinforcement of the hegemonic curriculum. From the historical record of wartime, we would perhaps do well to remember that collaboration, in this respect, is not always a virtue!

'Collaboration' and 'collegiality' carry a deceptive connotation of ideological neutrality, or even beneficence, with them. It is hard for us to imagine that they could be anything else but a good thing. Yet, we have seen that the political context of curriculum control in which these processes are fostered, gives them a very different meaning from one situation to the next. Teacher collaboration in the context of centralized curriculum control where curriculum content is tightly prescribed, amounts to something very different from collaboration in the context of more localized, school-centred innovation.

'Development' – be it teacher development or curriculum development – carries with it similarly deceptive connotations of neutrality or benificience. The important question the term begs is what is it that is to be developed. The argument of the first part of this book – particularly Chapter 3 – was that educational equality and opportunity is only likely to be significantly enhanced if the curriculum is developed beyond its present academic hegemonic limits. The academic curriculum builds upon and rewards forms of cultural capital in which middle-class parents and their children have a particularly strong investment and inheritance. It gives disproportiate weighting to academic, intellectual achievement above all others. By offering academic rigour only where there is little social or practical relevance, or relevance only where there is little intellectual rigour or challenge, it makes educational achievement all that more difficult to attain for many children coming from working class or a number of ethnic minority backgrounds. If improved educational equality or increased educational opportunity are among our chief educational goals, therefore, I have argued that this will require a curriculum which helps to *redefine* what is to count as cultural capital, which recognizes and rewards practical, aesthetic, and personal and social achievements, as well as intellectual and academic ones, and which combines rigour and relevance in the curriculum for *all* pupils, instead of offering rigour for some and relevance for others.

The hegemonic, academic curriculum nonetheless has a tenacious grip on the educational systems of most modern societies. It is not easy to develop alternatives. Alternatives threaten vested interests of middle-class advantage and inheritance, they threaten vested interests of political and economic control, and they threaten the vested interests of status and power enjoyed by academic subject communities within the educational system. The different models of curriculum development and teacher development that have already been considered will have done little and can do little to challenge this existing hegemonic curriculum.

School-based curriculum development combined with an individualistic culture of teaching allows the hegemonic curriculum to persist by default – curricular debate being restricted and inconclusive, bound by the culturally sanctioned limits of classroom experience. Centralized curriculum development, which imposes a mandatory curriculum of an academically dominated kind, is compatible with an individualistic culture of teaching and the academic subject interests such a culture fosters and protects. A centrally imposed academic curriculum is also not seriously challenged by a more collaborative teacher culture, since the scope for collaborative teacher judgement does not extend to the fundamentals of curricular judgement about purpose and value. This modern and increasingly pervasive combination leaves the hegemonic curriculum intact. We might anticipate that a fourth model – a centrally imposed curriculum which sought to redefine cultural capital beyond the academic domain – would be similarly ineffective in challenging the hegemonic curriculum, unless the culture of teaching and the powerful subject communities and divisions within it was itself reshaped.

So what alternative is there? What practical, if difficult course of action can be followed to mount a challenge to the hegemonic curriculum and to the forms of cultural capital which have traditionally underpinned it – as a way of securing greater educational equality and opportunity? It is tempting to resign oneself to the pessimistic, and arguably also realistic, conclusion that there really is no alternative; that the social, educational and historical forces sustaining the hegemonic curriculum are too powerful, too deeply entrenched to shift. I believe there is an alternative, however; a practical alternative, which, if implemented, would significantly increase and equalize the opportunities for success and achievement among young people from a wide range of social backgrounds. This alternative has four interrelated components – powerful and effective not in isolation, but in combination.

1. Contrary, to the popular trend among most Western societies, curriculum development and decision-making must be substantially decentralized. It must be given back to the teachers and the schools. School-based curriculum development must have sufficient scope to allow for meaningful teacher development. Unbound by tight, subject-based, content-loaded prescriptions, it should allow for flexibility and responsiveness to local needs and circumstances, to the cultural inheritance of what a school's pupils bring to the classroom as their starting point for learning. It should allow for teachers to value that essential engagement with their pupils' cultural and imaginative resources, in order to generate their motivation for, their interest in learning. This flexibility and responsiveness and sensitivity to individual and community needs has been one of the traditional strengths of the best primary school practice in decentralized systems, such as Britain's was until very recently.

2. However, decentralized processes of curriculum development must be accompanied by parallel changes in the culture and work of teaching. The individualism and variation that fostered excellent examples of primary practice in decentralized Britain, also tolerates and in many respects protects mediocrity and even incompetence in classroom teaching too. Moreover, as we saw in Chapter 2, if the nature of teachers' work and the balance of their duties continues to tie them almost exclusively in school hours to the world of the classroom, the classroom-centredness that results will restrict the scope and effectiveness of curriculum debate. It is in many ways a cruel irony that just when teachers are being provided with increasing opportunities to work together, talk together and share ideas within school time, the scope of what it is they can decide and develop is being narrowed by the centralization, the nationalization of curriculum

control. Yet a collaborative teacher culture, grounded in redefined conditions of teachers' work providing more time away from the classroom, could, in combination with a decentralized process of curriculum development, provide the potential for teachers to engage seriously and effectively in searching and wide-ranging discussions and decision-making about the very foundations of what they teach.

Even with this potent combination, we are still only talking of potential, however. A decentralized, collaborative process of curriculum development grounded in a reshaped teacher culture, provides no guarantee, of itself, that the hegemonic, academic curriculum will then be challenged. Not all teachers, not even most teachers, are motivated completely by altruism. Just like other workplaces, schools are places of politics, places where interests are protected, statuses defended, identities preserved. I have repeatedly noted that the academic subject is one of the most powerful sources of status, identity and material advantage (not least in terms of career) within the school system. Threats to the hegemonic curriculum will amount to threats to the status, identity and vested interests that come with academic subject membership also. This will be particularly true of secondary schools, but as the doctrine of subject specialism spreads downwards, of primary school too. Those many teachers who have vested interests in the continuing supremacy of specialized academic subjects cannot therefore be expected to embrace challenges to the hegemonic curriculum with unmitigated enthusiasm.

3. For this reason, there must be some limits to teacher discretion and independence in curricular judgement. Deregulation cannot be complete. We cannot return once more, our eyes romantically misted with nostalgia, to the individualistic schools and classrooms of the 1960s. In most places, that would lead only to reinforcement of the hegemonic curriculum, not redefinition. A *third* component of an alternative strategy is therefore needed: a set of centrally produced guidelines directing schools to provide a broad and balanced curriculum in a way which recognizes and rewards, in reasonably equal measure, a wide range of educational achievements and which does this for *all* pupils, not just some. These guidelines need not be very different from those which provided the basis of the counter-hegemonic curriculum which surfaced briefly in Britain in the early 1980s. Those guidelines defined different areas of educational experience and different forms of achievement to which all pupils had an entitlement. At that point, the guidelines failed to be influential because they were advisory, not mandatory; because their implications for practice were not spelt out; and because they were paralleled by more powerful statutory measures which reinforced the subject-specialist, academic curriculum. But guidelines for an alternative curriculum could have more teeth if they were mandatory rather than advisory; if they were accompanied by practical examples showing a range of possible interpretations at school level; and if they were implemented through a process of continuous inspection, review and supervision through such people as school

superintendents in North America, or the Inspectorate in Britain. The guidelines need not be specific about detailed content. They need not even be very specific about subject labels. In that sense they would have the necessary flexibility and scope required for substantial curriculum development and meaningful teacher development at school level. But the existence and statutory force of the guidelines would also lend an important sense of direction, overall purpose and definable change. Such clear directions and common purpose could not realistically be expected to evolve spontaneously from a community as diverse as the teaching profession. A little pressure, some centrally directed shift in curricular priorities, is in this sense necessary.

4. Pressure of itself will not, however, be sufficient to secure change. Teaching is and will continue to be a profoundly human business, conducted in the moment-by-moment process of human interaction, much of it in private, behind closed doors. Resistance will not be difficult. It will not be hard to comply simply with the letter rather than with the spirit of the law. For meaningful and substantial change to occur in the practical curriculum at classroom level, teachers themselves must see, feel and be committed to the necessity for such change, for the development of an alternative curriculum. Rational persuasion, brute sanity, will not be sufficient to secure this. Teachers must themselves feel – in the depth of their practice, in their grasp of their own effectiveness at a practical, concrete, day-to-day level – that something new, something better, is called for. This raises the *fourth* component of an alternative curriculum development strategy; one concerning the quality and character of classroom feedback.

I have discussed many weaknesses arising from the classroom-centred character of the culture of teaching – isolation, individualism, conservatism etc. But the great strength of teachers' classroom-orientation is in the psychic rewards they find in the classroom, in their contacts and relationships with children. Teachers rank their contacts with individual children highest in their work rewards. This is one of their major sources of satisfaction, particularly at primary level. They value what they do with their pupils, and they value what their pupils think of them.

This, I believe, is one of the richest, untapped reserves for securing educational reform. Teachers value what their pupils say, and think, and do, yet rarely are pupils involved in or consulted about the process of curriculum development. Teachers use feedback from their pupils as an indicator of their own success and effectiveness, yet as writers like Lortie have indicated, given that teachers deal with groups more than with individuals and that they do so amid a rapid and immediate ebb and flow of classroom interaction, the amount and quality of the feedback teachers get is often poor. As a rule, feedback from pupils is usually insufficient, uneven and unreliable.[1]

Part 2 examined new pupil-based assessment procedures designed to capitalize on the regard that teachers have for their pupils' judgements, perceptions and reactions. These were forms of pupil self-assessment, some-times known as pupil profiles, sometimes known as records of achievement, which included a regular one-to-one review between each pupil and their teacher, of progress, performance, experience and achievement. Such pat-terns of assessment and recording are relatively new in the United Kingdom, and virtually unheard of in North America, where pupil assessment is widely understood in terms of standardized test procedures administered to pupils by teachers and administration.

The periodic process of one-to-one review between teacher and pupil makes assessment part of learning, rather than a judgement passed on performance once the learning is over. It is designed to draw attention and give recognition to a wider range of achievements, experiences and pupil potential than has been customary in the conventional academic curriculum. It is intended to give pupils a sense of greater responsibility for their own learning now they have more say in what they do and how they do it. It is also meant to improve teachers' diagnoses of pupils' learning needs and difficul-ties. Supplied with more regular, systematic feedback by the pupils them-selves on their own progress, teachers can match work more appropriately to individual pupils' abilities, not only making it easier where pupils have experienced difficulty, but also making it more challenging where pupils are bored by unnecessary practice and repetition. In this way, teachers are better able to give their pupils more experiences of mastering new understandings or new skills. Similarly, once provided with more extensive information about a pupil's wider experience and interests, teachers are more able to make material relevant to their pupils and to gear into their practical lives or their imaginative preoccupations.

This fourth component of the alternative curriculum strategy therefore entails linking curriculum development and assessment development. More pupil-based assessment and recording procedures will lead to curriculum development which is more effectively geared to the needs of the individual pupil. By providing accumulated feedback across a series of unthreatening one-to-one encounters with individual pupils, teachers will also instigate curriculum development and change themselves as they begin to perceive, through their pupils, a need for change in their practice. In this way, these new patterns of pupil-based assessment develop the pupil, they develop the teacher and they develop the curriculum. Assessment development, pupil development, teacher development and curriculum development are there-fore deeply and inextricably intertwined. They form a mutually reinforcing system. To change one without the other is to move towards educational futility. The components go together. These kinds of assessment strategies will only prosper if the scope for curricular judgement, negotiation and adjustment at school level is wide and not too closely prescribed outside the school. They will also only prosper if the management and funding of teachers' work recognizes and encourages contact with individual pupils as a routine part of that work.

There is a desperate need for a coherent, alternative educational strategy which will tie together curriculum, assessment, teacher and pupil development in a persuasive reform programme which can promise and deliver greater educational equality and opportunity. In its reaffirmation of the hegemonic academic curriculum; in its tightening of central control to protect that curriculum; and in its extension of standardized testing and public examining as a way of institutionally entrenching that curriculum still further, the educational Right has certainly shown consistency and coherence in *its* reform strategies. In response, certainly in Britain, socialists and social democrats have reluctantly endorsed the idea of a National Curriculum, and held back from seriously challenging the hegemonic academic character of that curriculum. In this book, through my critique and reconstruction of modern patterns of curriculum and assessment reform, I have tried to lay out the bones of what a coherent alternative strategy for educational change might look like; a strategy in which the scarcely remembered ideals of equality and opportunity play a prominent part. That strategy combined four things: decentralization of curriculum development; administrative support for a collaborative teacher culture; mandatory guidelines requiring a broad and balanced curriculum and reinforced through the power of inspection; and a revamped assessment system designed to provide teachers with improved feedback about their pupils and their progress as a basis for curricular renewal. In present political climates, the realization of such an alternative strategy is improbable but not impossible. Yet while the distance between possibility and probability, between hope and expectation is great, it is not absolutely unbridgeable. More than anything what can bring these things closer together is the strength of our conviction about and commitment to something different, to an alternative educational vision. There *are* alternatives. I have tried to provide glimpses of some of them in this book's vision. It is time we began to assert them with greater confidence; with the hope and determination needed for their realization.

Notes and References

Critical introduction

1. Some of these points are made in a forthcoming book. Goodson, I.F. and Walker, R (1989). *Biography, Identity and Schooling*. New York, Philadelphia and London: Falmer.
2. See the introduction to Goodson, I.F. (1987). *School Subjects and Curriculum Change*. New York, Philadelphia and London: Falmer; and the introduction to Goodson, I.F. (ed.) (1988) *International Perspectives in Curriculum History*. London and New York: Routledge.
3. See Goodson, op. cit., note 2, Chapter 9.
4. Goodson, I.F. (1987). *School Subjects and Curriculum Change*. New York and London: Falmer.
5. Personal archive of Countesthorpe papers.
6. Gordon, T. (1986). *Democracy In One School*. New York, Philadelphia and London: Falmer.
7. Goodson, I.F. (1988). *The Making of Curriculum: Collected Essays*. New York, Philadelphia and London: Falmer, p. 22.
8. Goodson, op. cit., note 2.
9. Kliebard, H. (1986). *The Struggle for the American Curriculum 1893–1958*. Boston, London and Henley: Routledge.
10. Labaree, D. (1986). Curriculum, Credentials and the Middle Class: A Case Study of a Nineteenth Century High School, *Sociology of Education*, **59**, 54.
11. Tomkins, G.S. (1986). *A Common Countenance: Stability and Change in the Canadian Curriculum*. Scarborough, Canada: Prentice-Hall.
12. Connell, R.W. (1985). *Teachers' Work*. Sydney: George Allen and Unwin, p. 87.
13. ibid., p. 92.

Chapter 1

1. Lawton, D. (1980). *The Politics of the School Curriculum*. London: Routledge & Kegan Paul.
2. Dale, R. (1979). The politicisation of school deviance: reactions to William Tyndale. In Barton, L. and Meighan, R. (eds), *Schools, Pupils and Deviance*. Driffield: Nafferton Books.

3. Donald, J. (1977). Green Paper: noise of crisis. *Screen Education*, **30**; Halpin, D. (1981). Exploring the secret garden. *Curriculum*, **1** (2).
4. Eggleston, J. (1979). *School-Based Curriculum Development*. Paris: OCED; Eggleston, J. (1980). *School-Based Curriculum Development in Britain*. London: Routledge & Kegan Paul.
5. Skilbeck, M. (1976). School-based curriculum development and the task of in-service education. In Adams, E. (ed.), *In-service Education and Teachers' Centres*. Oxford: Pergamon Press.
6. For example see Warwick, D. (1975). *School-Based In-service Education*. Edinburgh: Oliver and Boyd; Henderson, E. (1979). The concept of school-focused in-service education and training. *British Journal of Teacher Education,* **5** (1); Henderson, E. and Perry, W. (1981) *Change and Development in Schools: Case Studies in the Management of School-Focused Inservice Education*. London: McGraw-Hill; Eggleston, J. (1980), op. cit., note 4.
7. Foremost amongst these is the *British Journal of In-Service Education* but the *British Journal of Teacher Education* has also devoted many of its pages to various aspects of SCI, and to school-based and school-focused INSET in particular.
8. See, for instance, *Curriculum*, **1**(1) (1980) and the *Cambridge Journal of Education*, **9**(2) and (3) (1979).
9. One of the best known of these was the *Priorities in In-Service Education* conference at La Sainte Union College of Higher Education, Southampton (1976).
10. Most notably the SITE project organized and co-ordinated by Bolam and Baker. See Bolam, R. (1979). Evaluating in-service education and training: a national perspective. *British Journal of Teacher Education*, **5**(1); Baker, K. (1979). The SITE project: an experiment in approaches to INSET. *Cambridge Journal of Education*, **9**(2) and (3); and the Open University IT/INSET project, organized by Ashton, P. and Merritt, J. (1979). INSET at a distance, *Cambridge Journal of Education,* **9**(2) and (3).
11. See Simmons, L.M. (1980). Staff development in schools. *Curriculum*, **1**(1), for a statement of this view.
12. For discussions of the role of SCI in a period of educational and economic recession see Lightfoot, M. (1978). The educational consequences of falling rolls. In Richards, C. (ed.), *Power and the Curriculum*. Driffield: Nafferton Books; Dennison, W.F. (1979). Falling rolls: teachers and shrinking schools. *Durham and Newcastle Research Review*, **IX**, 43; Hewitt, F.S. (1978). Teacher participation in planning and provision: the identification of pertinent factors. *British Journal of In-Service Education*, **5**(1); Harlen, W. (1977). A stronger teacher role in curriculum development? *Journal of Curriculum Studies*, **9**(1); Bradley, H. (1979). INSET now – taking stock. *Cambridge Journal of Education*, **9**(2) and (3); Hunter, C. and Heighway, P. (1980). Morale, motivation and management in middle schools. In Bush, T., Goodey, J. and Riches, E. (eds) *Approaches to School Management*. London: Harper and Row.
13. Reid, W.A. (1978). *Thinking About the Curriculum*. London: Routledge & Kegan Paul. For an interesting development of this view in relation to empirical data about teacher decision-making – see Walker, D.F. (1975). Curriculum development in an art project. In Reid, W.A. and Walker, D.F. (eds), *Case Studies in Curriculum Change*. London: Routledge & Kegan Paul.
14. For examples see Watkins, R. (ed.) (1973). *In-service Training: Structure and Content*. London: Ward Lock Educational; Warwick, D., op. cit., note 6; Partington, G. (1976). School-focused INSET. *British Journal of In-Service Education*, **3**(1); Jones, J.A.G. (1980) An in-school approach to in-service training. *Curriculum*, **1**(1); Golby, M. and Fish, M.A. (1980). School-focused INSET: clients and consultants. *British Journal of In-Service Education*, **6**(2).

15. Eraut, M. (1977). Strategies for promoting teacher development. *British Journal of In-Service Education,* **4**(1) and (2), 11.
16. Sayer, J. (1979). INSET strategy of a large comprehensive school. *Cambridge Journal of Education,* **9**(2) and (3), 95.
17. Sharp, R. and Green, A. (1975). *Education and Social Control.* London: Routledge & Kegan Paul.
18. Razzell, A. (1979). Teacher participation in school decision-making. *Education 3–13,* **7**(1), 5.
19. Henderson, E. and Perry, W. (1981), p. 14, op. cit., note 6.
20. Bolam, R. (1979), op. cit., note 10.
21. Alexander, R. (1980). Towards a conceptual framework for school-focused INSET. *British Journal of In-Service Education* **6**(2).
22. Examples of 'reflective' literature can be found in the collections edited by Eggleston, J. (1980) op. cit., note 4; Henderson, E. and Perry, W. (1981), op. cit., note 6; and articles by Broome, M. (1980). Professional self development through participation in curriculum development. *Curriculum,* **1**(1); and Keast, D.J. and Carr, V. (1978). School-based INSET – interim evaluation. *British Journal of In-Service Education,* **5**(3).
23. Bullock, A. (1980). Teacher participation in school decision-making. *Cambridge Journal of Education,* **10**(1); Richardson, D.A. (1981). Student-teacher attitudes towards decision-making in schools before and after taking up their first appointments. *Educational Studies,* **7**(1).
24. Ball, S. (1987). *The Micropolitics of the School.* London: Methuen.
25. One advocate of the grass-roots democracy view of SCI is Eggleston (op. cit., note 4). Halpin (op. cit., note 3) has presented an excellent critique of the central origin of the categories employed in local curriculum discussions. And Scarth, J. has documented an insightful study of an attempt to undertake whole school curriculum change where the head's initial policy document was framed within HMI's areas of experience. See Scarth, J. (1988). *Examination and Curriculum Decision Making.* London: Routledge & Kegan Paul.
26. Ideological features of this kind are by no means confined to SCI, but are common in educational discourse. For examples of their influence on writing about middle school education, for instance, see Hargreaves A. (1980). The ideology of the middle school. In Hargreaves, A. and Tickle, L. (eds), *Middle Schools: origins, ideology and practice.* London: Harper and Row; and Nias, J. (1980). The ideal middle school: its public image. In Hargreaves, A. and Tickle, L. (eds), *Middle Schools: origins, ideology and practice.* London: Harper & Row.
27. Cohen, D. and Harrison, M. (1979). Curriculum decision-making in Australian education: what decisions are made within schools? *Journal of Curriculum Studies,* **11**(3).
28. Rutter, M., Maughan, B., Mortimore, P., and Ouston, J. (1979). *Fifteen Thousand Hours: Secondary Schools and Their Effects on Children.* London: Open Books.
29. ibid., p. 126.
30. ibid., p. 138.
31. Her Majesty's Inspectorate (1979). *Ten Good Schools: a Secondary School Enquiry.* London: HMSO, p. 36.
32. Parlett, M. and Hamilton, D. (1976). Evaluation as illumination. In Tawney, D. (ed.), *Curriculum Evaluation Today.* London: Macmillan.
33. McDonald, B. (1974). Evaluation and the control of education. In *Innovation, Evaluation Research and the Problem of Control. SAFARI, CARE,* University of East Anglia.

34. Henderson, E. (1979), p. 24, op. cit., note 6. See also the work of the SITE team. See note 10.
35. Henderson, E. and Perry, W. (1981), p. 167, op. cit., note 6.
36. Abbs, P. (1980). Continuing curriculum change at Codsall School, in Eggleston, J. op. cit., note 4; Campbell, R.J. (1985). *Developing the Primary Curriculum*. Holt-Saunders: Eastbourne.
37. Carnie, J.M. (1980). IT-INSET: a school-focused programme of initial training and in-service education, *Curriculum*, **1**(1).
38. Ashton, P. and Merritt, J. (1979) INSET, op. cit., note 10.
39. Desforges, C. and McNamara, D. (1979). Theory and practice: methodological procedures for the objectification of craft knowledge. *British Journal of Teacher Education*, **5**(2).
40. Clandinin, D.J. (1986). *Classroom Practice: Teacher Images in Action*. Falmer Press: Lewes.
41. Kushner, S. and Norris, N. (1981). Interpretation, negotiation and validity in naturalistic research. *Interchange*, **11**(4), 30.
42. Elliot, J. (1980). Methodology and ethics, unpublished paper delivered to British Educational Research Association Conference, Cardiff.
43. Barton, L. and Lawn, M. (1981). Back inside the whale: a curriculum case study. *Interchange*, **11**(4).
44. Jenkins, D. (1978). An adversary's account of SAFARI's ethics of case study. In Richards, C. (ed.), *Power and the Curriculum*. Driffield: Nafferton Books.

Chapter 2

1. Lortie, D. (1975). *Schoolteacher*. London: University of Chicago Press; Jackson, P.W. (1968). *Life in Classrooms*. New York: Holt, Rinehart & Winston.
2. Jackson, op. cit., p. 146.
3. Lortie, op. cit., p. 77.
4. Waller, W. (1932). *The Sociology of Teaching*. New York: Wiley.
5. Hargreaves, A. (1981). Contrastive rhetoric and extremist talk. In Barton, L. and Walker, S. *Schools, Teachers and Teaching*. Lewes: Falmer Press.
6. On strategic compliance see Lacey, C. (1977). *The Socialization of Teachers*. London: Methuen Books.
7. Jackson, op. cit., note 1.
8. Elbaz, F. (1983). *Teacher Thinking*. London: Croom Helm.
9. Lukes, S. (1974). *Power: a Radical View*. London: Macmillan; Bachrach, P. and Baratz, M.S. (1963). The two faces of power, *American Political Science Review*, **57.**
10. See, for instance, Scarth, J. (1988), op. cit., Chapter 1, note 4; Gronn, P. (1983). Talk as the work: the accomplishment of school administration, *Administrative Science Quarterly*, **28**, (1–2).
11. The nature of grounded concepts is explained in Glaser, B. and Strauss, A.L. (1968). *The Discovery of Grounded Theory*. London: Weidenfield and Nicholson.
12. Cohen, S. (1973). *Folk Devils and Moral Panics*. St Albans: Paladin.
13. ibid., p. 44.
14. Durkheim, E. (1964). *The Rules of Sociological Method*. New York: Free Press; Taylor, I., Walton, P. and Young, J. (1973). *The New Criminology* London: Routledge & Kegan Paul.
15. Smith, D. (1978). K is mentally ill; the anatomy of a factual account. *Sociology*, **22**(3).
16. Hargreaves, D.H., Hester, S.K. and Mellor, F.J. (1975). *Deviance in Classrooms*. London: Routledge & Kegan Paul.

17. See Little, J.W. (1986). Seductive images and organizational realities in professional development, *Teachers College Record*, **1**(Autumn).
18. Keast, D. and Carr, W. (1978). School-based INSET – interim evaluation. *British Journal of Inservice Education*, **5**, 25–31.
19. Bolam, R. (1982). *School Focused Inservice Training*. London: Heinemann; Smith, L.M. and Keith, P.M. (1971). *Anatomy of Educational Innovation*. London: Wiley; Campbell, R.J. (1985). *Developing the Primary Curriculum*. London: Holt-Saunders; Fullan, M. (1982). *The Meaning of Educational Change*. Toronto, OISE Press.
20. Little estimates that two years is the minimum period of commitment required to see a development through and to overcome the hesitancies, false trails and senses of failure that often accompany the early stages of collaborative decision-making. See Little, J.W., op. cit., note 17.
21. Lortie, op. cit., note 1.
22. Gronn, op. cit., note 8; Hanson, E.M. (1981). Organizational control in educational systems: a case study of governance in schools. In Bacharach, S.B. *Organizational Behaviour in Schools and School Districts*. New York: Praeger; Burlingame, M. (1981). Superintendent power retention. In Bacharach, op. cit.
23. Hammersley, M. (1980). A peculiar world? Teaching and Learning in an Inner City School. Unpublished Ph.D. thesis. Manchester: University of Manchester.

Chapter 3

1. Stenhouse, L. (1980). *Curriculum Research and Development in Action*. London: Heinemann.
2. Lortie, D., op. cit., Chapter 2, note 1.
3. Jackson, P., op. cit., Chapter 2, note 1.
4. Lortie, op. cit.
5. Hargreaves, D. (1982). *The Challenge for the Comprehensive School*. London: Routledge & Kegan Paul, pp. 225–6.
6. Westbury, I. (1973). Conventional classrooms, open classrooms and the technology of teaching. *Journal of Curriculum Studies*, **5**(2); Sharp, R. and Green, A. (1975). *Education and Social Control*. London: Routledge & Kegan Paul; Woods, P. and Hammersley, M. (1977). *School Experience*. London: Croom Helm; Hargreaves, A. (1978). The significance of classroom coping strategies. In Barton, L. and Meighan, R. *Sociological Interpretations of Schooling and Classrooms: a Reappraisal*. Driffield: Nafferton Books.
7. Waller, W., op. cit., Chapter 2, note 4.
8. See Chapter 2, note 22.
9. Denscombe, M. (1985). *Classroom Control: a Sociological Perspective*. London: Allen & Unwin.
10. Richardson, D.A. (1981), op. cit., Chapter 1, note 23.
11. Goodson, I. (1987). *School Subjects and Curriculum Change*. Lewes: Falmer Press.
12. Ball, S. (1981). *Beachside Comprehensive*. Cambridge: Cambridge University Press.
13. Goodson, I. (1983). Subjects for study: aspects of a social history of curriculum. *Journal of Curriculum Studies*, **15**(4); Goodson, I. (1988). *The Making of Curriculum*. Lewes: Falmer Press; Cooper, B. (1985). *Renegotiating Secondary School Mathematics*. Lewes: Falmer Press.
14. See Chapter 5.
15. Bernstein, B. (1971). On the classification and framing of educational knowledge. In Young, M.F.D. *Knowledge and Control*. London: Collier-Macmillan; Lacey, C. (1977), op. cit., Chapter 2, note 6.

16. Ball, S. (1987), op. cit., Chapter 1, note 23; Burgess, R. (1983). *Experiencing Comprehensive Education*. London: Methuen Books; Hargreaves, D. (1980). The occupational culture of teaching. In Woods, P. *Teacher Strategies*. London: Croom Helm.

17. Ball, S. (1981), op. cit., note 12; Evans, J. (1985). *Teaching in Transition*. Milton Keynes: Open University Press; Barnes, D. and Shemilt, D. (1974). Transmission and interpretation. *Educational Review*, **26**(3).

18. Hargreaves, A. (1986). *Two Cultures of Schooling*. Lewes: Falmer Press.

19. Lacey (1977), op. cit., note 15; Hanson, D. and Herrington, D. (1976). *From College to Classroom: the Probationary Year*. London: Routledge & Kegan Paul; Bolam, R. (1982), op. cit., Chapter 2, note 19.

20. See Brown, S. and McIntyre, D. (1985). Research Methodology and New Policies for Professional Development and Innovation. Paper presented to the annual conference of the Scottish Educational Research Association. Also refer to the literature cited in Chapter 1 on this topic.

21. Pollard, A. (1984). Ethnography and social policy for classroom practice. In Barton, L. and Walker, S. *Social Crisis and Educational Research*. London: Croom Helm.

22. Olson, J. (1982). *Innovation in the Science Curriculum*. London: Croom Helm, p. 24.

23. ibid., p. 20.

24. ibid., p. 27.

25. Bernstein, B. (1973). *Class, Codes and Control*, Vol. 1. London: Paladin.

26. Apple, M. (1979). *Ideology and Curriculum*. London: Routledge & Kegan Paul; Apple, M. (1982). *Education and Power*. London: Routledge & Kegan Paul.

27. Apple (1982), op. cit.

28. See also Clandinin, J. (1986), op. cit., Chapter 1, note 40, and Elbaz, F. (1983), op. cit., Chapter 8, note 2.

29. See, for example, Labov, W. (1973). The logic of non-standard English. In Keddie, N. *Tinker, Tailor . . .* Penguin: Harmondsworth.

30. Dittmar, N. (1976). *Sociolinguistics*. London: Arnold; Rosen, H. (1974). *Language and Class*. London: Falling Wall Press.

31. On Australia, see Connell, R.W. (1985). *Teachers' Work*. London: Allen & Unwin; and on the United States see Labaree, W. (1986). Curriculum credentials and the Middle Class, *Sociology of Education*, **59**, 1.

32. The notion of cultural capital was developed by Bourdieu, P. in, for example, Cultural reproduction and social reproduction. In Karabel, J. and Halsey, A.H. (1977). *Power and Ideology in Education*. Oxford: Oxford University Press.

33. See, for instance, Halsey, A.H., Heath, A.F. and Ridge, J.M. (1980). *Origins and Destinations*. Oxford: Oxford University Press; and Hargreaves, D. (1983). The teaching of art and the art of teaching. In Hammersley, M. and Hargreaves, A. *Curriculum Practice*. Lewes: Falmer Press.

34. Her Majesty's Inspectorate (1979). *Aspects of Secondary Education*. London: HMSO. See also Gray, J., McPherson, A.F. and Raffe, D. (1983). *Reconstructions of Secondary Education*. London: Routledge & Kegan Paul.

35. This was in a speech delivered to the North of England Education Conference in January 1984.

36. Hargreaves, D., op. cit., note 5.

37. Her Majesty's Inspectorate (1977). *Curriculum 11–16*. London: HMSO, and (1983). *Curriculum 11–16: Towards a Statement of Entitlement*. London: HMSO.

38. Inner London Education Authority (1984). *Improving Secondary Schools*. London: ILEA.

39. See *Times Educational Supplement*, 7 August 1987.

40. A point made in the preface to Goodson, I. (1988). *The Making of Curriculum*. Lewes: Falmer Press.
41. The literature for this initiative is discussed in Chapter 4.
42. Fairbairn, D. (1987). Pupil profiling: some policy issues for school-based practice. *Journal of Education Policy*, **2**(3).
43. See chapter 7 for a more extended discussion of multiple innovation.
44. On the intensification of teachers' work, see Apple, M. (1986). *Teachers and Texts*. London: Routledge & Kegan Paul.
45. Harland, J. (1987). The new INSET: a transformation scene. *Journal of Education Policy*, **2**(3).
46. See Hargreaves, A. and Reynolds, D. (1988). Decomprehensivisation. In *Educational Policy: controversies and critiques*. Lewes: Falmer Press.
47. Radnor, H. (1987). *The Impact of the Introduction of the GCSE at LEA and School Level*, Final Research Report, Windsor, NFER, March.
48. National Commission on Excellence in Education (1983). *A Nation at Risk*. Washington: U.S. Government Printing Office.
49. Apple (1988), op. cit., note 44; Westbury, I. (1984). A nation at risk, *Journal of Curriculum Studies*, **16**(4).

Chapter 4

1. The paper from which this chapter is drawn was first presented to the Third International Conference on Teacher Thinking and Professional Action held at the University of Leuven, Belgium, 14–17 October 1986.
2. Department of Education and Science (1983). *Teaching Quality*, Cmnd 8836. London: HMSO.
3. Department of Education and Science (1985). *Better Schools*, Cmnd 9469. London: HMSO.
4. Department of Education and Science (1984). *Initial Teacher Training: Approval of Courses*, Circular 3/84. London: HMSO.
5. For more extended discussions of the deficit model of teaching, see the previous chapter.
6. HMI (1979), op. cit., Chapter 3, note 34.
7. HMI (1982). *The New Teacher in School*. London: HMSO.
8. See, for example, HMI (1978). *Primary Education in England*. London: HMSO; HMI (1983). *9–13 Middle Schools – An Illustrative Survey*. London: HMSO; and HMI (1985). *Education 8 12 in Combined and Middle Schools*. London: HMSO.
9. See, for example, Bennett, N. (1976). *Teaching Styles and Pupil Progress*. London: Open Books; Galton, M., Simon, B. and Croll, P. (1980). *Inside the Primary Classroom*. London: Routledge & Kegan Paul; Gracey, H. (1975). *Curriculum or Craftmanship: Elementary Teachers in a Bureaucratic System*. Chicago: University of Chicago Press; Barnes, D. and Shemilt, D. (1974), op. cit., Chapter 2, note 17; Westbury, I. (1973), op. cit., Chapter 3, note 6; Hammersley, M. (1976). The mobilisation of pupil attention. In Hammersley, M. and Woods, P. *The Process of Schooling*. London: Routledge & Kegan Paul; and Blenkin, G.M. and Kelly, A.V. (1981). *The Primary Curriculum*. London: Harper and Row.
10. Tye, B. (1985). *Multiple Realities: A Study of Thirteen American High Schools*. Lanham: University Press of America.
11. Tye, K. (1985). *The Junior High: School in Search of a Mission*. Lanham: University Press of America.
12. HMI (1982) (see note 7).
13. DES (1983) (see note 2).

DES (1985), p. 44 (see note 3).
15. ibid., p. 51.
16. See, for example, DES (1984) (see note 4).
17. Such points are made by McNamara in a more extended critique of the 'official' preoccupation with teachers' personal qualities. See McNamara, D. (1986). The personal qualities of the teacher and educational policy: a critique. *Journal of Curriculum Studies*, 12(1). See also Rudduck, J. (1988). Care and initial training. In Hargreaves, A. and Reynolds, D. (eds) *Educational Policy: Controversies and Critiques*. Lewes: Falmer Press.
18. DES (1983), p. 8 (see note 2).
19. DES (1985), p. 44 (see note 3).
20. HMI (1979) (see note 6).
21. HMI (1982) (see note 7).
22. HMI (1983), para. 3. 19 (see note 8).
23. DES (1983), para. 3.29 (see note 2).
24. ibid., para. 3.37.
25. ibid., para. 3.40.
26. Tye, B. (1985) (see note 10); and Tye, K.(1985) (see note 11).
27. See, for example, Wilson, S.M. and Shulman, L.S. (1987). '150 different ways' of knowing: representations of knowledge in teaching. In Calderhead, J. (ed.) *Exploring Teacher Thinking*. Eastbourne: Holt–Saunders.
28. See, for instance, the experimentally based work of David Berliner, which, while not so exclusively concerned with didactic teaching, nonetheless focuses on subjects in the intellectual-cognitive, rather than the practical or affective domains. For instance, Berliner, D.C. and Carter, K.J. (1986). Differences in processing classroom information by expert and novice teachers. Paper presented to the Third International Conference of the International Study Association of Teacher Thinking, Leuven, Belgium, 14–17 October; and Berliner, D. (1987). Ways of thinking about students and classrooms by more and less experienced teachers. In Calderhead (see note 27).
29. The classic example here is Flanders' recommendations concerning 'indirect' teaching which, because they were based on classroom interaction samples of the transmission type, could consider only variation *within* the transmission model, rather than possible questioning of the appropriateness of that model as a whole. See Flanders, N. (1970). *Analysing Teacher Behavior*. New York: Addison-Wesley.
30. Hammersley, M. (1980). Putting competence into action: some sociological notes on a model of classroom interaction. In French P. and Maclure M., *Adult-Child Conversation*. London: Croom Helm.
31. Hoetker, J. and Ahlbrand, W.P. (1969). The persistence of the recitation. *American Educational Research Journal*, **6**.
32. Westbury (1973) (see note 9).
33. Grace, G. (1978). *Teachers, Ideology and Control*. London: Routledge & Kegan Paul.
34. On the mobilization of pupil attention, see Hammersley (1976) (see note 9).
35. Edwards, A.D. and Furlong, V.I. (1978). *The Language of Teaching*. London: Heinemann.
36. Sinclair, J.M. and Coulthard, R.M. (1974). *Towards an Analysis of Discourse*. Oxford: Oxford University Press.
37. Hammersley, M. (1974). The organization of pupil participation. *Sociological Review*, **22**(3).
38. Thomas, C. (1984). An ethnographic study of sixth form life. M.Phil. thesis. Department of Educational Studies, University of Oxford.

39. Hammersley, M. (1977). The cultural resources required to answer a teacher's question. In Woods, P. and Hammersley, M., *School Experience*. London: Croom Helm.

40. The centrality of the notion of the 'collective student' within teachers' thinking and practice has been discussed by Bromme, R. (1987). Teachers' assessments of students' difficulties and progress in understanding in the classroom. In Calderhead (see note 27).

41. The most important work on 'steering groups' has been conducted by Dahllof, U. and Lundgren, U.P. (1970). Macro and micro approaches combined for curriculum process analysis: a Swedish education field project. Report from the Institute of Goeteborg, Sweden.

42. See Clark, C.M. and Peterson, P.L. (1980). Teachers' thought process. In Wittrock, M.C. (ed.), *Handbook of Research on Teaching*, 3rd edn. New York: Macmillan.

43. Webb, J. (1962). The sociology of a school. *British Journal of Sociology*, **13**(3).

44. Hargreaves, A. (1979). Strategies, decisions and control: interaction in a middle school classroom. In Eggleston, J. (ed.) *Teacher Decision Making in the Classroom*. London: Routledge & Kegan Paul.

45. Woods, P. (1979). *The Divided School*. London: Routledge & Kegan Paul.

46. Hargreaves, A. (1986), op. cit., Chapter 3, note 18.

47. See Payne, G. and Hustler, D. (1980). Teaching the class: the practical management of a cohort. *British Journal of Sociology of Education*, **1**(1).

48. See Willis, P. (1977). *Learning to Labour*. Farnborough: Saxon House; Woods (1979) (see note 45); Hammersley (1974) (see note 9); Hammersley (1976) (see note 37); and Hammersley (1977) (see note 30). A study of a comprehensive school with a secondary modern type intake presents similar evidence. See Beynon, J. (1985). *Initial Encounters in the Secondary School* Lewes: Falmer Press.

49. See Ball, S. (1981), op. cit., Chapter 3, note 12.

50. See Anyon, J. (1981) Social class and school knowledge. *Curriculum Inquiry*, **11**(3).

51. Blyth, W.A.L. (1965). *English Primary Education: A Sociological Description*, Vol 2: *Background*. London: Routledge & Kegan Paul.

52. Furlong, V.J. (1976). Interaction sets in the classroom: towards a study of pupil knowledge. In Stubbs, M. and Delamont, S. (eds), *Explorations in Classroom Observation*. Chichester: Wiley; Torode, B. (1978). Teachers' talk and classroom discipline. In ibid., Marsh, P., Rosser, J. and Harre, R. (1978). *The Rules of Disorder*. London: Routledge & Kegan Paul; Beynon (1985) (see note 48); Zeichner, K.M., Tabachnick, B.R. and Densmore, K. (1987). Individual, institutional and cultural influences on the development of teachers' craft knowledge. In Calderhead (see note 27).

53. Support for this point, and development of the concept of coping strategies more generally, is available in Hargreaves, A. (1978), op. cit., Chapter 3, note 6.

54. Woods (1979) (see note 45).

55. See Westbury (1973) (see note 9); Pollard, A. (1985) *The Social World of the Primary School*. Eastbourne: Holt-Saunders, p. 31 and Denscombe, M. (1985), op. cit., Chapter 3, note 9.

56. This they have done in a series of surveys of the effects of local authority expenditure policies on the education service in England and Wales.

57. HMI (1979) (see note 6).

58. Hargreaves, D. (1982), op. cit., Chapter 3, note 5.

59. Gray, J., McPherson, A.F. and Raffe, D. (1983). *Reconstructions of Secondary Education*. London: Routledge & Kegan Paul.

60. ibid.

61. See Hammersley, M. and Scarth, J. (1986). The impact of examinations on secondary school teaching. Unpublished research report, School of Education, Open University, Milton Keynes; and Scarth, J. and Hammersley, M. (1987). Examinations and teaching: an exploratory study. Unpublished paper. Milton Keynes: School of Education, Open University.

62. At the time of writing, Hammersley and Scarth are analysing their data with respect to some of these factors.

63. Weston, P. (1979). *Negotiating the Curriculum*. Windsor: NFER; Olson, J. (1982), op. cit., Chapter 3, note 22.

64. Turner, G. (1983). *The Social World of the Comprehensive School*. London: Croom Helm.

65. Sikes, P., Measor, L. and Woods, P. (1985). *Teacher Careers: Crises and Continuities*. Lewes: Falmer Press.

66. Scarth, J. (1983). Teachers' school-based experiences of examining. In Hammersley, M. and Hargreaves, A. (eds), *Curriculum Practice: Some Sociological Case Studies*. Lewes: Falmer Press.

67. Mortimore, J. and Mortimore, P. (1984). *Secondary School Examinations: The Helpful Servant, not the Dominating Master*. Bedford Way Papers No. 18, University of London Institute of Education.

68. HMI (1982) (see note 7).

69. National Union of Teachers (1984). *Teaching Quality*. London: National Union of Teachers.

70. HMI (1983) (see note 8).

71. National Union of Teachers (1984). *9–13 Middle Schools*. London: National Union of Teachers.

72. See Bernstein, B. (1971), op. cit., Chapter 3, note 15; Goodson, I. (1987), op. cit., Chapter 3, note 11.

73. A point made repeatedly in Goodson, I. (ed.) (1985). *Social Histories of School Subjects*. Lewes: Falmer Press.

74. Barnes and Shemilt (1974) (see note 9).

75. Ball (1981) (see note 49). See also Evans, J. (1985). *Teaching in Transition*. Milton Keynes: Open University Press; and Hargreaves, A. (1986) (see note 46).

76. Bernstein (1971) (see note 72).

77. A point revealed by Baglin, E. (1984). A case study of a social education department. Dissertation for the Special Diploma in Educational Studies, Department of Educational Studies, University of Oxford.

78. Examples can be seen in Sikes, Measor and Woods (1985) (see note 65).

79. Hargreaves (1986), p. 188 (see note 46).

80. Sikes, Measor and Woods (1985) (see note 65).

81. Hargreaves, D. (1983), op. cit., Chapter 3, note 33.

82. Ball, S. and Lacey, C. (1980). Subject disciplines as the opportunity for group action. In Woods, P. (ed.), *Teacher Strategies*. London: Croom Helm.

83. The quotation is from a United States middle school teacher, cited in Webb, R.B. and Ashton, P. (1986). Teacher motivation and the conditions of teaching: a call for ecological reform. Paper delivered to the International Sociology of Education Conference, Westhill College, Birmingham.

84. Hargreaves (1986) (see note 46).

85. Riseborough, G. (1981). Teacher careers and comprehensive schooling: an empirical study. *Sociology*, **15**(3).

86. For a critical discussion of teacher 'burnout', see Freedman, S. (1986). Weeding men out of woman's true profession. Paper delivered to the International Sociology of Education Conference, Westhill College, Birmingham.

87. These points are made by Lortie, D. (1975), op. cit., Chapter 2, note 1.

88. Denscombe (1985) (see note 55).
89. Lortie (1975) (see note 88).
90. On the culture of individualism within teaching, see Hargreaves (1982) (see note 58); Jackson, P.W. (1968), op. cit., Chapter 2, note 1; Jackson, P.W. (1977). The way teachers think. In Glickwell, J.C. (ed.), *The Social Context of Learning and Development*. New York: Gardner Press.

Chapter 5

1. Note, for example, the replacement of the School Certificate by 'O' levels, the implementation and expansion of the CSE, protracted discussions through the Waddell Committee and elsewhere about a possible system of common examining at 16+, the proliferation of new credentials in vocational education, and so on.
2. The list does not end here, of course. Others would include the expansion of the activities of the Assessment of Performance Unit into the monitoring of national standards; the increasing use of educational testing; the development of staff appraisal near to the point where it will almost certainly become a mandatory requirement of conditions of teacher service, the requirement through the 1980 Education Act that schools publish their examination results, the introduction of 'AS' levels as a way of broadening the sixth form curriculum, etc.
3. Balogh, J. (1982). *Profile Reports for School Leavers*. York: Longmans.
4. Her Majesty's Inspectoratre (1979), op. cit., Chapter 3, note 34; Burgess, T. and Adams, E. (1980). *Outcomes of Education* London: Macmillan; Hargreaves, D. (1982), op. cit., Chapter 3, note 5; Hitchcock, G. (1986). *Profiles and Profiling*. Harlow: Longman.
5. Goacher, B. (1984). *Selection Post 16: the Role of Examination Results*. York: Longmans; Jones, J. (1983). *The Use Employers make of Examination Results and other Tests for Selection and Employment: a Criteria Report for Employers*. School of Education, University of Reading.
6. Here, there have been remarkable similarities between the observations of Sir Keith Joseph, formerly Secretary of State for Education and Science in an influential speech to the North of England Education Conference at Sheffield in January 1984; and of David Hargreaves, the man who was soon to become Chief Inspector of the Inner London Education Authority, in an equally significant review of secondary education in the ILEA published in the same year – see Chapter 3, note 38.
7. Moon, R. (1984). A modular framework. *Forum*, **27**(2).
8. Hargreaves, A., Baglin, E., Henderson, P., Leeson, P. and Tossell, T. (1988). *Personal and Social Education: Choices and Challenges*. Oxford: Basil Blackwell.
9. For evidence of such influence in early profile schemes, see Her Majesty's Inspectorate (1983). *Records of Achievement at 16: Some Examples of Current Practice*. London: HMSO; and Goacher, B. (1983). *Recording Achievement at 16+*. York: Longmans, for instance.
10. For example, in Hitchcock, op. cit., note 4, p. 11.
11. Durkheim, E. (1979). *The Evolution of Educational Thought*. London: Routledge & Kegan Paul.
12. Habermas, J. (1976). *Legitimation Crisis*. London: Heinemann.
13. Foucault, M. (1977). *Discipline and Punish*. Harmondsworth: Penguin. These are by no means the only sources on which I have drawn. My interpretation has also been influenced by other writing on crisis developments in the modern state and on the nature of the capitalist state in general. Sample sources include Offe, C.

(1984). *Contradictions of the Welfare State*. London: Hutchinson; McLennan, G., Held, D. and Hall, S. (1984). *State and Society in Contemporary Britain*. Oxford: Polity Press; Dale, R. (1982). Education and the capitalist state: contributions and Contradictions. In Apple, M., *Cultural and Economic Reproduction in Education*. London: Routledge & Kegan Paul. See also Dale, R. (1989). *The State and Educational Policy*. Milton Keynes: Open University Press.

14. More expanded explanations of the first two crisis phases – of administration and reorganization, and curriculum and belief – can be found in the final chapter of Hargreaves, A. (1986). *Two Cultures of Schooling*. Lewes: Falmer Press.

15. As, for instance, in Ministry of Education (1954). *The Early Learning Report*. London: HMSO; and Central Advisory Council for Education (England) (1959). *The Crowther Report*. London: HMSO.

16. See Central Advisory Council for Education (1963). *The Robbins Report*. London: HMSO.

17. Central Advisory Council for Education (1967). *Children and Their Primary Schools*. London: HMSO.

18. Simon, B. (1985). *Does Education Matter?* London: Lawrence & Wishart.

19. In dealing with comprehensive reorganization and indeed the raising of the school–leaving age, the Ministry of Education and later the Department of Education would not sanction new school building projects occasioned by these initiatives only. (See Hargreaves, A., op. cit., note 14 for detailed evidence on this point).

20. ibid.

21. Within Marxism, there has been a great deal of discussion as to whether teaching is 'productive' or 'unproductive' labour. The point about education, however, as Habermas himself argues, is that it is neither directly productive nor unproductive, but *indirectly productive*. It has a loose and uncertain relationship with economic activity that is exceedingly difficult to trace. Consequently, when recession bites, a well-funded programme of state education can quickly come to be seen as a dispensable investment.

22. At the time of writing, there are signs of a resurgent interest in administrative reorganization on a grand scale, as a key solution to the educational problems of the age. But the policy context in which initiatives are being taken to let the fate of school survival be determined by a wide and unprotected market of parental choice, to permit schools to withdraw from LEA control, to establish City Technical Colleges and to maintain the Assisted Places Scheme, is of a very different order from the one in which administrative reorganization was first deployed. The policy context then was one of comprehensive commitment. Now it is one of commitment to increased selection and differentiation; to *decomprehensivization*, as I have called it elsewhere. See Hargreaves, A. and Reynolds, D. (1989). Decomprehensivization. In Hargreaves, A. and Reynolds, D. (eds) *Educational Policies: Controversies and Critiques*. Lewes: Falmer Press.

23. Cox, C.B. and Boyson, R. (1975). *Black Paper 1975*. London: J.M. Dent & Sons.

24. Gretton, M. and Jackson, R. (1976). *William Tyndale: Collapse of a School or a System*. London: Allen & Unwin.

25. Bennett, N. (1976). *Teaching Styles and Pupil Progress*. London: Open Books.

26. A term neatly used by Reid, W. (1978) in *Thinking About the Curriculum*. London: Routledge & Kegan Paul.

27. Williams, R. (1961). *The Long Revolution*. London: Chatto & Windus.

28. Hargreaves, op. cit., Chapter 3, note 5.

29. Boyson, R. (1975). Maps, chaps and your hundred best books. *Times Education Supplement*, 17 October.

30. Her Majesty's Inspectorate (1977), op. cit., Chapter 3, note 37.

31. For a searching critique of the 'areas of experience' model, see Halpin, D., op. cit., Chapter 2, note 10.
32. For empirical evidence on this point, see Scarth, J., op. cit., Chapter 2, note 10.
33. Her Majesty's Inspectorate (1983), op. cit., Chapter 3, note 37, pp. 14–15.
34. ibid., p. 13.
35. ibid., p. 14.
36. Torrance, H. (1987). GCSE and School Based Curriculum Development. In Horton, T. (ed.) *GCSE: Examining the New System*. London: Harper and Row.
37. Radnor, H. (1987), op. cit., Chapter 3, note 47.
38. For instance, in Her Majesty's Inspectorate (1985). *The Curriculum from 5 to 16*. London: HMSO.
39. McNay, I. (1987). GCSE and the new vocationalism. In Horton, T. (ed.), op. cit., note 36.
40. See Dale, R. *et al.*, TVEI: a policy hybrid. In Hargreaves, A. and Reynolds, D. (1988), op. cit., note 22.
41. Weston, P. and Harland, J. (1988). The lower attaining pupils programme: myth and messages. In Hargreaves and Reynolds, ibid.
42. Willis, P. (1977). *Learning to Labour*. Farnborough: Saxon House.
43. Gray, J. *et al.* (1983), op. cit., Chapter 4, note 59.
44. Raffe, D. (1986). Unemployment and school motivation; the case of truancy. *Educational Review*, **38**(1).
45. Her Majesty's Inspectorate (1983), op. cit., note 9.
46. Balogh, J. (1982), op. cit., note 3.
47. Goacher, B. (1983), op. cit., note 9.
48. Harrison, A. (1982). *Review of Graded Tests,* Schools Council Examination Bulletin 41. London: Methuen Education.
49. Department of Education and Science(1984). *Records of Achievement: a statement of policy*. London: HMSO.
50. Burgess, T. and Adams, E. (1985). *Records of Achievement at 16*. Windsor: NFER-Nelson.
51. See Moon, R. (1984), op. cit., note 7; and ILEA (1984), op. cit., Chapter 2, note 38.
52. Popkewitz, T. (1986). Educational reform and its millenial quality. *Journal of Curriculum Studies,* **18**(3), 277.
53. ILEA (1984), ibid.
54. Schools Curriculum Development Committee (1986). *Records of Achievement*. London: SCDC.

Chapter 6

1. DES (1983), p. 3.
2. ibid.
3. Department of Education and Science (1984), op. cit., Chapter 5, note 49, para. 11, my emphasis.
4. Habermas, J. (1976), op. cit., Chapter 5, note 12.
5. Department of Education and Science (1984), op. cit., note 3.
6. Goacher, B. (1985), op. cit., Chapter 5, note 5, p. 126.
7. See Hitchcock, G. (1986), op. cit., Chapter 5, note 4. A more extensive explanation of the types of profile with all their implications is presented in Hargreaves, A. *et al.*(1988), Chapter 5, note 8. Numerous practical examples have also been listed in Law, B. (1984). *The Uses and Abuses of Profiling*. London: Harper and Row.

8. Evaluation of the RPA scheme which reviews evidence of this sort, can be found in Swales, T. (1980). *Records of Personal Achievement: an independent evaluation of the Swindon RPA scheme*. London: Schools Council.
9. As found by Her Majesty's Inspectorate (1983), op. cit., Chapter 5, note 9.
10. Swales, op. cit., note 8.
11. Scottish Council for Research in Education (SCRE) (1977). *Pupils in Profile*. Edinburgh: Hodder & Stoughton.
12. See Jones, J. (1983), op. cit., Chapter 5, note 5.
13. Goacher, B. (1983), op. cit., Chapter 5, note 9. See also Education Resource Unit for YOP (1982). *Assessment in Youth Training: Made to Measure*. Glasgow: Jordanhill College of Education.
14. Goacher, B. (1983), op. cit., note 13, pp. 31–2.
15. Education Resource Unit for YOP (1982), op. cit., note 13, p. 14.
16. op. cit., note 1, p. 7.
17. Goacher, op. cit., note 13, p. 15.
18. Department of Education and Science (1984), op. cit., note 3, p. 6.
19. The particular document cited here is one that was used for pilot purposes only by the LEA involved, and that LEA has therefore not been identified here. Other examples of comment banks and their effects are listed in Hargreaves, A. *et al.* (1988), op. cit., Chapter 5, note 8.
20. Useful examples of such prompt sheets are provided in Oxford Certificate of Educational Achievement (1987). *Student Reviewing and Recording*. Oxford: International Assessment Services.
21. Oxford Certificate of Educational Achievement (1985). Newsletter, Spring, 3.
22. Department of Education and Science, op. cit., note 1, p. 7.
23. Balogh, J. (1982), op. cit., Chapter 5, note 1, pp. 41–42.
24. Burgess, T. and Adams, E. (1980). *Outcomes of Education*. London: Macmillan; and Burgess, T. and Adams, E. (1986), op. cit., Chapter 5, note 50.
25. Burgess, T. and Adams, E. (1984). Records of achievement for school leavers: an institutional framework. *Working Papers on Institutions*, No. 57. London: North East Polytechnic, p. 4.
26. ibid., p. 5.
27. Goacher, B. (1983), op. cit., Chapter 5, note 9, p. 35.
28. Waller, W. (1932), op. cit., Chapter 2, note 4, p. 196.
29. ibid., p. 9.
30. Hattersley, R. (1983). *A Yorkshire Boyhood*. London: Chatto & Windus, p. 147.
31. Sharp, R. and Green, A. (1975). *Education and Social Control*. London: Routledge & Kegan Paul; Hargreaves, A. (1977). Progressivism and pupil autonomy. *Sociological Review*, **25**(3).
32. Woods, P. (1976). The myth of subject choice. *British Journal of Sociology*, June; Ball, S. (1981), op. cit., Chapter 3, note 12.
33. Woods, ibid.; Ball, ibid.; Sharp and Green, op. cit., note 30; King, R. (1978). *All Things Bright and Beautiful*. London: Wiley.
34. Broadfoot, P. (1982). Alternatives to public examinations. *Educational Analysis*, **4**, 51.
35. Jones, J. (1983), op. cit., Chapter 5, note 5.
36. Gray, J. *et al.* (1983), op. cit., Chapter 4, note 59.

Chapter 7

1. See Swales (1980), op. cit., Chapter 6, note 8.
2. Pupils Personal Records Management Group (1984). *Pupils as Partners: Pupils Personal Records Handbook*, Swindon: PPR, p. 1.

3. ibid., p. 2.
4. ibid., p. 1.
5. Adams, E. and Burgess, T. (1982). Statements at sixteen: an example. *Working Papers on Institutions*, No., 29. London: North East London Polytechnic.
6. Burgess and Adams (1980), op. cit., Chapter 6, note 23.
7. Burgess and Adams (1984), op. cit., Chapter 6, note 24.
8. Oxford Certificate of Educational Achievement (1984). *The Personal Record Component: A Draft Handbook for Schools*. Oxford: OCEA, p. 4.
9. Foucault, M. (1977), op. cit., Chapter 5, note 13, p. 130.
10. Broadfoot, P. (1984). From public examinations to profile assessment: the French experience. In Broadfoot, P. (ed.) *Selection, Certification and Control*. Lewes: Falmer Press.
11. Foucault (1977), op. cit., note 9, p. 141.
12. ibid., p. 183.
13. ibid., p. 170.
14. ibid., p. 171.
15. ibid., p. 184.
16. ibid., p. 191.
17. Broadfoot, P. (1983). Assessment constraints on curriculum practice: a comparative study. In Hammersley, M. and Hargreaves, A. (eds) *Curriculum Practice: Some Sociological Case Studies*. Lewes: Falmer Press.
18. *Pan* – total, universal; *optic* – pertaining to sight.
19. Foucault (1977), op. cit., note 9, p. 201.
20. ibid., p. 206.
21. Hargreaves, A. (1977), op. cit., Chapter 6, note 30.
22. Bernstein, B. (1975) Visible and invisible pedagogies. In Bernstein, B. (ed.) *Class, Codes and Control, Volume 3*. London: Routledge & Kegan Paul.
23. Hargreaves, A. (1985). English Middle Schools: an Historical and Ethnographic Study Ph.D. Thesis. Leeds: University of Leeds, p. 466.
24. Foucault, M., op. cit., note 9, p. 227.
25. Department of Education and Science (1984), op. cit., Chapter 5, note 49, para. 41.
26. Balogh (1982), op. cit., Chapter 5, note 1; Goacher (1983), op. cit., Chapter 5, note 9; Broadfoot (1982), op. cit., Chapter 6, note 33; Mortimore, J. and Mortimore, P. (1984), op. cit., Chapter 4, note 67.
27. Her Majesty's Inspectorate (1983), op. cit., Chapter 3, note 37, p. 16.
28. Department of Education and Science (1984), op. cit., Chapter 5, note 49, Para. 41.
29. Stenhouse, L. (1975). Neutrality as a criterion in teaching: the work of the humanities curriculum project. In Taylor, M.J. (ed.) *Progress and Problems in Moral Education*. NFER: Windsor.
30. Baldwin, J. and Wells, H. (1979). *Active Tutorial Work Books 1–5*. Oxford: Basil Blackwell.
31. Barnes, D. and Shemilt, D. (1974), op. cit., Chapter 4, note 9.
32. Ball, S. (1981), op. cit., Chapter 4, note 49; Evans, J. (1985), op. cit., Chapter 4, note 75; and Hargreaves, A. (1986), op. cit., Chapter 4, note 46.
33. Bolam, R. and Medlock, P. (1985). *Active Tutorial Work-training and dissemination: an evaluation*. Oxford: Basil Blackwell.
34. Barnes and Shemilt (1974), op. cit., Chapter 4, note 9; Hargreaves, A. (1986), op. cit., Chapter 4, note 46.
35. Her Majesty's Inspectorate (1979), op. cit., Chapter 3, note 34; Hargreaves, D., op. cit., Chapter 3, note 5; Dore, R. (1976). *The Diploma Disease*. London: Allen & Unwin.

36. Olson, J. (1982), op. cit., Chapter 3, note 22; Weston, P. (1979), op. cit., Chapter 4, note 63.
37. Her Majesty's Inspectorate (1983), op. cit., Chapter 3, note 37.

Chapter 8

1. Broadfoot, P. (1979). *Assessment, Schools and Society*. London: Methuen Books.
2. Salter, B. and Tapper, T. (1987). Department of Education – steering a new course. In Horton, T. (ed.) *GCSE – Examining the New System*. London: Harper & Row.
3. Whitty, G. (1985). *Sociology and School Knowledge*. London: Methuen.
4. Roy, W. (1987). The teacher's viewpoint. In Horton, T., op. cit., note 2.
5. Radice, G. (1986). *Equality and Quality: a Socialist Plan for Education* Fabian Society Pamphlet No. 514. London: Fabian Society.
6. Socialist Education Association (1986). *Better Schools*. London: Socialist Education Association.
7. Radice, op. cit., note 5, p. 12.
8. ibid.
9. Gray *et al.* (1983), op. cit., Chapter 4, note 59.
10. Ranson, S. and Tomlinson, J. (eds) (1986). *The Changing Government of Education*. London: Allen & Unwin.
11. See, for example, Whitty (1985), op. cit., note 3.
12. Broadfoot, P. (1986). Assessment policy and inequality: the United Kingdom experience. *British Journal of Sociology of Education*, **17**(2).
13. Sikes, P., Measor, L. and Woods, P. (1985), op. cit., Chapter 4, note 65.
14. Scarth, J. (1983), op. cit., Chapter 4, note 66.
15. See Hammersley, M. and Scarth, J. (1986), op. cit., Chapter 4, note 61; and Scarth, J. and Hammersley, M., op. cit., Chapter 4, note 61.
16. See Hargreaves, D. (1982), op. cit., Chapter 3, note 5.
17. Tye, B. (1985), op. cit., note 10.
18. Scarth, J. (1987). Teaching to the exam? – the case of the Schools Council History Project. In Horton, T., op. cit., note 2.
19. Such perceptions are held, for instance, by Nuttall, D. (1984). Doomsday or a new dawn: the prospects for a new system of examining at 16+. In Broadfoot, P. (ed.) *Selection, Certification and Control*. Lewes: Falmer Press.
20. Hargreaves, D. (1982), op. cit., Chapter 3, note 5; Inner London Education Authority (1984), op. cit., Chapter 3, note 38.
21. Goodson, I. (1987), op. cit., Chapter 3, note 11.
22. Hargreaves, A. *et al.* (1988), op. cit., Chapter 5, note 8; Burgess, R. (1984),. It's not a proper subject: it's just Newsom. In Goodson, I. and Ball, S. (eds) *Defining the Curriculum*. Lewes: Falmer Press.
23. ILEA (1984), op. cit., note 20.
24. For such right wing accounts, see Cox, C. and Scruton, R. (1984). *Peace Studies: a Critical Survey*, Occasional Paper No. 7, Institute for European Defence & Strategic Studies. London; Alliance Publishers; Scruton, R., Ellis-Jones, A. and O'Keefe, E. (1985). *Education and Indoctrination*. London: Sherwood Press.
25. As in, for example, Centre for Contemporary Cultural Studies (1981). *Unpopular Education*. London: Hutchinson.
26. Torrance, H. (1985). Current prospects for school based examining, *Educational Review*, **37**(1); and Torrance, H., GCSE and school based curriculum development. In Horton, T., op. cit., note 2.
27. Harrison, A., op. cit., Chapter 5, note 48; Her Majesty's Inspectorate, op. cit.,

Chapter 5, note 9; Murphy, R. and Pennycuick, D., Graded assessments and the GCSE. In Horton, T., op. cit. note 2.

28. Her Majesty's Inspectorate (1985). *Report by HM Inspectors on a Survey of Work in Modern Languages in 27 Schools in the Leeds Metropolitan District Taking Graded Tests of Defined Objectives in Modern Languages*. London: HMSO.
29. Graded Assessments in Mathematics (GAIM) (1986). *Newsletter 4*, Spring Term.
30. Apple, M. (1982), op. cit., Chapter 3, note 26.
31. Sutton, R. (1986). *Assessment in Secondary Schools: the Manchester Experience*. York: Longmans.
32. Dunn, R. (1986). Speech to the London Education Business Partnership, 11 November.
33. Hargreaves, A. *et al.* (1988), op. cit., Chapter 5, note 8.
34. Inner London Education Authority (1985). *Profiling in ILEA Secondary Schools*. London: ILEA.

Conclusion

1. Lortie, D. (1975). *Schoolteacher*. Chicago: University of Chicago Press.

Author Index

Subject Index